THE FOOTBALL FITNESS BIBLE

Copyright © 2020 Matchfit Football Limited. All rights reserved.

No part of this publication may be reproduced or distributed in any form or by any means, electronic or mechanical, including photocopying, recording or any other information storage and retrieval system, without the written permission of the author.

Disclaimer

This book is for educational purposes. The publisher and authors of this instructional book are not responsible in any manner whatsoever for any adverse effects arising directly or indirectly as a result of the information provided in this book. If not practiced safely and with caution, working out can be dangerous to you and to others. It is important to consult with a professional fitness instructor before beginning training. It is also very important to consult with a physician prior to training due to the intense and strenuous nature of some of the techniques, methods and strategies in this book.

The publisher and the author advise you to take full responsibility for your safety and know your limits. Before practicing the guidance described in this book, be sure that your equipment is well maintained and do not take risks beyond your level of experience, aptitude, training and comfort level.

Although the publisher and the author have made every effort to ensure that the information in this book was correct at press time and while this publication is designed to provide accurate information in regard to the subject matter covered, the publisher and the author assume no responsibility for errors, inaccuracies, omissions, or any other inconsistencies herein and hereby disclaim any liability to any party for any loss, damage, or disruption caused by errors or omissions, whether such errors or omissions result from negligence, accident, or any other cause.

This publication is meant as a source of valuable information for the reader from the experiences and education of the authors, however it is not meant as a substitute for direct, bespoke expert assistance. If such level of assistance is required, the services of a competent professional should be sought.

CONTENTS

ABOUT THE AUTHOR 8

THE MATCHFIT MISSION 10

FITNESS

THE IMPORTANCE OF MASTERING FUNCTIONAL MOVEMENTS 15

THE DIFFERENT TYPES OF STRENGTH 19

THE BENEFITS OF STRENGTH TRAINING FOR FOOTBALL PERFORMANCE 22

HOW TO FIND YOUR 1 REP MAX 25

CAN YOUNG ATHLETES TRAIN WITH WEIGHTS? 29

CAN YOU INCREASE MUSCLE MASS USING ONLY YOUR BODYWEIGHT? 31

KEY PRINCIPLES OF CORE STRENGTH TRAINING 33

HOW TO ACTIVATE YOUR GLUTES & WHY 37

HOW TO INCREASE STRENGTH AROUND THE KNEES 41

THE BENEFITS OF TRAINING BAREFOOT 44

THE EFFECTS OF BAD POSTURE 48

HOW TO IMPROVE YOUR BALANCE 50

THE BENEFITS OF TRAINING ON UNSTABLE SURFACES 53

HOW TO INCREASE SHOT POWER 55

HOW TO INCREASE THROW-IN LENGTH 58

HOW TO HAVE MORE POWERFUL HEADERS 60

SHOULD FOOTBALLERS USE OLYMPIC LIFTS? 62

- BLOOD FLOW RESTRICTION (BFR) TRAINING: CAN YOU BENEFIT? 64
- WHY YOUR PERFORMANCES PLATEAU 66
- HOW TO AVOID TRAINING INTERFERENCE 69
- KEY PRINCIPLES OF PRE-SEASON TRAINING 71
- STRENGTH TRAINING DURING THE SEASON 73
- HOW TO TRAIN STAMINA IN A FOOTBALL SPECIFIC WAY 75
- THE PRO'S & CON'S OF TREADMILL TRAINING 78
- TRAINING STAMINA IN THE POOL 80
- HOW TO TRAIN STAMINA FOR FOOTBALL IN THE GYM 82
- CAN TRAINING MASKS MAKE YOU FITTER? 85
- KEY PRINCIPLES OF SPEED TRAINING 88
- THE ESSENTIALS OF AGILITY TRAINING 90
- HOW LONG DOES IT TAKE TO IMPROVE FROM PLYOMETRICS? 94
- HOW TO SPEED UP YOUR FOOTWORK 96
- WILL ANKLE WEIGHTS GIVE YOU FASTER FEET? 99
- HOW TO BECOME QUICKER AT TURNING 101
- HOW TO DECELERATE FASTER 104
- THE BENEFITS OF UPHILL SPRINTS 107
- WHEN TO UTILISE DOWNHILL SPRINTS 109
- HOW TO INCORPORATE SLEDS & PARACHUTES 112
- ANALYSING RONALDO'S SPRINTING TECHNIQUE 114
- KEY STRETCHES FOR ENHANCED PERFORMANCE 117
- HOW TO RELIEVE HAMSTRING TIGHTNESS 121
- WAYS TO IMPROVE HIP MOBILITY 124

HOW TO OVERCOME IT BAND TIGHTNESS 127

HOW TO SPEED UP THE RECOVERY OF SORE LEGS 130

USING BATHS TO AID RECOVERY 134

DO EPSOM SALT BATHS AID RECOVERY? 138

THE IMPORTANCE OF SLEEP AND SCHEDULING RECOVERY TIME 140

WHY DO YOUR JOINTS CLICK? 143

HOW YOUR INJURY RISK CHANGES POST-MATCH 145

MAINTAINING FITNESS WHEN YOU'RE INJURED 147

GETTING BACK TO MATCH FITNESS POST-INJURY 151

NUTRITION

CAN YOU OUT-TRAIN A BAD DIET? 156

THE IMPORTANCE OF NUTRITION FOR ADAPTATIONS TO TRAINING 159

THE CONNECTION BETWEEN NUTRITION & MENTAL PERFORMANCE 161

WHAT'S THE DEAL BODY FAT %? 164

HOW TO LOSE FAT DURING THE SEASON 167

SHOULD FOOTBALLERS DO INTERMITTENT FASTING? 170

SHOULD FOOTBALLERS EVER FOLLOW A LOW CARB DIET? 173

IS CARB CYCLING GOOD FOR FOOTBALLERS? 175

THE PRO'S & CON'S OF A VEGAN DIET 178

THE PRO'S & CON'S OF EATING MEAT 181

ARE NUTS REALLY THAT HEALTHY? 185

IS BREAD BAD FOR YOU? 188

IS COWS MILK BAD FOR YOU? 191

UNDERSTANDING SUGAR	194
THE DIFFERENT TYPES OF WATER	197
PRE-MATCH NUTRITION	199
HALF-TIME NUTRITION	202
POST-MATCH NUTRITION	205
UNDERSTANDING DEHYDRATION	208
THE EFFECTS OF ALCOHOL ON RECOVERY	211
NUTRITION DURING RAMADAN	214
NUTRITION FOR GOALKEEPERS	217
GREAT FOOD OPTIONS WHEN YOU'RE ON THE ROAD	219
WHAT TO BUY WHEN YOU'RE ON A BUDGET	222
FOOTBALL "SUPERFOODS"	224
HOW BEETROOT JUICE CAN AID STAMINA	226
KEY SUPPLEMENTS FOR FOOTBALL PERFORMANCE	229
WHICH SUPPLEMENTS ARE SAFE TO TAKE?	232
WHAT SUPPLEMENTS CAN YOUNG PLAYERS HAVE?	235
WHEN TO USE PROTEIN POWDERS	238
THE BENEFITS OF CREATINE	242
COLLAGEN SUPPLEMENTATION	245
SHOULD YOU BUY BCAA'S?	247
WHAT'S IN A "PRE-WORKOUT"?	250
THE TRUTH ABOUT "FAT-BURNERS"	252
ENERGY DRINKS	255
CAN AN ALKALINE DIET ENHANCE PERFORMANCE?	258

WHAT TO EAT TO STAY HEALTHY 261

THE BENEFITS OF BROTHS 265

STRENGTHENING YOUR IMMUNE SYSTEM 267

WHAT TO EAT WHEN YOU'RE INJURED (TO AID REPAIR) 270

WHAT TO EAT TO PREVENT & REDUCE JOINT PAIN 273

NUTRITION TO PREVENT CRAMP 276

WHY PROTEIN POWDERS CAN CAUSE STOMACH UPSET 278

STOMACH ISSUES FROM COFFEE? 281

ABOUT THE AUTHOR

JAMES DONNELLY

As a player I spent 9 years at English pro club Wycombe Wanderers FC and represented England Schoolboys U18's before suffering (what I was told was) a career ending labral tear hip injury aged 19.

From the moment the doctor informed me that I would never play again, I became obsessed with proving him wrong. That's how my strength and conditioning journey began in 2008.

Since then, not only did I make a miraculous comeback to semi-pro football after 4 years out of the game thanks to a programme I was able to create with my new-found training knowledge, I also:

- Went on to work 1-1 privately with hundreds of footballers, passing on what I had learnt about the benefits of strength and conditioning to take their performances to the next level
- Continued to study and specialise in football-specific strength and conditioning, eventually earning a Masters from the Football Science Institute and being mentored by some of the world's top football scientists
- Launched Matchfit Football in 2016, and built a team of specialist coaches, including a sports nutritionist and sports psychologist, to help me train players at a deeper level and at greater scale

Together we've now coached over 50,000 footballers worldwide, many of whom have been able to step up to pro and international level after applying much of what you'll discover in this book to their training.

KEY BOOK CONTRIBUTORS:

- James Donnelly: https://www.linkedin.com/in/jdmatchfit/
- Shaun Ward (Sports Nutrition): https://www.linkedin.com/in/shaunwardnutrition
- Yianni Kyriacou (Strength & Conditioning): https://www.linkedin.com/in/yianni-kyriacou/

KEY LINKS:

For training programmes, head over to:

- bit.ly/matchfitfootball

If you're interested, here's where you can learn more about my personal story:

- bit.ly/my-matchfit-story

THE MATCHFIT MISSION

The reason I wanted to write this book is simple.

At the highest level, the game has reached an extraordinary standard over the last 15-20 years. On the one hand this can be put down to improvements in coaching, equipment and facilities, on the other we can look at how more attention has been paid to the development of footballers who are not only technically brilliant, but also possess incredible athletic abilities.

Here's the current issue. With every passing day, the gap widens between the players at the top level who are guided by sports science experts on a daily basis and the many talented players outside of the professional environment, who have the technical ability to play at the highest level, but lack the knowledge and support in terms of athletic development to make it realistically possible.

Indeed, having high levels of technical ability provides only a fraction of the qualities you need to possess in order to play at the highest level. One of the biggest challenges? Having a body which allows you to stay on the pitch and not break down.

A world class football athlete is pre-conditioned to be able to cope with highly demanding workloads season after season, whilst limiting the risk of injury setbacks from overuse. They possess the capacity to impact matches in the way that they wish to in their minds, rather than within the limits of what their bodies will allow. This takes years of compounding daily smart, science-backed training efforts and optimal nutrition to achieve.

Of course, there's more to fitness and nutrition than simply avoiding injury. It has the potential to unlock a level of performance and expression of skill which would simply never be realised without it.

My goal is to make you excited about the fact that you can become a dramatically more effective footballer without even touching a ball and to awaken the realisation that without strength and conditioning you will almost certainly never fulfil your true footballing potential. I want you to think "my god, I wish I knew all this 10 years ago!"

No matter if you're currently an amateur, semi-pro or pro player, if you apply what you're about to uncover in this book you will take your performances to a new level not possible by training your technical ability alone.

Yes, continuing to develop your technical game is a crucial part of your success, you've got to have elite technical ability to stand any chance of playing at the highest level and a "football brain" which makes smart decisions on and off the ball. But what you're about to learn will further enhance the results of your training efforts and allow your technical and mental talents to flourish on the pitch to a much higher degree.

What's in front of you right now is a wonderful opportunity to develop a highly influential aspect of your football performance which will directly impact the level which you are able to play at. Much of what you're about to discover is still overlooked, misunderstood and under-utilised by millions of players (by no fault of their own).

If you want to become a world class pro, you need to train and have the lifestyle habits of a world class pro. The sooner you start the better, it's as simple as that.

This is a process which requires years of compounding smart training efforts and eating habits, it's why players who join top professional clubs from a younger age have a significant advantage over gifted players outside of that environment. The vehicle they have to express their talents from is simply more developed. As a result, they:

- Are more resilient to common football injuries
- Are stronger on the ball
- Adapt to and recover from training faster
- Can maintain high intensity efforts for longer
- Possess more advanced levels of athleticism
- Can react and move more efficiently at a higher level of their speed capacity

...to name just few qualities. Notice how none of them directly involve the ball? All of these things are in your control, if you have access to the knowledge required to achieve them.

So, with the internet giving almost every footballer on the planet access to unlimited scientific studies which reveal all of this knowledge, why is it that so many players are still not applying␣t to their game and reaping the rewards? I believe it comes down to two main things:

1. Coaching
2. Confusion

It's one thing knowing what the research says, it's another thing all together being able to apply that knowledge successfully to your training when there are endless scenarios to consider and elements of performance to juggle and cram in.

This is where specialist fitness and nutrition coaches come in, to remove confusion and allow the player to focus on what they do best, playing football. Access to these coaches however is by no means cheap or widespread. Which leads us to the situation we are in now. The only players who can capitalise on this knowledge are the ones who:

1. Are at a top pro club and can be guided by experts
2. Have and can afford access to coaches in their local area
3. Have self-educated (which takes years of study and often means sacrificing a professional football career to go to university)

Our mission with this book is to give players, football coaches and parents (who are outside of the top professional club environment) simple and practical fitness and nutrition strategies which can be easily applied to any training schedule to unlock a higher level of performance. We've focused on the key areas which players, football coaches and parents have repeatedly told us that they are struggling with and unsure about over the last 5 years and hope that the 1-1 coaching style this book is written in inspires you to take action!

Throughout my playing years I saw many talented footballers get released or not "make the cut" for reasons that had absolutely nothing to do with their technical ability. I also saw players who were nowhere near as technically gifted, but fantastic athletes, go on and achieve incredible things in football. Imagine the possibilities if you possess both qualities!

I strongly believe that if you want to fulfil your true footballing potential, then you need to understand and appreciate the pivotal role that fitness and nutrition plays in unlocking elite performance. I'm not talking about a debatable 1 or 2% difference here; I'm talking about completely transforming the level of impact you're able to consistently have in matches. Ultimately, the goal of any footballer should be to fuse peak performance with a low injury rate. What you'll learn inside this book will get you closer to achieving that whilst bridging the gap between where you are now and what's required of your body at the highest level of football.

At the end of this book you'll find a list of references and further reading. Please remember that whilst scientific studies give us a great insight, there is no greater insight than research performed on yourself. For this reason, I encourage you to test and monitor all of the strategies you learn in this book on yourself to see how your body adapts and find what works best for you. This is why many professional clubs run in-house studies and tests (guided by previous research) to attain data which applies specifically to their players.

This book is a melting pot of knowledge sourced from the experiences and education of the Matchfit Football coaches, we pride ourselves on our ability make the seemingly complex and overwhelming, simple and actionable for players. Essentially, if you came to us in person right now and said you wanted to become a world class footballer, this is what we would teach you...

FITNESS

THE IMPORTANCE OF MASTERING FUNCTIONAL MOVEMENTS

Good fundamental movement skills are associated with health, wellbeing and high-level sports performance. These movement skills are developed from childhood and become integrated in various movements which make up real life sporting movements. All sport specific movement patterns can be seen as an extension of good fundamental movement skills and this justifies their emphasis in strength and conditioning programmes.

It's not by chance that the best players in the world are all great movers. Having sound movement mechanics enables you to have greater balance, move faster and more gracefully, use energy more efficiently and perhaps most importantly be more resilient to injury thanks to a greater capacity to safely absorb and distribute force throughout the body.

Ensuring sound movement mechanics before adding weight or resistance to the movement is of paramount importance. Performing movements such as the bodyweight squat with poor technique and then adding weight is a recipe for disaster in terms of further increasing injury risk and hindering the benefits which could come from performing the exercise with additional load in the first place.

Without mastering functional movement skills, your ability to perform athletic movements with stability, speed and precision will be affected, which could in turn determine the level of football you can achieve. The higher the level of football, the more athletic the players and the more complex movements they can perform well.

Think about Ronaldo's stepovers, Zlatan's overhead kicks or Messi's pirouettes on the ball. It's all made possible through sound movement mechanics along with possessing a vast catalogue of movement patterns that can be accessed in the blink of an eye. This can best be developed in younger players by ensuring that they take part in a wide variety of sports which demand different types of movement. Specialising in one sport too early could limit the opportunity to acquire movement skills which will be required to make it to the highest level of the sport you want to specialise in.

Functional movement skills can be split into 4 categories: Movement, Manipulation, Stabilisation and Locomotion.

Movement	Manipulation	Stabilisation	Locomotion
Squat	Throw	Balance	Run
Lunge	Catch	Co-ordination	Jump
Push/Pull	Kick	Posture	Skip
Hinge	Strike	Core Stability	
Rotate		Joint Stability	

A great way to regularly brush up on your functional movement technique is to include some of the exercises in your training and match day warm ups. Most people have heard of the RAMP warmup method (raise, activate, mobilise, potentiate), below we have provided a warm up example which follows the RAMP method and incorporates some of these key functional movements. By doing this you can ensure you're perfecting these movements at least 2-3 times per week:

RAISE

Elevates body temperature, heart rate, respiration rate, blood flow and joint fluid viscosity.

EXAMPLES:

- 5 mins low intensity cycling, jogging, rowing or skipping (has the added benefit of a plyometric stimulus)
- Dribbling with the ball at 50% intensity ensuring lots of changes of direction, stop-starts and using every part of both feet

ACTIVATE AND MOBILISE

Activate key muscle groups and mobilise joints and ranges of motion (ROM) used in the sporting activity.

EXAMPLES:

- Lunges, single leg deadlifts, inchworms, bear crawls, overhead squats
- Heel kicks, knees up, open/close gates, kick throughs, kickbacks, kicks across the body, lateral leg swings

POTENTIATE

Increase the intensity of exercise to a point at which it feeds into the intensity of the training session or match they are about to perform. This could involve selecting activities which may contribute to a super-maximal effect and therefore increase performance via a post-activation potentiation (PAP) effect.

EXAMPLES:

- Pogo jumps, box jumps, knee tuck jumps, skipping, lateral hop and holds
- 20m sprints. Sprints with changes of direction
- Up for a header and sprint in different direction, up for a header and pause still upon landing before turning and sprinting, lay flat on the floor and press yourself up to standing before sprinting to a cone

As you can see, the RAMP method provides a great structure that you can follow to ensure a thorough warm up for both pitch and gym work. For match days and pitch sessions you should also incorporate multi-directional ball work through activities such as:

- Pass and move
- Rondo's
- Keep ball
- Position specific work like shooting, heading and long/short ball passing and receiving

BREAKDOWN OF A SQUAT

The first movement listed in the table above is the squat. This refers to the bodyweight version of the exercise. The reason this movement is first and valued so much is due to its multi-joint nature. By performing an overhead squat (squat with arms raised in the air), we can include all key joints of the body and use the exercise as a movement screen to identify common movement faults. You'll find a video analysis of the overhead squat in the fitness section of the Matchfit Conditioning app.

COMMON OVERHEAD SQUATTING FAULTS:

- Heel comes off the floor = Foot and ankle mobility issue
- Knees cave in = Knee stability issue

- Lack of depth and tightness or pinching in the front of the hip = Hip mobility issue
- Rounding of the lower back = Lumbar spine stability issue
- Unable to extend through upper back = Thoracic spine mobility issue
- Arms falling forwards = Shoulder mobility issue

KEY POINT

An issue in any of the areas or movements listed above can have a knock-on effect throughout the body, limiting athletic performance and increasing injury risk. It's worth mentioning that even if you've never really struggled with injuries, consider yourself very athletic and are already playing at a high level, identifying a weakness through the overhead squat movement screen and addressing it could unlock an even higher level of athleticism for you.

THE DIFFERENT TYPES OF STRENGTH

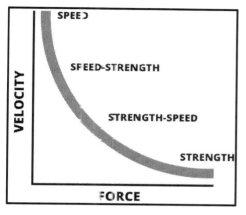

Different types of strength training can develop different aspects of your football athleticism. There are many different categorisation methods for the strength curve, the one below is the simplest.

We can see that movements which require maximal speed and provide less time to exert force belong at the top left of the graph (sprinting for example), whilst movements which require maximal force and are therefore performed slower belong at the bottom right of the graph (a one rep max squat for example).

The recommended goal in terms of strength training for a footballer would be to become well rounded across the entire spectrum of strength and then work towards being able to produce greater force at speed, which translates to power and explosiveness on the pitch.

Of course, once a good baseline level has been established across all types of strength, players may look to focus on one area of the strength curve which they feel would further enhance their performance specific to their style of play or position.

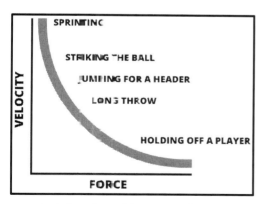

On the left we have outlined a few examples of football movements on the force velocity curve. More explosive actions are at the higher end of the curve and slower actions like holding a player off are at the lower end.

A simple way to demonstrate putting this curve into practice in a weekly training schedule is by doing different types of work at specific times so as not to negatively interfere with your performance in team training and matches.

If you play every Saturday, you are likely to be fatigued on a Sunday and Monday. This makes Tuesday as the first big training day. On Tuesday, you are fresh but also far enough from Saturday that any fatigue will subside by game day. This means that strength and strength-speed work is perfect for this day. Thursday is the last training opportunity you have to do intense work, but you cannot afford to cause fatigue that may hinder you on game day. This makes it the perfect time to do speed and speed-strength work. This training could even have a potentiating affect, priming your body to perform on game day.

The schedule mentioned may not apply to you but the principles are simple. Do the work that causes fatigue far enough away from game day as possible whilst still doing good quality work. If you do that, your training week will organise itself and all the parts will fall into place. Below are some exercise examples which work the curve:

SPEED (< 30% 1RM):

- Sprinting, overspeed sprinting, light resisted sprints, plyometrics with very short ground contact times

SPEED-STRENGTH (30-60% 1RM):

- Light-medium resisted sprints, plyometrics with longer ground contact times, light-medium loaded jumps, med ball throws, lifts using light-medium loads with max intent. Peak power which is the equal combination of speed and strength would sit at the centre of the curve and represent 30-80% 1RM

STRENGTH-SPEED (80-90% 1RM):

- Heavy loaded jumps, Olympic lift alternatives (kettlebells), lifts with accommodating resistance such as bands or chains, heavy prowler pushes

MAXIMAL STRENGTH (90-100% 1RM):

- Barbell squat 1RM, maximal isometrics, slow eccentrics

KEY POINT:

- Train all parts of the force-velocity curve
- Focus on specific parts of the force-velocity curve to improve specific qualities

- Plan different types of work so as not to negatively affect your team training and match performance

THE BENEFITS OF STRENGTH TRAINING FOR FOOTBALL PERFORMANCE

Strength is often seen as the major quality which enables players to be tough to knock off the ball, strong in the tackle and dominant in the air. Whilst these are all great examples of strength being utilised on the football pitch, there are many more often overlooked benefits of increasing your strength.

In sport, strength is the maximal force you're able to apply against a load and power is being able to apply that force at speed. Strength and power go hand in hand, this means you can only be as powerful as you are strong. So, if we're talking specifically about speed for example, a lack of strength can limit your true potential when it comes to acceleration, deceleration and performing sharp changes of direction.

DIRECT BENEFITS

Increased lower body strength can aid both your jumping and sprinting ability on the pitch. Studies have shown a strong correlation between high 1RM (one rep max) weights on squats or deadlifts and the ability to jump high or run fast in semi-pro and pro footballers.

Improvements in speed from strength training alone are likely to be more noticeable in young or undeveloped players. In more experienced players with plenty of gym experience, simply getting stronger won't necessarily further increase speed, but it will allow for greater force production. An increase in force will allow any player to keep progressing their power and it's that ability to produce force at speed which will lead to a heightened ability to move faster and jump higher on the pitch.

In terms of upper body strength, one of the major benefits is an increased ability to hold off players and protect the ball when you're being challenged. Using progressively heavier weights in exercises such as the bench press or barbell row can help to develop general upper body strength across a range of muscle groups.

KEY POINT

Simply increasing strength can lead to progressions in speed in less trained players. However, in players with more strength training experience, further improvements in speed from strength training alone will be minimal. For these players, increases in speed can be made possible by following strength training with power-based training.

INDIRECT BENEFITS

Research has shown that strength training can reduce the risk of overuse injuries by 50%. This gives you a greater chance of being consistently available for matches, which in turn means you can continue to progress your form and hone your craft (instead of experiencing repeated set-backs, which prolong your journey to elite performance and may be the determining factor in you never fulfilling your true potential).

Availability is extremely important in football. Top players become top players because they play often. A good example is Ronaldo. His career has been largely free of serious, long term injuries so he's been able to train more often, play more often and continue to improve as a result. Contrast that with someone such as Daniel Sturridge, who has missed over 700 days and 123 matches through injury since 2013.

KEY POINT

If you're always getting injured, you're not only missing matches (which scouts will attend), you're also missing the opportunity to improve at every training session and become a better player.

Greater levels of strength will enable you to recover quicker after matches. In fact, studies in rugby have shown that stronger players return to pre-match levels of readiness quicker than players with lower levels of strength.

Faster recovery means a faster return to training. Training and playing more with a lower risk of injury puts you in a better position to keep improving, compared to a player who spends more time in recovery or out of action through injury.

Finally, by increasing strength you'll also decrease your normal level of fatigue in the dying stages of a match. In simple terms, the greater your 1RM, the lesser percentage of effort every step you take running or walking on the pitch represents compared to a player with a lower 1RM. The greater your strength, the lower your effort, the lower your level of fatigue as the game progresses.

Every action you take, whether it's a sprint, a pass, or a shot, is going to cause you less fatigue than a weaker player. This means your energy levels will be more sustained throughout the entire 90 minutes, whilst other players start to fade.

Compared to other sports, football players are not typically the strongest athletes. This is an important point to remember because the player that can lift the heaviest weights is not necessarily the better footballer. It's relative strength which is important, how strong you are in relation to your own bodyweight.

Whilst strength is just one aspect of football athleticism, a good base level of strength can help to maximise performance and boost recovery times after training or a game.

KEY STRENGTH EXERCISES

Numbers are arbitrary, but bodyweight can be used as a guide for optimal strength levels for players.

- **1 Rep Max Back Squat:** 1.5 to 2 x your bodyweight
- **1 Rep Max Deadlift:** 1.5 to 2 x your bodyweight (perhaps a little more if you're using a trap-bar rather than a straight-bar)
- **1 Rep Max Bench Press:** 1 to 1.5 x your bodyweight

Going heavier for the sake of boasting bigger numbers is engrained in many gym-training cultures, but for footballers a line needs to be drawn to avoid training like power lifters. Focusing on lifting more than 1.5 – 2 x your bodyweight is unlikely to produce significant further gains in terms of football performance and is likely to take you away from training more influential aspects of your performance.

FOOTBALL PERFORMANCE

The key exercise guidelines set out above should be considered solid strength-training foundations. From this base, you can progress to the next level of training and hopefully stay injury free as you begin to focus on more advanced exercises over time that will keep you progressing and further enhance your impact on the football pitch.

HOW TO FIND YOUR 1 REP MAX

Finding your 1RM (one rep max) in key compound exercises such as the back squat, deadlift and bench press is a good way of tracking upper and lower body maximal strength changes over time and calculating the loads required depending on the strength adaptation you are looking for in your training.

SAFETY FIRST

Safety must be your first concern. If you are going for a 1RM, always have a spotter with you. It might be possible to squat without a spotter if you're in a squat rack and the safety is set at a height that would let you bail out safely and you might be okay in a deadlift if you're on a surface that would allow you to just drop the bar, but never attempt a 1RM bench press without a spotter.

CALCULATING YOUR 1RM

By using a 1RM tool on a website such as bodybuilding.com, it's possible to get a rough idea of your potential 1RM by punching in the weights and reps that you know you can lift. This is a useful tool for footballers who generally don't train with maximum weight loads and don't know their true 1RM.

For example, if you know that you can bench press 80kgs for 10 reps, putting this information into the online calculator will give you a guide to an estimated 1RM. It's not an exact science, but it gives you a good estimation of the loads you should be using in various aspects of your strength training.

GOING FOR A NEW 1RM

KEY POINT

Before lifting any weights, you must work through a dynamic warm-up routine to limit the potential for injury. Even in a 1RM session, work through the same warm-up you would use before any other weight-training session in the gym.

BACK SQUAT

Before any kind of lift, it's always a good idea to nail your technique in the warm-up. In the back squat, this means using just the bar for a warm-up set of 10 reps and then progressively adding weight until you're close to your estimated 1RM. The aim is to prepare your body for a maximal lift but keep the targeted muscles fresh in the process. As the weight increases, the number of reps performed decreases.

For example, if your estimated back squat 1RM is 100kgs, you might progress as follows:

- Bar only (20kgs) for 10 reps
- 40kgs for 10 reps
- 60kgs for 5 reps
- 80kgs for 3 reps
- 90kgs for 1 rep
- 95kgs for 1 rep, or make the jump straight to 100kgs for 1 rep

Going for a 1RM is as much about building confidence as it is strength. Once you're close to your predicted max weight, it's better to add weight in small increments.

If 95kgs feels good, go for 100kgs and if that feels good, go for 105kgs. When you reach a weight that you're unable to lift successfully, leave it there. It's tempting to give it another try, but once you've missed a rep, you're getting into an area where injuries are much more likely to occur. Leave it there until your next 1RM training session.

KEY POINT

This is not about power lifting. Your priority is to stay strong and fit for football, so don't push it and risk an injury.

DEADLIFT

The grip you use to deadlift will depend on your strength. A double overhand grip might work for you if you're strong and some power lifters favour an alternate grip with one hand in an overhand grip and the other in an underhand grip. However, it's worth pointing out that many power lifters using this grip also end up with torn biceps, so for this reason it's safer to use straps. Grip strength is not key to football performance, so don't let it become an issue. Use straps rather than risk an injury.

If your estimated deadlift 1RM is 120kgs, you might progress as follows:

- Bar only for 10 reps to nail your technique
- 40kgs for 10 reps
- 60kgs for 5 reps
- 80kgs for 3 reps
- 100kgs for 1 rep
- 110kgs for 1 rep
- 115kgs, then 120kgs for 1 rep and if it feels good, you might try 122kgs

The closer you get to your estimated max weight, the smaller the weight increments should be. When the load is getting heavy, big jumps in weight are going to make it less likely that you'll reach your maximal weight. Go for small increases and keep going until you can no longer lift the load – this will give you a truer 1RM result.

Another useful training aid is to video your lifts. When you film yourself, you're able to gauge the quality and speed of each lift. By definition, a 1RM is going to be a slow lift and when you watch yourself on video, you might notice that you're moving fast enough and smoothly enough to suggest that you're not done yet.

KEY POINT

With squats and deadlifts, relatively big jumps in weight can safely be made in the warm-up sets and then the reps should be reduced as the weight increases and you get closer to your predicted 1RM.

BENCH PRESS

Your bench press maximum weight is going to be much lower than your squat and deadlift maximum weight. If not, you've got some imbalance issues to address. For this reason, the weight increments will be smaller between each warm-up set. Remember, you must always have a spotter and ideally it should be the same person each time so that you're not thrown off by having a different spotter do something differently.

If your estimated 1RM is 80kgs, you might progress as follows:

- Bar only for 10 reps

- 40kgs for 10 reps
- 50kgs for 5 reps
- 60kgs for 3 reps
- 70kgs for 1 rep
- 75kgs or 80kgs for 1 rep

SET RULES IN PLACE

Measuring your 1RM is a means of tracking your strength-training progress, so set some rules in place to ensure you're measuring like-for-like each time. The squat, deadlift, or bench press lift you use as a measure of your 1RM must be completed with the same good form you've used in all other warm-up lifts.

For example, if you normally complete a full squat with a neutral spine and your hips dip below your knees at the bottom of the move, a rep that leads to an excessive curve in your spine and your hips staying above the line of your knees is not a valid squat in terms of claiming a 1RM.

The same can be applied to bench pressing; if good form in your warm-up reps takes the bar from touching your chest to straight arms, a lift that doesn't touch your chest or finish with straight arms can't be considered a valid 1RM.

Set rules in place that define your valid lifts and make a note so that you can accurately track your progress. Stick to the rules and make every lift a good quality, safe lift. After all, it's progress your tracking, not your ability to cheat on an exercise.

CAN YOUNG ATHLETES TRAIN WITH WEIGHTS?

In the past, it was often considered harmful to use weights in a young person's training programme. Today, this is an outdated concern that has been proven unfounded.

The current NSCA (Nation Strength and Conditioning Association) position statement on youth resistance training reads as follows:

"Despite outdated concerns regarding the safety or effectiveness of youth resistance training, scientific evidence and clinical impressions indicate that youth resistance training has the potential to offer observable health and fitness value to children and adolescents provided that appropriate training guidelines are followed and qualified instruction is available."

The key sentence in the statement is "provided appropriate training guidelines are followed and qualified instruction is available."

COMPETENCY-BASED TRAINING

If you send a bunch of kids into the gym and tell them to do what they want without keeping an eye on them, then it's fair to say that weight-training could prove dangerous.

In a supervised environment, resistance training is perfectly safe provided the training programme is competency-based rather than age-based. For example, if a young player is 5 years old and able to follow instructions, he or she is more competent than a 10-year-old player who can't follow instructions. Exercises must always be age-appropriate, but it's competency rather than age that dictates how safely the exercises can be performed.

KEY POINT

A resistance training programme for a young player must be designed around what they have shown themselves to be capable of doing, rather than their age alone. Depending on resistance training experience, a 15-year-old may be more capable than a 19-year-old for example.

THE BENEFITS OF YOUTH RESISTANCE TRAINING

Resistance training can strengthen muscles, tendons, ligaments and even bones. Improving bone density is a major benefit for young footballers, it enables players to safely absorb high force and be heavier to push off the ball.

Children who regularly jump off swings or climb trees and drop to the ground are going to have more than their bodyweight going through their bones when they do this. Being subject to the forces which are experienced in activities such as these also leads to increases in bone strength and density. So, in effect, many children are already doing a form of resistance training, it's just taking a different form. And just like in football, if they're unable to deal with these forces, injuries will occur.

It's therefore logical that strength training in a controlled environment will help to further increase bone strength and density in young players just as it does in more mature players. This can be done at the same time as teaching optimal and safe landing mechanics. In this sense, not using resistance training in a young footballer's training programme is far more dangerous than using it.

MYTHS AND MISCONCEPTIONS

The previous concern over the safety of weight-training with young athletes was based on the misconception that growth plates would be negatively affected. This is simply not true and unless a youngster is lifting excessively heavy weights without supervision, no damage is being done.

Another related myth is that lifting weights at a young age will stunt growth. This is a myth that has been perpetuated by the short stature of many Olympic weightlifters. In reality, the reason for the success of shorter lifters over taller lifters is that they have less distance to cover when moving a heavy weight from the floor to an overhead position. Weight lifting doesn't lead to being short, being short is an advantage for weightlifters and this is perhaps why shorter athletes succeed.

CAN YOU INCREASE MUSCLE MASS USING ONLY YOUR BODYWEIGHT?

Lifting heavy weights at the gym is generally considered the way to go when the aim is to add lean muscle mass. However, for beginners it is possible to make gains in muscle mass using just bodyweight.

MAKING GAINS

For a footballer it makes sense to focus on compound exercises first. Exercises such as squats, lunges, press ups and pull ups all train multiple joints and muscle groups simultaneously. This is exactly what occurs on the football pitch, muscle groups work together to exert and absorb force.

No matter the exercise, time under tension should be a central focus (which means performing the exercise in a slow and controlled manner) and it must be made progressively harder over time in order to maintain the adaptation of hypertrophy (increase in the size of the muscle fibres). This can be achieved in a number of ways, most commonly:

- Increasing the number of sets
- Increasing the load
- Increasing the difficulty of the exercise (single leg vs double leg for example)
- Increasing time under tension

Essentially all ways of increasing muscular stress.

It makes sense to perfect exercise form and technique, as well as explore the range of exercise variations (for example forward lunges vs side lunges vs reverse lunges vs diagonal lunges) before adding any further weight or resistance to the exercise. However, the difficulty comes when the athlete reaches a certain level of proficiency, has explored many exercise variations and experimented with tempos to increase time under tension and now cannot efficiently train for hypertrophy for a given exercise using only their bodyweight.

Exercises such as squats for example using just bodyweight can be quite easy, making it increasingly hard to trigger the mechanisms of muscle growth. Progressive overload is required to increase muscle mass, once a good base level of strength has been achieved through bodyweight training, training different aspects of the strength curve can be done more efficiently by utilising added weight or resistance.

KEY POINT

Bodyweight training can be used to increase muscle mass, but it will only get you so far. If you're new to strength training then gains in muscle mass are possible using your bodyweight alone, but you will eventually hit a point where creating enough of an overload to keep triggering muscle growth becomes difficult and a switch to weights and gym training will eventually be needed to make further gains in football specific strength and power. This will also enable you to train all aspects of the strength curve in an efficient and varied way.

It's also important to note that many players skip straight to training with weights and miss out on all of the possible benefits of bodyweight training, which can be equally as detrimental. A good phrase to refer to here is "the wider the base, the higher the peak". In short this means that if you focus on squeezing as many possible benefits as you can from the more basic exercises, then greater benefits will be waiting for you when you reach the sexier, more advanced exercises further down the line.

This goes hand in hand with earning the right to progress any exercise. To give an extreme example, if you cannot repeatedly perform a simple bodyweight squat with correct technique, then trying to perform barbell back squats with chains hanging from either end of the barbell would be doing yourself a huge injustice. If we can use subtle but effective increments to keep increasing the difficulty of an exercise, then you are building the foundations for a much higher peak of performance in the future whilst addressing the immediate training goal.

KEY PRINCIPLES OF CORE STRENGTH TRAINING

Good core strength is an essential element of maintaining good posture, but improvements made through consistent training can also boost your football athleticism thanks to an enhanced capability to transfer force throughout the body.

Your core muscles help to maintain balance as you move. Increased core strength will also enable you to resist motion to a greater extent which in turn unlocks the ability to apply and absorb force more efficiently as you move, therefore allowing for increased performance in movements such as sprinting, cutting, kicking and throwing for example.

RESISTING MOTION

The main motions your core muscles work to resist are extension and rotation.

EXTENSION

Extension increases the angle between two bones at a joint, so elbow extension straightens your arm, knee extension straightens your leg and in a football example, your spine extends as you bend backwards to take a throw-in. Being able to resist extension in your spine allows you to put full force into the throw.

An example of a core-strengthening anti-extension exercise is the dead bug exercise:

- Lie on your back and bring your knees up to a 90-degree angle (knees above your hips)
- Raise your arms so that your hands are in line above your shoulders (pointing at the ceiling)
- Push your spine into the floor so that there's no gap for your hand to fit underneath
- Slowly lower your right arm and straighten your left leg towards the floor
- Keep your spine pushed flat to the floor as you move and stop the movement just before your hand and foot touch the floor
- Return to the start position and repeat with your left arm and right leg

Keeping your back flat and resisting the temptation to let your spine arch from the floor is resisting extension.

ROTATION

Rotation is essentially turning to the right or left through your spine. An example of resisting rotation in football might be holding your posture when being pushed by another player. Without good posture, you're more likely to get pushed off balance. You also need to be able to resist rotation to put full force into every stride as you run and sprint.

An example of a core-strengthening anti-rotation exercise is the Pallof press:

- Stand parallel to a cable machine (or a band fixed at chest height) and hold the handle in both hands
- Position your feet hip-width apart and keep a slight bend in your knees
- Start with the handle against your chest and press out slowly to a straight-arm position
- Slowly return to the handle to your chest
- Complete 8-10 reps and then switch sides to repeat

Resisting the pull of the cable or band (trying to turn you towards it) is resisting rotation

CORE STRENGTHENING

The above exercises provide good examples of using resistance to movement, to improve the strength and stability of your core muscles, but variety is the key. Once the anti-extension and anti-rotation boxes are ticked, there are numerous other exercises that can be used to condition the trunk muscles involved in the core movements of extension, rotation and flexion.

FLEXION EXERCISES

Any form of sit-up can be considered a flexion exercise. You could progress the sit-up by using a decline, straightening the legs or by adding a weight overhead for example. These exercises work well with anti-extension exercises to add power to your throw-ins.

When you throw a ball, you're going to go through extension, then flexion and often rotation at the same time. You need strength in these movements to be able to produce the force into the ground that adds power to your throw.

A simple alternative is leg raises:

- Lie on your back on the floor with straight legs
- Keep your legs together and raise them from the floor until the soles of your feet are facing the ceiling
- Slowly lower your legs (keep them straight) until they almost touch the floor
- Hold for a few seconds and then raise them to repeat the exercise
- Maintaining a flat back to the floor as you lower your legs also makes this an anti-extension exercise

EXTENSION EXERCISES

Most gyms have some form of back extension machine or equipment. Back extensions not only strengthen the lower back, but also the glutes, which both help to produce force when accelerating and sprinting. Increasing lower back strength also reduces the potential for injury when you start training with heavier weights in exercises such as squats and deadlifts etc.

ANTI-ROTATION EXERCISES

A useful alternative to the Pallof press is the bird dog exercise:

- Position yourself on the floor on your hands and knees
- Raise your right arm and straighten out your left leg simultaneously
- Keep your head in line with your spine and maintain a neutral curve (avoid sagging) in your back
- Hold for 3 or 4 seconds and resist the rotational forces that could lead to losing your balance
- Return to the start position and repeat with your left arm and right leg

TRAINING PROGRAMME

Increasing your core strength is going to directly boost your athletic performance on the pitch and also allow you to safely lift heavier loads when training for strength and power in the gym, so it's important to include them in both you in-season and pre-season training programmes.

If you don't have time to do them as a stand-alone session (in a circuit for example), a great time to schedule them is at the end of both pitch and gym training sessions, choosing a few core exercises and switching them up for variety each week.

For example, if you're training 3 times per week in the gym:

- Session 1: Dead bugs for 3 x 10 reps and back extensions for 3 x 15-20 reps. Superset by completing 1 set of each exercise alternately
- Session 2: Bird dogs for 3 x 10 reps and straight-leg sit ups for 3 x 10 reps
- Session 3: Pallof presses for 3 x 10 reps and leg raises for 3 x 10 reps

An alternative is to take the above exercises and cycle them in a circuit. You would complete 10 reps of each of exercise or keep going for 30 seconds on each one for a full circuit, take a short rest and then repeat until 3 circuits have been completed.

PROGRESSION

Core muscles should be trained just like any other muscle group. Start with 1 or 2 sets of 10 reps and then progress to 3 or 4 sets before looking for ways to add weight or load the exercises.

Just as you wouldn't continue to train your legs using bodyweight only, follow the same rules of progression. Start low and then finds ways to add to the workload, making the exercises progressively more challenging.

HOW TO ACTIVATE YOUR GLUTES & WHY

In simple terms, glute activation is waking up your gluteal muscles (glutes) by getting your brain to send a "get fired up" message to the muscle group in preparation for a training session or match. Lack of activation generally results from a lack of activity – too much time spent sitting down – so it can become an issue for footballers who regularly sit in front of the TV when they're not training or playing.

THE IMPORTANCE OF STRONG GLUTES

One important role played by the glutes is hip extension, meaning any movement that involves your leg extending behind you. In football, this could be running, sprinting or bringing your leg back in preparation to strike a ball.

When your glutes are activated and firing properly, they add power to all of these movements (essentially unlocking a greater % of the potential power that you already have within you). However, when they don't fire as they should, not only is power lost but other muscles are recruited to compensate and take some of the load. This not only means that your power output is lower than it could be but also increases the risk of overuse injuries occurring in the muscles which are being recruited to compensate.

Glute strength not only affects movement around the hip joint, but also the lower back, knee and all the way down to the ankle. Without good strength and control in your glutes, you'll lack stability in all of these areas, again making you much more susceptible to injury.

TEST YOUR GLUTE STRENGTH

If your glute muscles are already weak, having them activated and fired-up is going to have limited impact on your performance. In this case you should place additional emphasis on glute strength training whilst also working on glute activation.

The simplest way to test your current glute strength is the double-leg glute bridge exercise.

- Lie on your back with your knees bent and feet flat on the floor
- Bring your heels in close enough to your backside to be able to reach them with your hands

- Lift your hips up from the floor by pushing down into your heels, creating a straight (diagonal) line from your knees down through your hips and shoulders to the floor
- Keep your knees in line with your hips (avoid letting them splay out or fall inwards) and focus on squeezing your glutes as you lift
- Hold the bridge position for 30 seconds
- If you have no difficulty holding the bridge, then your glute strength is at a decent level. If you do feel it excessively in your lower back, hamstrings or quads then this indicates glute weakness and highlights that these muscle groups are being recruited to compensate for a lack of glute strength

To improve your glute strength, work on building up to 20 reps of the double-leg glute bridge exercise with a squeeze-hold of 3 or 4 seconds at the top of the bridge position each time before lowering to the floor and repeating.

To progress the exercise, switch to the single-leg glute bridge. To do this, get into the double-leg bridge position as above and then lift one leg from the floor to hold the squeeze for 3 or 4 seconds before lowering to the floor to repeat, alternating the leg being lifted from the floor each time.

GLUTE ACTIVATION EXERCISES

Exercises to get your glutes fully activated and fired up should be done as part of your warm-up routine before training and matches. There are many exercises that target the glutes, but it's important to keep things football-specific and focus only on those that offer the greatest bang for their buck in terms of football performance and convenience.

The three gluteal muscles you're targeting are the gluteus maximus, gluteus medius and gluteus minimus.

GLUTE MAX

This muscle is involved in hip extension, but it really kicks into action when you're running and sprinting. To be able to power into a sprint and accelerate quickly, you need this muscle to be fully activated.

Activation exercise: Double-leg and single-leg glute bridge

GLUTE MED

This muscle is involved in stabilising your hip as you move, including running and kicking actions. Without full activation, other muscles groups will be recruited to take the strain, putting you at risk of picking up injuries.

Activation exercise: Clamshells, with or without a resistance band, or monster walk with a band around your ankles or knees.

CLAMSHELLS:

- Lie on your left side with your left arm under your head and both knees bent to around 90 degrees (right leg on top of left leg)
- Position your knees so that your feet are below your backside and in line with your hips
- Keeping your feet together, raise your right knee (mimicking a clamshell opening) as high as you can without your left hip rolling or your left knee lifting from the ground
- Hold the open clamshell position for 3 or 4 seconds at the top of the move and focus on squeezing your glute muscles
- Slowly lower your knee to the start position and repeat
- Complete 20 reps and then switch positions to repeat on the other side
- The clamshell exercise can be progressed by looping an exercise band around your thighs

MONSTER WALK:

- Loop an exercise band around your ankles (or just below your knees) so that tension can be felt when your feet are slightly beyond hip-width apart
- In a semi-squat position (around a 30-degree bend in your knees and hips) begin to "monster walk" around by stepping laterally right and left, keeping the tension on the band

GLUTE MIN

This muscle works along with the glute med to stabilise your hip, preventing your pelvis from dropping toward the opposite swinging leg when you're running. Lack of activation will once again lead to other muscles being used to compensate.

Activation exercise: Donkey kick-back

DONKEY KICK-BACK:

- Position yourself on the floor on your hands and knees, with your head in line with your spine, hands under your shoulders and knees under your hips
- With one leg, kick back (in the way a donkey might) and aim your foot towards the ceiling
- At the highest point of the kick, squeeze your glute muscles, making sure you maintain good posture in your stomach and back (neutral spine with no sagging) throughout each move
- Return to the start position and repeat, completing 20 reps on each leg

GLUTE ACTIVATION AND WARM-UPS

If you want to make sure your glutes are fully activated before a training session or match, pick 3 of the above exercises and work through them before getting into your normal dynamic warm-up routine. This is particularly important before a lower body training session in the gym to ensure that the lower back, hamstrings and quads won't be overcompensating if the glutes aren't firing as they should.

HOW TO INCREASE STRENGTH AROUND THE KNEES

Building strength around the knee involves developing strength in the main muscles and muscle groups supporting the movement of the joint. These are the quadriceps, hamstrings and the gastrocnemius (a muscle of the calf which crosses over the back of the knee.)

In terms of injury prevention, the most functional exercises can be split into 3 categories:

DOUBLE-LEG EXERCISES

Double-leg squats can be loaded with both dumbbells and barbells and performed as front squats or back squats. Double-leg deadlifts can be performed with either a barbell or trap bar.

These exercises are highly functional in terms of their cross over to football. Squats and deadlifts will help to develop maximal strength qualities that will transfer well to your running, jumping, cutting and sprinting performance.

SPLIT EXERCISES

Both static split squats and variations of lunges can be loaded with dumbbells or barbells. For a more dynamic option which will further test stability and movement mechanics, walking lunges are a perfect progression.

These exercises are great options for improving strength around your knees. The split position transfers well to running and for this reason, split exercises are slightly more functional than double-leg exercises for football (although it makes sense to ensure that you are proficient at the double-leg version of an exercise before progressing to a split stance variation).

TRUE SINGLE-LEG EXERCISES

Single-leg squats are very useful from an injury prevention point of view, helping to more clearly highlight strength imbalances between each leg and also reveal mobility or stability issues within the feet, ankles, knees, hips or lower back.

Single-leg deadlifts help to further stabilise the knee as the focus is on maintaining a position rather than creating movement around the knee.

Single leg exercises are considered the most difficult to perform well, many players will struggle to perform these exercises with quality even using only their bodyweight. For this reason, again it makes sense to utilise them only after you are capable of performing the double-leg and split stance variations well, however you could perform them with assistance to reduce the load (performing a single leg squat whilst holding onto a TRX for example is a great option.)

GYM MACHINES

Gym-based options such as leg extension, hamstring curl and leg press machines can also be useful in certain situations, if the focus is on hypertrophy (increasing muscle mass) for example or if an injury is preventing you from using free weights. The main disadvantage here is that gym-based machines increase the stability of the movement, which means you'll be able to lift a heavier weight with greater ease whilst not activating as many stabilising muscles to control the movement. This reduces the exercise' functionality for football, when you're on the pitch your stabilising muscles are constantly required to control movement and apply force.

To give a simple example, if your 1RM on the leg press machine is 150kg, your 1RM for a barbell back squat will be nowhere near this high. For this reason, it makes sense to use free weights in your everyday training as much as possible, and limit using gym-based machines to when you have no better alternative or you're testing maximal strength without a spotter.

DEVELOPING SYMMETRY

Single-leg exercises not only help to promote better balance and stability around the knee, but also better symmetry across the body. Developing equal strength in both legs is important, but it's also important to work on developing symmetry between opposing muscle groups such as the quads and hamstrings.

Research centred on ACL (anterior cruciate ligament) rehab has concluded that the closer your quads and hamstrings can be in terms of strength, the lower the risk of re-injury. It can be difficult to develop hamstring strength to match quad strength, so depending on the severity of your strength imbalance it could make sense to schedule some additional training time which is focused purely on increasing hamstring strength.

Trying to get both sides of your body to match across the board can go a long way in terms of lowering your risk of injury. Being able to play with both feet for example helps to ensure strength and stability is more closely matched within each leg. In players who are very one footed, it's often found that although the kicking leg is stronger, it's far less stable than the other leg. This is because the other leg is supporting the kicking leg every single time a ball is struck.

The kicking leg is missing out on all of this stability training if the opposite foot is never used in training and match play (and also partly explains poorer kicking performance in the first place when using the weaker foot, because there is a lack of balance throughout the kicking action, which then effects power and the quality of the connection made with the ball).

KEY POINT

It's also worth noting that the muscles surrounding your hip have an important role to play in helping to maintain the strength and stability of your knee. The gluteus medius is involved in externally rotating the hip and thereby keeping the knee in a good position when you run and land after a jump. Working on glute strength will assist the quads, hamstrings and gastrocnemius muscles in their knee support role. This ultimately outlines the importance of having a well-rounded programme which includes compound movements that work multiple muscle groups simultaneously.

THE BENEFITS OF TRAINING BAREFOOT

Barefoot training in the gym can help to strengthen the muscles in your feet, ankles and lower legs, which in turn helps to lower the risk of picking up injuries when playing football. This makes going barefoot a good thing, but care must be taken to train appropriately.

THE PROBLEM WITH SHOES

There are 26 bones, 33 joints and over 100 muscles, tendons and ligaments in each foot, all designed to keep us upright, support our weight and allow us to move.

The problem with shoes is that they lead to all of these structures being crammed into a small, generally tight-fitting space, severely limiting the natural flexing and bending movements needed for feet to do their job.

Try holding one of your football boots or trainers next to a bare foot to compare the difference in shape and you'll notice that your foot is much wider than the boot, especially in the toe box area at the front. This means your feet are being squeezed into a narrower shape than their natural form, making the joints much less mobile and restricting the movement of muscles, tendons and ligaments.

Boots, trainers and most other shoes you wear on a regular basis all change the shape of your feet and, over time, the changes can become permanent. So, in a nutshell, the more you wear shoes, the more your feet begin to adapt to the restricted space and the more difficult it becomes for your feet to do the job they were designed to do.

The narrow space and restricted movement can lead to weaknesses in the arches of your foot, the toes and around your ankles. This increases the potential to suffer injuries such as:

- Plantar fasciitis
- Shin splints
- Achilles tendonitis
- Knee pain

...when training and playing.

KEY POINT

In an ideal world, shoes would literally fit like a glove. A glove is shaped to fit around the fingers and the thumbs, but we expect our feet to mould into the shape of the shoes we're squeezing them into.

THE BENEFITS OF GOING BAREFOOT

Just like any other part of your body, your feet need to be exercised to stay strong. When they're being held tightly in place by shoes, they're unable to work through a full range of movement, which leads to weakness.

When you go barefoot, you give the muscles, tendons, ligaments and joints the freedom they need to function as nature intended. There's more space between your toes and the ball of your foot can spread as it connects with the ground, giving you a much wider base of support. This in turn can lead to improvements in balance, shock absorption and propulsion from the ground when running and jumping.

The efficiency of strength or power training sessions in the gym can also be improved by going barefoot. For footballers, this type of training involves putting as much force into the floor as possible. Training shoes with foam soles or other spongy materials absorb much of that force, making it difficult to push off the floor in exercises such as loaded squat jumps. Imagine trying to jump high from a crash matt and you'll understand the limitations of spongy soles. Similarly, if you were doing a series of jumps, a spongy sole would be aiding your ability to jump high as it absorbs force and then springs you into your next jump.

As mentioned, these types of soles aid in absorbing landing forces, this is great for a long-distance runner who wants to limit joint impact whilst out on a run, but as a footballer in the gym this is an opportunity to increase your body's natural ability to absorb force safely and efficiently which is being lost.

The relationship that your foot has with the ground is also vitally important when it comes to proprioception. This is your body's awareness of its position in relation to the ground upon contact. If for example you're running and place one foot partially into a pothole, proprioception enables your foot to quickly react, activating muscles and changing the position or posture of your body to protect you against injury. This split second of initial feedback which your foot receives from the ground could be the difference between continuing unscathed or tearing multiple ankle ligaments.

The sole of a shoe also acts as a barrier between your foot and the ground, delaying the time it takes for the message from the ground to reach your foot whilst also dumbing down that message once it's received. Yes, we're talking about a split second and fractional differences here, but that alone could make all the difference.

Of course, when you're playing in a match you can't play barefoot but at the same time the soles of football boots aren't as spongy as your everyday trainer (sneaker). So, it makes sense to find a balance between scheduling some barefoot time to reap the benefits outlined but also wear appropriate protective footwear depending on the situation.

TRAINING CONSIDERATIONS

Training barefoot in the gym brings with it all the benefits of doing foot-strengthening exercises without having to devote time to following a separate programme. With strong feet and ankles, you should be able to jog, sprint and perform strength training, plyometric and agility exercises without trainers, however you may need to progress to this in steady stages.

To get the most out of barefoot training, you must listen to your body. Without shoes, your feet and ankles are free to function as they were meant to, but if you're used to wearing shoes, it's going to take time for the weakened muscles, tendons and ligaments to adjust, adapt and strengthen. If going barefoot is causing you pain during training or afterwards, you need to back off and build up gradually by steadily increasing the amount of time spent barefoot each week.

If it's simply not possible for you to train barefoot in your gym, then wearing a minimalist shoe such as the Vibram five fingers is a great option (you still must be very careful around heavy weights with these on), or you could go to a matted area of the gym and work through a full dynamic warmup barefoot. This might include movements such as lunges, squats, single-leg deadlifts or similar, before putting your shoes back on.

If you're ready to start running barefoot, you should begin by using low volume, low intensity running, with the emphasis on learning to run more on the ball of your foot. Getting up on the ball of your foot as you run is more efficient when it comes to applying force and generating speed, whilst also ensuring stability with each step. The more your toes and the ball of your foot can spread naturally as your foot hits the ground, the wider your base of support and the less chance you have of going over on an ankle or twisting a knee.

KEY POINT

Barefoot running on a treadmill is not recommended. Make use of lightly padded gym floor space or indoor athletics tracks where possible. You could also run barefoot and do agility drills or grass in areas where you can be sure there are no sharp objects.

THE EFFECTS OF BAD POSTURE

Poor posture can be an indicator of over-tight or over-lengthened muscles, it's not the posture itself which is going to necessarily hinder your performance, it's what's going on beneath the surface. Over-tight or over-lengthened muscles, the imbalances which can result as well as the impact this could have on altering your movement mechanics can all put you at greater risk of injury.

SUB-OPTIMAL POSTURE

A common postural issue is anterior pelvic tilt or lower cross syndrome. In simple terms, this is the result of tight hip flexors and lengthened hamstrings causing your pelvis and hips to tilt forwards, also leading to weakness in your abdominal and trunk muscles. An athlete with this postural issue will often have an exaggerated curve in their lower back which in turn leads to a rounded appearance of the belly.

Sub-optimal posture won't necessarily affect your overall performance as a footballer and athletes in other sports demonstrate that it needn't be a barrier to elite performance. Usain Bolt is a good example. Images of him in action show evidence of anterior pelvic tilt, but this clearly didn't affect his ability to outperform all other sprinters at Olympic level.

Poor posture may not prevent you from playing well, but overly-tight or overly-lengthened muscles (which will negatively impact passive tissues such as tendons and ligaments) will put you at greater risk of injury. Common postural issues such as anterior pelvic tilt can be corrected with appropriate training, so taking the time to focus on making postural improvements may prevent time being lost to injuries further down the line.

KEY POINT

Sub-optimal posture may not affect your top performance, but it could limit you in other ways. In other words, it might not stop you from running fast, but it could put you at higher risk of picking up a hamstring injury when you do.

CHECK YOUR POSTURE

Stand in front of a mirror and look at the position of your shoulders in relation to the rest of your body. If they appear rounded (hunched forwards) and therefore out of line with the rest of your body, it suggests tightness in your pecs (pectoral muscles) and weakness in the lats (latissimus dorsi), traps (trapezius) and rhomboids. This can sometimes be the result of overcoing the bench-press exercise. To a certain degree, this may not be an issue, but in extreme cases it's going to put you at greater risk of injury which will then impact your performance

Next, check the position of your hips. If your pelvis is tilted forwards, creating an exaggerated curve in your lower back that makes your belly stick out, it could indicate tight hip flexors and overly-lengthened hamstrings. Again, this puts you at greater risk of picking up injuries in training and matches.

The bottom line is that the effect of posture on football performance may be minimal, but noticeable issues shouldn't be ignored when corrections that could lower the risk of injury can be made.

HOW TO IMPROVE YOUR BALANCE

Your centre of gravity (COG) is a hypothetical point around which your weight is centred to help you maintain your balance. In theory, this is going to be around your belly button if you're standing still in an upright position. Of course, in football, you're not standing still, you're moving, so the COG is constantly changing.

Another factor that can affect the location of the COG is your height, but in terms of balance, it's your base of support (BOS) that determines how stable you are. To use extreme examples, a tall person with a narrow base of support is going to be less stable than a short person with a wide base of support, but whatever height you are, it's maintaining a low athletic stance which helps to improve your stability as a player. This involves placing your feet wider than hip-width apart and keeping your hips and knees flexed.

KEY POINT

A good example of a low athletic stance can be seen in tennis players as they wait for their opponent to serve. From this stance, you can produce powerful movements and move quickly and efficiently without losing your balance.

EXERCISES FOR BALANCE AND STABILITY

If you feel you lack balance, you need to do two things:

- Single-leg stability and strength work
- Core stability and strengthening work

Good examples of single-leg stability exercises are single-leg squats and single-leg deadlifts. These exercises can be done with resistance, but dynamic exercises such as hop and holds over hurdles, or continuous hops travelling forwards, backwards and laterally are also useful.

HOP AND HOLD:

- Using your right or left leg, hop forwards and hold the landing position for 3 or 4 seconds

- Keep the landing knee bent and aim to stay low and balanced as you hold the landing position
- Hop again, changing direction to move backwards or to the side
- Build up to 10 hops on one leg, then repeat using the other leg, aiming to complete 3-5 sets in total

With practice, you will become more stable in a low hold position on each leg, resulting in improved balance in a low athletic stance.

CORE STRENGTHENING EXERCISES

If you're a taller, less stable player, you're going to be dealing with higher rotational forces when you're making quick changes of direction on the pitch. Working on being able to resist these forces by strengthening your core will help to improve your balance and stability.

KEY POINT

To improve your stability as a player, you need to work on:

- Achieving a wider base of support
- Maintaining your balance in a low position on one leg
- Strengthening your core to be able to resist rotation

TRANSFER TO FOOTBALL

Better balance brings with it a reduced risk of developing injuries and the above exercises will help you to develop qualities that transfer well to football. As well as developing better stability around your COG, you'll be able to make faster changes of direction, remain balanced as you turn and more efficient at powering out in a new direction. By being able to resist the rotational forces, you not only improve your turning speed, but also your ability to hold your ground when being tackled.

IMPROVING YOUR GAME

Football commentators often refer to Messi's low centre of gravity when he's demonstrating speed and skill on the pitch, but it's important to realise that his short stature and therefore lower COG is not the be-all-and-end-all in terms of his abilities as a player. Messi is a skilled player because he practices those skills. Lowering your COG will not automatically improve your game unless you're putting in the practice needed to improve every element of your game.

THE BENEFITS OF TRAINING ON UNSTABLE SURFACES

Unstable surfaces can be provided by balance cushions, BOSU balance trainers, or anything that's less stable than flat ground. It's a strategy commonly used in a rehab setting but the benefits can extend into other aspects of football conditioning. The main areas targeted when training on unstable surfaces are the feet, ankles, knees, hips and lower back. Improving stability and mobility in these areas can help to limit the potential for injuries to occur and improve force production and application.

Because they're all connected in a chain, weakness in one joint can lead to issues within another. For example, pain in the knees during movement due to a lack of stability in the knee joint could directly relate to tightness at the ankles and hips. Therefore, if we can improve mobility at the ankles and hips and improve knee stability, then we can lower the stress placed upon the knee and ensure it remains within its optimal range of movement. Tightness at the ankles and hips combined with instability at the knee could result in the knee collapsing inwards upon a landing in an effort to absorb force, this inward tracking of the knee is common in ACL injuries.

Think of the joints of the body as layers of stability and mobility, helping to produce and absorb force. The joints of the feet allow stability, the ankles provide mobility, the knees supply stability, the hips provide mobility, the lower back provides stability and the mid to upper back gives mobility. Using this simple guideline, we can see how an issue in one area can directly impact another in the chain.

BEYOND REHAB

In a rehab setting, unstable surface exercises can form the bulk of a session, but there's also much to be gained from including these exercises in a non-rehab training programme as part of a warm-up or in movement preparation work.

Studies have shown that only 60% of the force you can produce on solid ground can be achieved on an unstable surface. For this reason, if you're aiming to build strength and power using exercises such as barbell squats jumps, you should remain on stable ground. However, this doesn't mean to say that unstable surfaces can't be utilised to aid subsequent power performance.

"You can't fire a cannon from a canoe."

You can't fire a cannon from a canoe is an expression that can be applied here. Out on the pitch there is less emphasis on your combined leg strength and power because running is essentially a single-leg exercise.

If you watch a 100-metre sprinter in slow-motion, it becomes clear that only one leg at a time is in contact with the ground. So, to improve your running speeds, you should aim to be just as strong, powerful and stable on one leg as you are on two. Increasing your single leg stability can therefore enable you to apply more force to the ground every time your foot comes into contact with it, it will also enable you to change direction more explosively too.

If you lack single leg stability, in effect you're trying to "fire a cannon from a canoe" every time you attempt to powerfully push-off into a new movement. In other words, you're unable to fully utilise the strength and power you possess within that limb and transfer it into faster sprinting, turning and dodging movements.

KEY POINT

Training on unstable surfaces can be useful at every stage of training, you don't need to have had an injury to benefit. It can help to:

- Increase muscle activation and the recruitment of stabilising muscles (increases production and betters the application of that force)
- Build greater resilience to injury (through enhanced joint stability and proprioception)
- Enable greater control in your movements

HOW TO INCREASE SHOT POWER

To work on increasing your shot power, you need to work on each component and movement involved in producing a powerful shot. These are balance and stability, knee extension and hip flexion.

BALANCE AND STABILITY

The first thing we need to address is the stability of the leg you're standing on when taking a shot. For example, if you're right-footed, you need to plant your left leg and it needs to be stable to help you keep your balance as you swing your right leg.

Without balance and stability, you're unable to produce the force needed to strike the ball with power.

Static balance exercises can help:

- Stand on one leg with a slight bend in the knee
- Aim to hold your balance for 30 seconds and work towards a full minute
- Progress the exercise by doing it with your eyes closed or throwing and catching a ball as you balance

Once you're able to balance on each leg for 30 seconds to 1 minute, add some ball work to the exercise. For example, if you're a right-footed striker of the ball, a good drill would be to volley a ball back to a teammate with your right foot (keeping it off the ground) while you balance on your left foot, continue volleying for a set number of kicks or length of time.

This is great for balance, with the additional bonus of it being football specific.

KNEE EXTENSION

Knee extension is straightening your leg, so it takes a strong, forceful knee extension to be able to strike a ball with great force.

Improving your quad strength will help you to produce a more powerful strike of the ball. Double-leg exercises such as squats and deadlifts can be used to build quad strength, as can single-leg supported exercises such as split squats and lunges or any variation that involves stepping forward onto one leg and then pushing back as powerfully as you can.

The leg extension machine in the gym is another option. Not all strength and conditioning coaches favour leg extensions as some believe it's not a functional movement. However, the angle of the knee in this exercise is able to mimic the angle of your knee when taking a shot, so there's strong potential for a cross-over into developing a stronger, more powerful strike.

ADDING SPEED TO KNEE EXTENSION

The next step after increasing the force which each of the muscles involved in kicking can apply is to add speed to the movement, that combination of increased strength and increased speed leads to increased shot power.

This can be achieved using free-weight exercises such as box squats, where you descend slowly to the box and then power back out of the squat position at speed to return to a standing position. However, for more advanced athletes in the gym, adding accommodating resistance can be useful. In squats or deadlifts for example, adding chains or bands to the bar will make the exercise easier towards the bottom of the movement and then harder towards the top. This can help to produce more power than regular lifts by removing the need to decelerate at the top.

Using regular back squats as an example, there's a need to slow down towards the top of the movement to avoid finishing with a jump. With accommodating resistance however, you can power up from the bottom to the top at speed without the need to slow down.

KEY POINT

Accommodating resistance exercises should only be used once you have a good base of strength and power. If you can back squat 1.5 x your bodyweight, you'll benefit from using accommodating resistance in training.

HIP FLEXION

Bringing your knee up to your chest is a movement that demonstrates hip flexion. One training option is to use a hip flexion machine, but a more accessible exercise is to use a short, looped resistance band.

- Loop the band under your left foot to stand on it and put your right foot inside it
- Lift your right knee as high as you can against the resistance of the band

This exercise should be done with a light band initially to master the movement and control your balance. Increasing the resistance with a stronger band will then help to build strength.

The next progression is to return to a lighter band and add speed to the lifts, using a running arm movement to help maintain balance and rhythm as you develop power in the moves.

Hip flexor and groin pain can be an issue for footballers, so begin with a light band for no more than 2 or 3 sets of 5 reps. If you're pain free, progress to a stronger band and gradually increase the reps to 10 or 15. When you then begin working on speed, return to a lighter band and around 5 reps per set.

SHOOTING PRACTICE

Working on stability, balance, knee extension and hip flexion will help to increase your shot strength, but shooting practice is equally as important. If you want to improve your shot strength, you need to practice striking the ball with a good connection and with as much force as possible. To increase stability throughout the movement further, try tensing your stomach as you strike the ball, you'll be amazed at the difference such a simple strategy can make on your striking power and quality.

Hard striking of the ball should be treated as a power exercise and should only be done following a thorough warm up. Power training, such as sprinting, requires extended rest periods and shooting practice should be no different. It makes sense to go for quality rather than quantity to avoid fatigue limiting your performance, therefore every shot should be as strong as possible with rest scheduled between each strike.

Imagine it in terms of percentage, if you can kick a ball at 100% maximum power, there's no point practicing kicks that only equate to 75% of your maximal power due to fatigue.

Shoot, go and get the ball, relax a minute and then take another shot. If you limit the number of shots you take to no more than 5 and take a rest of 30 seconds to a minute between them, you're going to get closer to maximal power and you'll get more speed on the ball.

HOW TO INCREASE THROW-IN LENGTH

If you want to be the next Rory Delap, able to throw the ball distances of 30 to 40 metres at speeds of 60 kph (37 mph) with every throw, you need to practice your throw-in technique regularly. If you don't have time to make it a stand-alone session each week, you need to at least include throw-in practice somewhere within your existing training, going for maximum distance with every throw.

INCREASING LOWER-BODY POWER

It goes without saying that your upper-body is involved in a throw-in and you're going to be releasing the ball with your hands, but a lot of the strength and force that goes into a throw is produced by the lower-body muscles and transferred through your trunk to the upper-body muscles.

Rory Delap was a champion javelin thrower in his school days and just as a javelin thrower works on lower-body strength and power to maximise their throwing ability, the same can be applied to a footballer working on increasing their throw-in length.

Two ways to develop lower-body power for throw-ins are:

SPLIT SQUATS AND LUNGES

By making squats and lunges dynamic instead of static exercises, it's possible to mimic the run-up element of a throw-in, so they become transferrable to moves used in football. Simply travel forwards with each lunge step instead of staying in one spot.

DOUBLE-LEG AND SINGLE-LEG BOX JUMPS

Training for power with double-leg and single-leg box jump exercises can help in terms of being able to produce force quickly. The increase in force will transfer through the trunk to the upper-body, thereby helping to increase throw-in length.

MEDICINE BALL THROWS

Specific throwing exercises using medicine balls can be utilised once a good base of full body strength and power has been developed.

Overhead med ball throws can be progressed in 3 stages:

1. Begin with both knees on the floor (kneeling position) and throw the medicine ball as powerfully as possible into empty space or at a wall. This position will limit the involvement of the lower body, but it's a good starting point to perfect the throwing action of the arms whilst further engaging the muscles of the trunk to stabilise the movement. A medicine ball of 1kg to 3kgs is heavy enough, you don't want to change what the throwing action looks like. Focus on throwing as hard as you can for 2 or 3 sets of 5 reps
2. Progress to a half-kneeling position
3. Progress to a standing position, then include a run-up

KEY POINT

The biggest mistake made with med ball exercises is not throwing with maximum intent. Just as running slowly will not help develop your sprinting speed, throwing softly or slowly will not help you to throw a ball harder, faster or further. Every throw must be performed with maximal intent, which means ensuring enough recovery time between each set of throws so that fatigue doesn't hinder your power output.

HOW TO HAVE MORE POWERFUL HEADERS

The most effective way to improve your heading strength is simply to practice heading a ball with power and precision. Working on exercises in the gym may assist the neck strengthening process, but regularly practicing the skill of heading the ball before or after training is always going to be the most useful and effective way to get stronger and better at doing it.

NECK STRENGTHENING EXERCISES

There are limited options available in terms of specialist equipment for training the neck muscles, but there are some simple exercises which can help. These include neck isometrics and band or cable exercises.

Training your neck muscles in isolation is not something you're likely to be well-practiced at compared to training other muscle groups, but the same training principles apply. Begin with controlled movements using light resistance and high reps, as the strength and size of the targeted muscles increases, you'll move to progressively heavier loads using lower reps of 5 or less. The next stage is to build power by decreasing the load and adding speed to each movement, aiming to mimic the movement patterns used when heading a ball.

NECK ISOMETRICS

This type of training is used in rugby to minimise the risk of concussion, but it transfers well to heading in football.

In a seated or standing position, get someone to put their hand on your forehead. As you try to move your head, they will resist the movement to create an isometric exercise. Movements include:

- Try to move your head so that your chin drops down and in to create a double-chin effect
- Try to get your ear to drop towards the shoulder on the same side
- Try to move your head backwards so that your chin lifts and your head tilts towards your spine.

The hand on your forehead should resist these movements for 5 seconds each time, giving you a 5 second rep. You can begin with 3 sets of 5 reps, keep each rep at 5 seconds and add variety by using different movements in each set. Build up to 3 sets of 10 reps.

BANDED OR CABLE EXERCISES

Using isometric exercises to work your neck in all directions will strengthen the muscles. When you become well-practiced, you can progress to banded or cable exercises.

Working on cervical spine flexion (the movement of tucking your chin in and angling your forehead towards the floor) is going to provide the biggest transfer over to heading performance.

In boxing, there's a specialised piece of equipment that's used to develop neck strength which can help in resisting blows to the head. A strap goes over the head from which a weight can be suspended. Then, lying on your back on a physio or weights bench, position yourself so that the weight is dangling over the edge.

Allow the weight to take your head back as far as you comfortably can without causing pain, then slowly resist the load to bring your chin in towards your chest. Although this is used in boxing training, it's essentially training the same muscles used in the heading movement but with an external load. This can also be replicated in an upright position by using an anchored resistance band or a specialised attachment on a cable machine.

KEY POINT

When working on neck strength, the trap muscles (trapezius) can try to take over. If they're taking the load they may become tight, so it's important to find ways to release any muscle tension to avoid injury (such as self-massage using a tennis ball against a wall or a massage gun).

For each of the above exercises, ensure that your set up is safe and always begin with very light loads, progressing slowly and in small increments to avoid injury.

SHOULD FOOTBALLERS USE OLYMPIC LIFTS?

It's common to see weightlifters in the gym working on Olympic lifts, but these lifts are rarely included in weight training programmes for footballers. Olympic lifts develop lower body power (an element of fitness that's crucial for elite performance in football) so does that mean you should include them in your programme?

The short answer is no and this is for two main reasons:

1. Olympic lifts are complex to learn
2. There are numerous simpler alternatives

COMPLEXITY AND SAFETY

Olympic lifting is a sport in itself and it takes a huge amount of time to become technically proficient enough to fully reap the training benefits. The lifts themselves are not inherently dangerous, but the complexity of the movements required makes injury an ongoing concern in athletes who have not yet mastered them.

The need to focus on technique also makes it difficult to use Olympic lifts in a group training environment. A strength and conditioning coach might have 25 players coming into the gym on the first day of pre-season and with it taking anything from 8 weeks to 3 months to gain even a basic level of competency in most lifts, they'd find themselves well into the season without having gained much in terms of improving football performance.

KEY POINT

There's a risk of injury if the lifts are not performed with correct form and not all footballers have the level of mobility required to achieve correct form.

ALTERNATIVE EXERCISES

Olympic lifting can be a useful lower-body power training tool, helping to develop aggressive triple extension in the ankle, knee and hip. This is a key element of sprinting and jumping performance in football, but there are numerous alternative exercise options capable of achieving the same outcome without the need to master complex techniques.

These include:

- Loaded jumps using dumbbells, a trap bar or a barbell, jump up as high as you can from a bent-knee starting position. It's easy to load these exercises and it's a simple way to focus on producing maximum force without any technical issues to complicate things
- Medicine ball throws: hold a medicine ball in both hands and then bend your knees to lower it towards the ground before jumping up as forcefully as you can to throw it up into the air. Another bonus of this simple exercise is that it can be done pitch-side

These exercises help to develop aggressive triple extension in the same way as an Olympic lift would and they can be safely used by players who lack the mobility to get into a deep squat position. They're simple to learn (so they can be done from the first day of training) and they provide the benefits you're looking for without increasing the risk of getting injured.

Olympic lifts can have their place, but for football, alternative exercises produce the same power gains without lengthy teaching times or heightened injury risk.

BLOOD FLOW RESTRICTION (BFR) TRAINING: CAN YOU BENEFIT?

The concept of BFR training is that by restricting venous blood flow (the return of blood to the heart), some of the mechanisms believed to be involved in hypertrophy (muscle growth) can be stimulated and exaggerated so that growth can be triggered without the need to lift heavy loads.

HOW IT WORKS

It's done by wearing a restrictive wrap around the upper portion of a limb. Ideally it would be a specialised BFR training cuff-like device that can precisely measure the pressure being applied. The wrap is tightened to allow arterial blood flow to be maintained (allowing oxygenated blood to continue to flow to the muscles) but whilst simultaneously restricting the return of blood to the heart. This has a blood "pooling" effect.

WHY IT WORKS

The pooling of the blood causes a build-up of waste products such as lactic acid, this promotes a hormonal response which stimulates muscle growth. The body is also "tricked" into believing the muscles are working much harder than they actually are, so its natural adaptation response is to build more muscle to cope with the increased workload.

THE BENEFIT OF BFR

The benefit of BFR training is the ability to make effective gains in muscle growth without the arduous task of lifting heavy weights. For example, instead of lifting 70% of your 1RM (one rep max), you can lift 20-30% of your 1RM and hopefully create the conditions for roughly the same amount of hypertrophy to occur. This can make a big difference in your training loads, especially when your programme includes multiple elements of fitness which need to be trained.

BFR IN YOUR TRAINING PROGRAMME

Achieving muscle growth with lower weight loads holds an obvious attraction for bodybuilders dealing with fatigue, but for footballers, BFR can only really be utilised during an intense pre-season period or in a rehab setting (to increase muscle mass and then strength without having to put the previously injured area under a big load).

During the season, the central aim of strength training is to maintain the strength and power you've developed in the prior pre-season to ensure peak performance. Certain elements of fitness must be prioritised over others during the season to allow for enough recovery time and in order minimise injury risk and be fresh for matches. Of course, if you wanted to add muscle mass during the season then BFR could help you to do that whilst minimising the training load, however this is training time that could probably be better utilised.

BFR IN REHAB

BFR training has become a regular feature in the rehab world. If you're rehabbing an injury, getting back to the workloads you were accustomed to pre-injury can take a long time as you need to build-up very gradually. Using BFR, you're effectively able to jump straight back into building muscle using lighter loads, thereby limiting the amount of muscle you lose.

Is BFR beneficial in football training? There are benefits in a rehab setting and it can be useful in pre-season training to reduce muscular workload whilst still achieving a degree of hypertrophy, however, for most players who follow a well-planned out programme, BFR training does not need to be utilised.

WHY YOUR PERFORMANCES PLATEAU

Your performance can hit a plateau in many ways. If you have plateaued, you'll notice that the gains you've been making in training have halted. Maybe you've been making steady progress in terms of weight increments in the gym or sprint speed on the pitch and now you seem to have hit a glass ceiling. Or perhaps you're just not feeling as sharp on the pitch or as strong and powerful in the gym as you normally do. Performances plateau for different reasons but pinpointing the cause may lead to a quick and easy fix. The main causes are generally:

- Over-training
- Inadequate sleep, nutrition and recovery
- Psychological stress

OVER-TRAINING

The first thing to look at is your workload. Let's say you're playing Tuesday and Saturday (and have to travel a long way to matches), training with the team three times per week and also scheduling strength-based gym sessions. Sudden spikes in workload without careful consideration can cause a lot of stress to your body and even lead to illness.

If this resonates with you, the simplest solution is to be smart and reduce your workload until you return to feeling energetic and healthy, especially during the season. Begin by taking the least important activities out of your weekly schedule. Of course, the most important ones are always your team matches and training sessions.

KEY POINT

If you think overtraining may be the cause of your performance plateau, make sure you have at least one, ideally two rest days each week and consider ways to reduce your workload without negatively affecting your overall performance. During the competition period when you're playing lots of games, it comes down to doing the minimum amount of work to get the maximum amount of gains. This is also referred to as the minimum effective dose.

INADEQUATE SLEEP, NUTRITION AND RECOVERY

If the above doesn't apply to you and your workload is appropriate, your performance plateau could be the result of inadequate sleep, poor nutrition, or a lack of recovery time after games or training.

SLEEP

The general advice is to aim for an 8-hour sleep every night, but anything from 7 and a half up to 10 hours could be the right amount for you. Sleeping for 10 hours might be a luxury you can't justify, however, getting as much sleep as you can is going to lead to feeling better in training and matches.

NUTRITION

Having sufficient protein and carbohydrates in your daily diet will also have a positive impact on your performance. As a general guide, this should be 2g of protein per kg of bodyweight and 4g-5g of carbohydrate per kg of bodyweight per day (although you may eat less on rest days).

RECOVERY

Maintaining flexibility, tissue quality and joint mobility is essential in terms of boosting recovery and staying injury free. Foam rolling and stretching are the most effective strategies to use and any tight areas should be released consistently to keep you performing at your best. Being able to sit into a deep squat position comfortably is a good indicator of having the flexibility and mobility required to move well on the pitch.

PSYCHOLOGICAL SOURCES

When you're training in the gym, the weights, reps and sets in your programme make it easy to identify a progression or regression in your body's condition. If you notice that you're no longer making gains or you're not able to lift as much as you did in the previous week, you have a clear indication of a performance plateau or dip. As mentioned, in gym training it's simple to measure and monitor your performance objectively, but monitoring your performance in a football training session becomes much more subjective.

With objective measures, a dip in progress lets you know that you need to pull back somewhere in your training schedule and reduce your workload, but when measures are subjective, it's harder to evaluate your performance and know whether you've really plateaued. One way to help with this is to use the RPE scale (rate of perceived exertion), it's a simple 0-10 scoring system where you give the perceived intensity of your session a score, we outline how to use this in both our testing guide and true tracking system. You can then combine your RPE score with the number of training minutes to give an overall training units score. For example, if you had just finished a training session which was 60 minutes long and you perceived the intensity to be a 7/10 (very hard), then your training units for that session would be 60 x 7 = 420.

AVOIDING IN-SEASON PLATEAUS

Hitting a plateau in training is a normal part of your body's adaptation process. Gradually increasing the workload in steady increments and allowing appropriate recovery between sessions promotes steady improvements, however, it's natural to plateau at times when your body needs additional time to adapt to new stresses.

Athletes in all sports hit performance plateaus at some stage in training and in competition. Olympic sprinters might achieve a PB in one race, but they're not going to keep on improving on that PB in every race that follows. Olympic weightlifters might lift a new WR weight in one round, but they're not going to keep on breaking that record in every consecutive round. Plateaus occur and by following a progressive training plan and continually monitoring yourself, further improvements will be achieved over time.

As a player, reaching peak fitness for crucial games and avoiding in-season plateaus is important. The most important games tend to come towards the end of the season when teams are chasing cup finals or trying to avoid relegation, so improving in pre-season and then maintaining your performance levels throughout the season is key. Plateauing when you're in the form of your life is one thing, but experiencing a dip in your performance mid-season is another.

KEY POINTS:

- Monitor your progress objectively in the gym
- Monitor your progress subjectively in football training
- Make sure you're doing everything in your power to optimise your performance at every stage by sleeping well, eating well and boosting recovery by maintaining your flexibility, tissue quality and joint mobility

HOW TO AVOID TRAINING INTERFERENCE

Interference describes the potential negative effect of attempting to train multiple elements of fitness at the same time.

In football, you need stamina to stay out on the pitch for 90 minutes and you also need speed to keep up with the game and make an impact. You need both stamina and speed, but the training required to improve each of these elements is very different.

Training for stamina usually involves using a combination of low, medium and high intensity actions and movements with the aim being able to sustain these efforts over time. Training for speed, on the other hand, involves short, fast-paced sprinting to develop fast-twitch muscle fibres and improve the phosphagen and glycolytic energy systems.

The two interfere with each other if trained at the same time. If you're doing a lot of stamina training, your energy and nervous systems are going to be taxed, inhibiting your ability to produce maximal sprint speeds.

An extreme example would be an Olympic athlete trying to train to win both the 100m and the marathon at the same time. Their marathon training would be inhibiting their potential to become a faster sprinter and vice versa. They are two different qualities which must be developed separately from one another if progress is desired.

As a result, this athlete is likely to become average at both and world class at neither, despite having the potential to be world class. Of course, during the season, the goal shifts to simply needing to maintain the gains made during pre-season. This is why you will often see teams combining many different elements of training into one session during the season.Linear Periodisation

It goes without saying that footballers need a combination of all elements of fitness in order to be effective on the pitch, which is why things can become puzzling. So how can somebody like Ronaldo display incredible levels of speed, stamina and strength all at the same time?

The truth is that to become an elite football athlete like Ronaldo, it takes years if not decades. It's a repeated cycle of producing the right stimulus and allowing enough recovery time (combined with optimal nutrition) for adaptations and progress to occur. You cannot speed up time, but what you can do is ensure you're training in the most optimal way (and not wasting precious time).

The order in which you train various elements must make sense. For example, in gym training, the common order would be to train for hypertrophy first and then strength. With hypertrophy training you would be increasing your muscle mass, which would then enable you to lift a greater load in the strength phase. Increased strength means a greater ability to produce force, so after the strength training phase you'd move onto power training, learning how to apply that force at an increased speed i.e. explosiveness.

You train one thing which makes the next thing better and then you train the next thing because it makes the thing after that better. This is known as linear periodisation or block periodisation.

STRUCTURE YOUR SEASON

You're always going to get better long-term gains when you concentrate on one element of fitness at a time and combine that with complimentary elements.

There are some fitness elements that can be trained for at the same time. For example, sprint training works well alongside power training in the gym and muscular endurance training goes well with stamina training on the pitch. Categorising your training into field-based or gym-based in this way can help to identify elements that will complement each other.

Planning which elements of fitness are most important for each period of the season allows you to structure your training in a way that makes sense and linear periodisation makes it possible to improve as a player with each block of training potentiating the next block, building on existing gains to create further improvements.

FILLING YOUR GLASS

Avoid overfilling your glass by putting too many fitness elements in there all at once. Add one element at a time and consider the most beneficial order to pour them in.

KEY PRINCIPLES OF PRE-SEASON TRAINING

Whether to ease into pre-season training or go hard from day one is a question many players ask.

If you rush into pre-season training, either by launching into intense training straight away or by giving yourself too short a period of preparation time, your injury risk is going to be higher.

TRAINING LOAD

Training load is the term used to quantify the amount of work you're doing in a session or over the course of a week. Dr Tim Gabbett has carried out extensive research on the topic and his acute:chronic ratio is now widely used in a variety of sports to help athletes achieve peak fitness without increasing the risk of injury.

The current week's workload is your acute load and the workload of the previous four weeks is your chronic load. If the acute load is 1.4 times greater (or more) than the average week of the chronic load, the risk of injury increases significantly. For example, let's say that over the last 4 weeks your workloads have been 100, 120, 130 and 135. Add these together and divide by 4 to get your average chronic load of 121.25. This means that if this week's workload goes above 1.4 x 121.25 (169.75) then your risk of injury will greatly increase.

KEY POINT

If you go straight from being on holiday or doing nothing into a high training load, the spike in workload increases your potential to pick up injuries. It's simply a matter of adhering to the tried-and-tested principle of progressive overload. Gradually increasing the difficulty of an exercise leads to gradual improvements as the body adapts to cope with the increase in workload.

ADAPTATION TIME

Changes and improvements in physical qualities can't take place overnight. One huge session in the gym won't trigger the body into producing hypertrophy, it takes repeated efforts with progressive loads to bring about adaptation and muscle growth.

During pre-season, you're training multiple elements of fitness at the same time. It may take only a few speed sessions to refine your technique and make improvements in terms of sprint performance, but training for lasting hypertrophy is going to be a longer process.

In beginners, strength gains are primarily from neural gains rather than actual muscle growth. Gains in muscle mass become noticeable at around 8 to 10 weeks into a progressive programme, so this gives an indication of the time frame needed in pre-season to make improvements that will transfer into performance gains out on the pitch.

KEY POINT

Adding muscle or improving strength is not something you can do with just two weeks of pre-season. You might be able to get a bit of a "pump" on, but the transfer of this to improvements on the pitch will be limited.

PROGRESSIVE OVERLOAD

Easing into pre-season training is going to give you maximum benefits with minimum risk of injury. A sensible time frame to allow is 10 weeks, essentially giving you time to rest at the end of one season and then gradually return to peak fitness for the next season. Allowing time to follow a progressively overloaded programme will ensure you make the improvements that will boost your performance in training and matches and stay injury free. In terms of preparing for the football season ahead, slow cooking wins over microwaving every time.

STRENGTH TRAINING DURING THE SEASON

At the highest level, strength training during the season is an essential component which builds towards success at the business end of the season. As we've outlined previously, strength is a key factor in athletic performance due to:

1. Greater ability to apply force which then leads to the potential to become more powerful and explosive
2. Reducing overuse injuries by as much as 50%
3. Greater strength levels lead to greater movement economy. Each step you take is less of a % of the force you can produce and therefore increased strength can improve endurance

The primary goal of strength training during the season is to maintain the gains which have been made during the off/pre-season, without creating additional muscle soreness and fatigue.

The key to making strength work simple in-season is to keep the intensity high (heavy loads of up to 80% 1RM) and volume low (2 sets of 6-10 reps for example). With this in mind, the concept of micro-dosing can be extremely useful. Micro-dosing is simply applying a stimulus that is big enough to produce a positive adaptation while at the same time being small enough to avoid negative effects such as muscle soreness and fatigue.

We advise following a structured programme rather than performing random strength sessions throughout the season. This way each strength session:

1. Directly relates to previous and future strength sessions
2. Is programmed in relation to other aspects of your in-season training for the week (such as speed or stamina)
3. Is part of a bigger plan which ensures that all planes of movement are being addressed over time

When it comes to scheduling, if you play one game per week on Saturday's, you could structure your week as follows:

- Monday: Light field session and injury prevention

- Tuesday: Intense field session and strength or strength-speed training
- Wednesday: Off
- Thursday: Light field session and speed-strength or speed training
- Friday: Light field session
- Saturday: Match Day
- Sunday: Day off/Active Recovery

KEY POINT

Maintaining your strength throughout the season is crucial to ensuring high levels of performance, resilience to injury and protecting the strength and power gains which have been made during the off season. Don't swerve the strength sessions during the season if you want to be lifting silverware at the end of it, however in the same breath don't go overboard and risk creating unwanted soreness and fatigue which could leave you feeling stiff and sluggish come match day. Remember the importance of scheduling enough recovery time and eating well.

HOW TO TRAIN STAMINA IN A FOOTBALL SPECIFIC WAY

In terms of stamina training for football, it's important to train for the pace of the game rather than the length of the game. A game is 90 minutes long, so it goes without saying that you need an appropriate level of endurance, but being able to run for 90 minutes is not necessarily a match for the demands of 90 minutes of football.

Running and reacting faster than your opponents will always have more impact than simply running further. In fact, the ability to repeat bursts of speed is a strong differentiator between Premier League and Championship players. Maximum velocity work also has an important role to play in conditioning the hamstrings to not only unlock greater levels of speed but also become more resilient to injury.

Football is an intermittent sport. It's all about repeated bouts of short duration exercise interspersed with long periods of active and passive recovery. There will be intense actions, then the ball might go out for a throw-in and you get 5 seconds of standing still or walking to a position.

In those periods of intense action you're not simply running in straight lines, you're running in curves, rapidly accelerating and decelerating into short sprints and quick turns (a midfielder can make up to 1000 turns in a game) and there will be jumping, kicking and tackling...it's far from a 90-minute steady run.

KEY POINT

In football, the brief periods of intense action are essential to the outcome of the game. Generally, low intensity actions won't affect the final score, but brief, high intensity actions will.

SPORT SPECIFIC TRAINING

In terms of football fitness, training using long distance running will bring little benefit other than perhaps aiding recovery between those periods of intense action. The average length of a sprint in football is 17 metres, with players in fullback positions perhaps sprinting up to 30 metres to assist with overlaps for example. This indicates that your main focus in training should be on producing repeated short bursts of sprint speed.

INCREASE SPEED

One way to do this is to work on increasing your top speed, so that it becomes easier to repeat absolute speeds. For example, if your top speed is 9 metres per second, then sprinting 7 metres per second in repeated bouts with quick changes of direction should be possible.

If you think of it in weight training terms, being able to bench press 100kgs will make it easier to increase the number of reps you can produce with 80kgs and the same training principle applies to running.

INTRODUCE THE BALL

The ball should only be introduced into pace training once you've successfully increased your top speed and improved your ability to produce repeated high intensity efforts. This could be done by keeping a ball at your feet in only some of your runs and adding in a passing and shooting element too. For example, you could make a quick change of direction, sprint towards the goal, take a shot (partner setting up the ball) and then continue with your next high intensity effort.

It's important to strike a balance between physical training and technical training, ensuring that one doesn't negatively impact the other. Physical training will improve the efficiency of the phosphagen and glycolytic energy systems, but if you reach a point of fatigue, your technical ability might suffer, leading to bad habits creeping in. Practice makes perfect, but if you practice doing something badly, you get better and better at doing that something badly. Train to increase your top speed and to produce repeated efforts of speed and only introduce the ball if it's not going to limit what you gain from the drills.

IS THE 5KM TEST RELEVANT TO FOOTBALL?

5km runs predominately challenge the aerobic energy system, which of course is an important element of football fitness. This however does not make the 5km test a good choice for footballers when it comes to indicating levels of performance. As outlined above, football is multi-directional in nature and demands the ability to repeat intermittent bouts of high-speed running over short distances without a significant drop off in the speed of those runs across the 90+ minutes of a match.

Given that a 5km run is not multi-directional, is steady state and taxes predominately only one energy system, it's effectiveness in predicting football performance is extremely limited. i.e. you could get a great 5km test score, but that doesn't indicate that you're going to be able to have more impact in a match than a player with a lower test score. As previously mentioned, what is a key indicator of football performance however is the ability to repeat high intensity efforts, for this reason the yo-yo intermittent recovery test level 2 (Yo-Yo IR-L2) is a far more appropriate stamina-based fitness test for footballers. If you score poorly in this test, it is a good indicator that you're going to struggle to have your desired impact at elite level.

THE PRO'S & CON'S OF TREADMILL TRAINING

Treadmill training is a popular choice for many. You get to stay indoors when the weather is bad and it's really easy to set interval times so that you don't need to watch the clock, but there are several reasons why treadmill training is a sub-optimal choice for footballers (when you also have the option of training out on the pitch).

CONS OF RUNNING ON A TREADMILL:

- Limited hip extension
- Less effort than running on grass
- No directional changes

LIMITED HIP EXTENSION

Optimal movement in your hips is crucial to performance. The strength of your glutes is an important factor in terms of injury prevention as they influence the movement of your lower back and your knees. Running on a treadmill tends to shorten your stride length, preventing your hips from extending and moving as they would on grass.

Depending on the treadmill design, this change in running style is often due to safety concerns (especially at speed) and changing your running technique can have a detrimental effect on your performance when you're back on grass.

LESS EFFORT THAN RUNNING ON GRASS

Treadmills can be quite bouncy. They're designed this way to limit the risks of repetitive impact, but the downside of this is that each step on the treadmill will return more energy than a step on grass or astroturf would.

This means you're putting in less effort to achieve the same speed or distances you'd expect on solid ground, which could negatively impact your running economy and your performance on the pitch. To become stronger, more powerful or more efficient, your body needs to adapt to progressive overloads in training. Treadmill running lightens the workload compared to running on grass, making it a sub-optimal choice if repeatedly used to develop football specific fitness.

NO DIRECTIONAL CHANGES

To be effective, stamina training should be sport specific. In football, this needn't involve dribbling a ball in every move, but it should mimic the demands of the sport in terms of directional changes.

Decelerating and accelerating in and out of turns provides a much greater (and more football specific) stimulus than running in straight lines. Without this stimulus in training, you'll be limiting your potential for improved athleticism in matches and increase your risk of picking up injuries.

So, should treadmills be avoided? Treadmill training is a sub-optimal choice for footballers, but it can serve a purpose. If you can't get access to a pitch, or if you're in an area where snow and ice make it difficult to run on grass or on the street at times, then running on a treadmill is a good plan B. However, if you do have access to a pitch and have opted for doing all of your pre-season running using a treadmill instead, you're actively making a decision to use your training time in a less functional, less efficient way than you could be.

TRAINING STAMINA IN THE POOL

Swimming pool sessions can provide a way of adding variety to your training and offer an alternative to pitch and gym-based stamina work.

Pool work can be of great benefit in a few situations:

If you're returning from injury: if you're not quite ready to get back to running-based workouts, swimming pool sessions offer a means of getting a cardio workout without the impact.

If you've got a little niggle: adding extra running-based work to your training schedule to help build stamina might not be the best thing if you've got an on-going or recurring niggle. Cycling or rowing in the gym would be an option, but if you prefer running, swimming pool sessions allow you to run with a much-reduced load on your joints.

If your match and team training workload is already high: if you're either training or playing matches every day and you're not getting much recovery time, doing extra running-based work to gain an edge in stamina will put you at greater risk of getting injured. Pool sessions let you work on stamina without adding an extra load to your joints, thereby helping to minimise this risk.

POOL-BASED STAMINA WORK

If you're a strong swimmer, you may be able to use swimming intervals to create a cardio workout, but there are other pool training exercises that don't require any swimming ability.

RUNNING ON THE SPOT

This is probably the most effective exercise to do in the pool. You don't need to be able to swim, you simply run. The faster you move, the greater the intensity of the exercise, but make sure you're pumping your arms and lifting your knees as high as you can, just as you would if you were running on the spot out of the water.

The following work to rest ratios provide a stamina workout that transfers to the type of effort required on the football pitch. There are three options:

1. 10 secs work: 20 secs rest (working at 100% intensity)

2. 15 secs work: 15 secs rest (working at 90% intensity)
3. 30 secs work: 30 secs rest (working at 80% intensity)

These work to rest ratios could be applied to swimming or running on the spot. Begin with 2 sets of 4 minutes using whichever work to rest ratio you choose. Stick to the same ratio for the entire session. Progress by adding 1 minute to each set until you have built up to around 6 to 8 minutes. Once you're there, you'll probably hit a ceiling where you can't improve much more and this is when you would drop the length of the sets and increase the number of sets.

For example:

- Build up to 2 sets of 6 mins
- Drop to 3 sets of 4 mins
- Build up to 3 sets of 6 mins
- Drop to 4 sets of 4 mins

To keep things varied, you could change the work to rest ratio you use each session.

Keeping your training as football-specific as possible is always the ideal, football is a running-based sport and includes sharp changes of direction, but if too much running-based work is putting you at risk of injury, then pool work can be an alternative way to increase your stamina.

KEY POINT

Pool work can help you to increase your stamina without adding extra loads to your joints, but you need to plan it. Pick your work to rest ratio and pick the number of minutes you're going to keep going for.

HOW TO TRAIN STAMINA FOR FOOTBALL IN THE GYM

Your body can provide energy using three energy systems and football utilises all of them. They are:

The phosphagen energy system: used in high intensity efforts of 0 to 10 seconds.

The glycolytic energy system: used in efforts of 10 seconds up to 2 minutes.

The aerobic energy system: used in efforts extending beyond 2 minutes.

At any given time, all three systems are at play, but one will dominate depending on what you're doing. It's important to note that high intensity actions are almost always responsible for game-changing moments (such as goals, clearances etc), so as mentioned previously it's important to focus on training for the pace of the game rather than the length.

PHOSPHAGEN

The phosphagen energy system is used to fuel very short, high intensity efforts, so training in the gym should involve pushing yourself as hard as you can for bouts of 5 seconds up to 15 seconds. In football, it's this energy system that's going to fuel acceleration into a maximal effort sprints and speedy changes of direction (it's these movements which often lead to game-changing moments, directly effecting whether you win, lose or draw a match).

Training the phosphagen energy system revolves around short, high intensity efforts. As an example in the gym, this could be done using intervals on an assault bike or regular bike:

- 10 to 15 seconds of all-out effort
- 50 to 45 seconds of recovery
- Repeat to complete a 4-minute set
- Allow 1 to 2 minutes of rest
- Repeat the set

- Up to a total of 4 sets is reasonable

GLYCOLYTIC

The glycolytic energy system kicks-in after 10-15 seconds and fuels efforts of up to 2 minutes. An all-out effort is going to be tough to maintain beyond 30 seconds, so pushing too hard is going to result in a drop-off in your performance before the end of your training session. For this reason, aim for an effort level of 7 or 8 on a scale of 1-10.

Treadmills lend themselves quite nicely to training the glycolytic energy system, however it's important to remember that there tends to be more bounce on a treadmill than you'd experience on the ground. So, whether you're conditioning the phosphagen or glycolytic system using a treadmill, it's worth using a 1-degree incline to mitigate this.

An example glycolytic energy system training session might be:

- 30 second's all-out run
- 30 seconds recovery
- Repeat to complete a 4-minute set
- Allow 1 or 2 minutes of rest
- Repeat the set
- Up to a total of 4 sets is reasonable

Most treadmills take a long time to change from a fast to a slow speed and vice versa, so standing on the sides is an easier option for rest periods.

Another glycolytic energy system training option is a rowing machine:

- Use a 500m interval programme and a 1:1 work to rest ratio
- Aim to push hard for 500m at around 80-90% of max effort
- Allow the time taken to complete the 500m as a recovery period
- Repeat to complete a 4-minute set
- Build up to 4 sets with 1 to 2 minutes of rest between sets

RUNNING V CYCLING AND ROWING

Football is a running sport, so it stands to reason that using the treadmill instead of a bike or rower will help to keep your gym training more football-specific. However, using other pieces of equipment which offer a lower impact alternative can help to give your joints and muscles a break and add variety to avoid mental staleness. Even battle ropes and boxing can provide a great option for a gym-based stamina training, especially when struggling with a lower body injury.

CAN TRAINING MASKS MAKE YOU FITTER?

Training masks were initially billed as altitude or elevation training masks. Eventually, due to ambiguous performance benefit claims, they have become known simply as training masks. Their popularity increased through marketing campaigns showing various elite athletes wearing them whilst training, but is the endorsement of an elite athlete enough to show that they are a useful tool for your day to day training?

First, let's start with what altitude training is and why it works. At elevations greater than 1200 metres above sea level, there is reduced partial pressure of oxygen in the atmosphere. This causes the body to increase its pulmonary ventilation (which is simply breathing frequency). There is also an increase in tidal volume, which is the amount of air that moves in and out of the lungs in one respiratory cycle.

These changes contribute to an increased demand for blood flow, to maintain adequate oxygen delivery for the body's tissues. Within 10-14 days at a given altitude there's an increase in red blood cell production, which brings pulmonary ventilation and tidal volume back down to normal levels. The following adaptations are maintained for around 1 month after the return to sea level:

- Increased formation of haemoglobin (generally 5-15% increase, although higher values have been reported) and red blood cells (30-50% increase)
- Increased diffusing capacity of oxygen through the pulmonary membranes
- Increased capillarization

Living and training at altitude above 1200 metres does cause positive adaptions which are generally associated with aerobic performance. That is settled. So, can a training mask really mimic this environment and create the same adaptations?

In short, as a training mask does not reduce the partial pressure of oxygen, it therefore cannot replicate training at altitude. To achieve this, the mask would need a mechanism similar to what is found in a hypobaric chamber. Even if this could be done, the impact would still be unknown if only worn for short periods of time.

Altitude training regimens are recommended as being at least 10-14 days for a positive adaptation to occur. Therefore (if we follow the logic) wearing a mask which could replicate the same conditions but only for the duration of a training session, would still likely be ineffective.

So, altitude training adaptations aside, could a mask be used as a clever way to strengthen your respiratory muscles?

Wearing a training mask may potentially induce respiratory muscle fatigue and increase strength, which could impact lung capacity and oxygen efficiency. However, with the research related to this being limited, it's not currently known whether increasing the strength or endurance of respiratory muscles has an impact on exercise capacity or the body's ability to process and use oxygen. So, for the moment, this one remains in the balance.

What about using a training mask purely to increase training intensity? If you could match the same intensity whilst wearing a training mask, which essentially is restricting your oxygen intake, would this make that intensity without the mask easier? Before considering this, we have to think about whether this is really necessary.

Let's say you're doing a basic speed endurance session, aiming to repeat 10 x 30 metre sprints, with 30 seconds rest in between each sprint and as little drop off in the speed of each sprint as possible. If you wanted to increase the intensity you could achieve this very easily without a training mask, simply by adjusting some of the other parameters of the workout. For example, the number of sprints, length of each sprint or rest time between the sprints.

If, however we're looking at reaching a certain heart rate quicker in an effort to train with more efficiency (i.e. reducing the training time through reaching a desired training heart rate quicker) then yes, wearing a training mask would likely achieve this. However, in reality and in a football specific environment, reaching a high heart rate quicker will be very low on the list of priorities any coach is likely to have for a session. But of course, it could have its time and place depending on the specific goal of the session.

We also can't overlook the psychological aspect of using a tool such as a training mask.

Like it or not, some players may feel they can train with greater focus whilst wearing a mask and can get more "in the zone". There could also be a psychological edge gained from knowing you are training in a way that most players aren't.

The mental aspect of training and performance is incredibly powerful and should not be overlooked, it's the same reason why some players perform certain rituals before stepping onto the pitch or have bigger biceps so they look stronger, the benefits gained in terms of football performance are purely mental, but for that reason alone still have merit.

This mental edge however could arguably still be achieved with simply creating a training environment where you can focus and by consistently following training principles which have been tried and tested for decades. Ultimately, it's going to come down to personal preference.

KEY POINT

To conclude, it's clear that the use of a training mask is not going to be the difference between you playing in the Premier League or Sunday League. Your team mate isn't going to get signed by a pro club over you because they've been training with a mask on and you haven't.

From experience, excessive use of unnecessary training tools and equipment can often overcomplicate, confuse and distract players away from consistently doing the basic things which will really move the needle for them and have been proven to work time and time again.

This therefore feels like an appropriate moment to refer to the K.I.S.S acronym, which should always be at the forefront of your thinking when planning a programme or session: "Keep It Simple Stupid".

KEY PRINCIPLES OF SPEED TRAINING

If you want to be fast, then you need to train fast! It's for this reason that speed training should only be done when you're feeling fresh and not already fatigued from other training.

THE PURPOSE OF SPEED TRAINING

Speed training is the time to work on perfecting your movement mechanics. With optimal movement mechanics, you can move faster and more efficiently simply by correcting movement deficiencies which are not only slowing you down but also sapping your energy stores. To improve your speed, you ultimately need to run at maximal intensity but with sound technique first and foremost. Therefore, you should first practice movements at submaximal speed with 100% focus on your mechanics (you could do this as part of your warm up) and then look to build up to maximal speed, ensuring full recovery between each rep. There's little point in practicing moving at maximal speed but with poor movement mechanics, training like this will limit your progress.

MAXIMUM FORCE

Much of the supplementary work done around speed training involves putting maximum force into the ground, however if you're already fatigued from another training session then this is going to hinder your ability to do that. If you want to train smart and get the most bang for your buck out of every speed session, then perform your speed training before any type of strenuous training and schedule enough time to allow for full recovery between each set.

NO MIDDLE-GROUND

In football, the moments that win games are most often high intensity. In the gym or in football training, the way you're going to get better is to train in a way which mirrors these moments of high intensity. Training at low intensities also provides an opportunity to recover from high intensity training, but training at a medium intensity offers neither of the above. If you spend most of your time training at a medium intensity, then it's likely going to lead to average playing performance.

KEY POINT

This "no middle ground" rule applies heavily to speed training. To gain maximum benefit, you need to work at maximum speed (after a thorough warm up practicing your technique). Moderate intensity training will lead to getting well-practiced at producing moderate results.

SCHEDULING SPEED SESSIONS

As outlined previously, the best time to do speed work is before a training session or a gym session. This is more time-efficient than scheduling a stand-alone session and will fire up your neuromuscular system which will aid performance in any subsequent sessions. After a team training or gym session however, you will likely already be physically and mentally fatigued, this will greatly reduce your ability to train speed with maximal intent which, as discussed, is required if you want to unlock a higher level of speed in response to your training.

KEY POINT

Working through a warm-up and then a speed session before training will not only help you to increase your maximum speed, but also ensure you're physically and mentally prepared to get the most out of your subsequent team training session.

In summary, endurance and stamina-based work could be done after training, but speed work requires 100% effort and maximum sprint speed in every rep. For this reason, it should only be done when you're fresh, when you're well recovered from the previous day's session and before doing any other exercise. Before training is ideal, but if you're unable to work it around other training sessions, then speed training should be a stand-alone session.

THE ESSENTIALS OF AGILITY TRAINING

Agility in football gives a player the ability to stop, start and make changes of direction at speed without losing their balance. This is achieved using a number of fitness elements, so agility training can't be singled out as one stand-alone aspect of fitness. It requires a combination of exercises, including drills designed to build both strength and power.

ECCENTRIC STRENGTH

Out on the pitch, you need good lower-body eccentric strength to be able to decelerate at great speed. Without it, you're going to struggle to slow down or stop to make sudden changes of direction. It's about training your body to absorb force and this can be done using bodyweight alone or with weights in a gym.

BODYWEIGHT EXERCISE

Drop lands from a box or step are a useful eccentric strength-based exercise that requires only bodyweight.

- Stand on a box that's around knee height
- Drop down to the floor from the box with both feet
- As you land, try to freeze in the bent-knee landing position for 3 or 4 seconds before straightening your knees and preparing for your next rep

WEIGHTS EXERCISE

Barbell back squats or any other squat variation can be used as a tempo exercise to develop eccentric strength.

- With weight in place, go from the top to the bottom of the squat in a slow, controlled four-second count
- Explode out of the bottom of the squat back to the top at speed

KEY POINT

Eccentric focused training exercises (the lowering phase of a lift) cause greater muscle damage compared to other forms of exercise, so you may experience greater muscle soreness as a result. For this reason, it's best to schedule this type of training into the earlier part of your week if you have a game on a Saturday. Pre-season is also a good time to place additional emphasis on increasing your eccentric strength. Avoiding muscle soreness during the season is a top priority but during pre-season muscle soreness can be accommodated to a greater degree due to being outside of the competitive part of the year.

CONCENTRIC STRENGTH

Once a good level of lower-body eccentric strength has been developed, it's time to focus on producing greater concentric strength. Out on the pitch, concentric strength gives you the explosive power to accelerate quicker, so when combined with eccentric strength, you'll be better able to sprint, stop, turn and burst away from your opponents to a higher level.

BODYWEIGHT EXERCISE

Double-leg and single-leg box to box jumps provide a useful progression to drop lands.

- Drop down from a box with both feet as described in the drop lands exercise above, but immediately power out of the bent-knee landing position to jump up onto another box
- Alternatively, drop down onto one foot and power out of the landing using the same leg to jump up onto another box

WEIGHTS EXERCISE

In the gym, exercises such as the clean pull can be used to develop concentric strength that will transfer into movements needed in football. Explosive lifts like this which involve your heels powerfully lifting from the floor help to develop the ability to power out of a stop and turn on the pitch.

LATERAL MOVEMENTS

Of course, explosive moves in football aren't always upwards, they're much more likely to be rapid changes of direction from one side to the other. This means agility training in football must include lateral movements. Options include:

1. Advance the above single-leg box jump to directional box jumps. Instead of jumping straight up onto another box, jump sideways onto another box, making sure to repeat the exercise using the other leg
2. Use a landmine attachment in the gym (or a barbell positioned in the corner) to work on side lunges. From a standing start, step out into a side lunge and then push hard to return to the start position

AGILITY DRILLS

The last stage of progression in terms of agility training for football is to practice agility drills. These can be split into closed or open drills:

CLOSED AGILITY DRILL

Closed drills are the best way to begin as they generally involve just one predetermined change of direction. An example would be running out to a cone and running back. In this type of drill, you already know where you need to change direction, so your focus is on technique and making the change in as few steps as possible. Fewer steps followed by a big push out to switch direction is the aim of the exercise. If it takes you 8 or 9 steps to switch direction after running into the cone, your eccentric strength needs work.

OPEN AGILITY DRILL

Closed drills can be progressed to include more than one cone, but the changes of direction remain predetermined. In an open drill, the number of changes and the direction of the changes remains unknown until instructions are called out.

For example, you might begin by standing in a box marked out on the pitch with different coloured cones in the corners. A teammate then calls out one of the colours and you must sprint out around that cone and back to the centre of the box.

Colours will continue to be called out at random, so the number of sprints or the direction of the sprints will never be known in advance, bringing in a cognitive element.

The faster your mind can register the instruction, the faster your body can react, making open drills closer to actual play on the pitch. However, the rapid reactions needed in open drills require a good level of eccentric and concentric lower-body strength, so it's always advisable to begin with closed drills and advance to open drills when you're able to change direction at speed with great technique.

THE BOTTOM LINE

Agility is not a stand-alone element of fitness. To be agile, you need balance, coordination, speed, strength and quick reflexes. This means that the best approach to agility training is to follow a training plan that brings all of these elements together. Keep it progressive and you'll see gradual improvements month on month as well as lowering your risk of picking up injuries.

HOW LONG DOES IT TAKE TO IMPROVE FROM PLYOMETRICS?

Compared to making gains in strength or muscle growth, your body needs a relatively short period of time to adapt to plyometric and agility exercises, meaning improvements can be seen quite quickly. However, it makes sense to establish a solid foundation of general strength and speed before adding plyometric and agility work to your training programme to ensure you're getting the most bang for your buck from your training time.

MEASURING IMPROVEMENT

Some of the biggest improvements made in plyometric and agility exercises are going to be due to improving technique. For example, the pro-agility test (or 5-10-5 agility test) is used by many football teams as a means of measuring change of direction speed. The test involves sprinting 5 metres either left or right from a centre point, touching a line, sprinting back past the centre to point to touch a line 5 metres on the other side (10 metre sprint in total) and then sprinting 5 metres back to the start point.

The set pattern format means that practicing the specific movements involved in the test will very quickly lead to improvements in the time taken to perform them, resulting in an improved test score. This same principle can be applied to practicing and perfecting other common movements involved in football.

Another test used in football is the reactive strength index or RSI. This involves a drop jump from a box with the goal being to achieve as high a vertical jump as possible immediately after landing. The results of this test give an indication of change of direction speed, acceleration speed and agility in footballers, but as with the pro-agility test, initial improvements may be due to practice and familiarity with the movements rather than long-term adaptations.

PROFICIENCY

Making technical improvements is a starting point from which you can go on to make real improvements that will transfer to the pitch. However, if you already have sharp ground contact times then you'll benefit most from plyometric and agility focused sessions once you have reached a good level in other elements of fitness such as strength and power. As an example, if you are unable to squat your own bodyweight, then this should be your priority before looking to benefit from plyometric and agility focused workouts.

KEY POINT

Plyometric and agility sessions should be considered the icing on the cake in terms of priority in your training programme. It makes sense to focus on strength training first (which will also improve muscle activation) and then condition that new strength and increased ability to produce force to be applied at greater speed using plyometric exercises, leading to your become a more explosive, powerful player.

PROGRAMMING

In pre-season gym training, the main focus of your will be strength, power and hypertrophy due to there being limited opportunity to progress these elements during the season. Once a solid base has been established, plyometric and agility exercises can be added in the final 3 or 4 weeks, again to condition that increased strength and mass to be applied explosively.

Technical improvements will be achieved quickly and, provided the volume is not overly high, you can work on plyometric exercises every 1 to 2 days and agility exercises every 2 to 3 days. Being able to do this type of training more frequently than strength training makes progress quicker and longer-term improvements are going to be made within a 3 or 4-week block towards the end of your pre-season training programme.

KEY POINT

Remember that every time you play football you are already performing many plyometric actions and actively training your agility in open play. Therefore, if you want to improve your agility further, it makes sense to shift your focus to developing your strength in the gym (which will improve force production as well as muscle activation levels) prior to devoting additional time to plyometric and agility sessions. If you are already experienced in the gym, then schedule your plyometric training in a block as part of a periodized programme or utilise plyometric exercises in strength training supersets, for example a set of heavy deadlifts followed by a few rebound depth jumps reps.

HOW TO SPEED UP YOUR FOOTWORK

It's fair to say that the mention of footwork brings images of speed or agility ladders to mind, but in terms of improving foot speed and coordination for football, hours spent on ladder drills needn't be the central focus.

FOOTBALL FOOTWORK

Efficient footwork in football is enhanced when you can more effectively separate the movements of your lower body from those of your upper body. Imagine a player jockeying another player on the pitch. They're not jumping in for a tackle, they're just trying to slow them down or guide them to wherever they want to go.

To do this, the upper body needs to hold a strong and stable position and your arms need to provide balance whilst the feet quickly shift into whatever position or angle is required to keep up with the opposing player. Hip mobility is a key component of creating this hinge effect, allowing your lower body to move at speed independently from your upper body.

An excellent exercise that works on hip mobility, balance, lateral speed and footwork quickness and coordination is the carioca drill:

- From a standing start, step to the left with your left leg
- Cross your right leg over in front of your left leg to continue travelling left
- Step to the left with your left leg
- Cross your right leg behind your left leg to continue travelling left
- Step to the left with your left leg and repeat the pattern
- Aim to get up on your toes and pick up the pace
- Switch direction to repeat the pattern with your right leg leading the way and left leg crossing over in front and behind

EFFICIENT MOVEMENT

Football specific footwork is fast-paced and this means the lower body needs to produce a lot of force in a short period of ground contact time to be able to move around the pitch efficiently.

One way to improve efficiency is to use plyometric exercises. These include static or dynamic jumps that focus on using the minimum amount of ground contact time to jump as high or as far as possible. To transfer into football, these jumps need to mimic the sideways, backwards and forwards movements required in a game, not just vertical leaps from the ground. For example, instead of doing pogo jumps on the spot, jump around to different positions to reflect the 360-degree range of movement needed on the pitch.

HURDLES

The aim of a plyometric exercise is to improve the ability to move explosively by training ankle stiffness, utilising a mechanism called the stretch shortening cycle which stores elastic energy in the rear of the lower leg. When optimal ankle stiffness can be achieved (not too stiff to limit movement but not too loose to result in lost energy and prolonged ground contact times) you increase your potential to move more explosively. Hurdles are not necessary for this type of work in their truest sense, however using them can increase the intent in each push-off or landing which is crucial for effective plyometrics.

Plyometric exercises using hurdles and conditioning the stretch shortening cycle mechanism include:

- Two footed hurdle jumps
- Single leg hurdle hops
- Multi-directional hops and jump
- Hurdle run throughs and many more

DIFFERENT SPORTS AND DIFFERENT POSITIONS

Exposing yourself to different sports brings with it a range of different footwork and movement patterns. The more experience you have of different patterns, the more movement literate you become, making it easier to adapt to changing situations in a game of football.

An example of this might be finding yourself with muddled feet when up against an attacker using a new skill to try and get passed you. The bigger your background in terms of playing other sports, the quicker you can adapt to the movements needed in any given situation.

> **KEY POINT**

Playing different sports can be used as an element of a football warm up at training. Several football teams incorporate other sports into training. Basketball is a popular one and also the England team has been seen playing with a Nerf American football.

The same effect can also be gained through playing in different positions. A striker's movement patterns are quite different to those of a left back, but there can be times in a game when a striker is in the left back position. This can mean being exposed to different or unknown types of movement, so by putting yourself in different positions in training or in practice games, you gain the experience needed to be able to adapt and deal with changing situations.

LADDER DRILLS

A broad knowledge of different types of footwork will feed into improvements in the specific footwork patterns needed in your position. If you struggle with movement patterns or find it difficult to coordinate the footwork in drills such as the carioca at speed, then ladder drills can be beneficial as they help to develop a better understanding of where your limbs are as you move.

As with all types of speed work, good movement mechanics are essential when using ladders too. There's no point in adding speed to a movement which is already being performed inefficiently. This will not only limit your speed potential but result in you moving fast without balance, fluidity and control. Perform all ladders movements at sub-maximal speed first to ensure sound mechanics and then gradually try to increase the speed whilst maintaining that form.

> **KEY POINT**

In terms of developing your speed of footwork for football, ladders and hurdles are a useful training tool but try to think more towards open play activities which require different types of speedy footwork if possible. If you can build up your footwork encyclopaedia from a young age then you'll be better prepared to succeed in footballing moments which require fast and more complex footwork patterns. The higher the level you reach, the more athletic and well-rounded the players you'll be competing against will be.

WILL ANKLE WEIGHTS GIVE YOU FASTER FEET?

The use of ankle weights to improve stepover speed is a training method used by some footballers, but it's not a method that's (as of the time of writing this) backed by any science, so the benefits of doing so remain anecdotal at this stage.

It's rumoured that Ronaldo used ankle weights in training during his time at Manchester United and stepover speed is a bit of a signature for him, but without research it remains unclear whether it's something that could be useful to all players or whether it's an individual thing.

As with other training methods, these things are often intuitively created by coaches based on their principles and then research catches up when benefits become evident. Once a scientific reason for improvements has been identified, methods can then be finetuned to ensure they're used effectively. As it stands, not enough players use this method to merit any research, so its effectiveness remains a grey area.

HOW IT (POTENTIALLY) WORKS

In theory, adding ankle weights creates the need to put more effort into achieving the same foot speed you'd achieve normally. This means when the weights are removed, there will be an improvement in speed in the same way that adding resistance such as a light sled can lead to improvements in sprint training.

FOOTBALL SPECIFIC

In terms of sport-specific improvements, becoming faster at running in straight lines and being able to make quicker changes of direction will probably have a bigger impact on your game than improving your stepover speed. This is not to say that adding ankle weights won't lead to increases in speed, but the increases are likely to be small and therefore less impactful than making improvements in other elements of training.

INJURY RISK

Ankle weights aren't commonly used in football training and one of the main concerns is injury risk. If the weights are too heavy or if they're used too frequently, there's an increased risk of injury in the ankle, knee and even the foot.

To avoid injury:

- Use ankle weights of 1kg or less
- Train with ankle weights no more than once a week
- Try and limit their use to just a few minutes at a time

An ideal time to practice stepovers with ankle weights would be a few short, sharp sets before training, immediately followed by a set without the weights.

RISK VS REWARD

Without scientific research to back it up, it's unknown whether this training method is effective. By limiting the time you devote to it, you're limiting the potential to pick up injuries and reducing the time it takes you away from other proven training methods.

DELIBERATE PRACTICE

Getting out to practice stepovers at real game speed and with 100% intensity is going to have a big impact in terms of skill development. This type of deliberate practice has been proven effective in many other aspects of training, so with or without ankle weights, it's the practicing of the stepover movement at speed with or without the use of weights which holds the key to getting quicker and better at them.

THE BOTTOM LINE

With or without weights, this should only be a small element of your training. Adding ankle weights to stepovers could have a positive transfer to football, but it's more of an individual choice than a proven method. The best plan would be to try it out, see if it increases your stepover speed or encourages you to be a little more aggressive and faster and if so, it might be something that's useful for you. If you try it and find it makes no difference at all then concentrate on making improvements in other areas of your game instead.

HOW TO BECOME QUICKER AT TURNING

In football, rotation is a movement which helps you to turn quickly and make speedy changes of direction. The muscles in your legs are largely responsible for the rapid decelerations and accelerations needed to make a quick turn, but training the muscles involved in rotating your torso will help to make those turns even more efficient.

ROTATIONAL EXERCISES

Any movements which are commonly used on the pitch should be mimicked in your training to ensure that the muscles directly involved in these key actions are developed in terms of strength and power to make them as efficient and effective as possible.

Compared to sports such as tennis, footballers have less emphasis on making rotational work a big part of their training schedule, but it can be a useful to include it.

CABLE MACHINE

A good example of a rotational exercise using a cable machine is the wood chop:

- Stand sideways on to a cable machine
- Hold the handle (set at waist height) in both hands at arm's length in front of you
- Keeping a slight bend in your knees, rotate to the side (away from the machine)
- Control the weight on the way back and repeat the rotation without letting the weights rest
- Aim for 8-10 reps and then repeat the exercise on the other side

This exercise can also be performed with the cable set in a high position and then moved from a high to low position whilst rotating, or it can be set in a low position to then rotate from low to high. An alternative to the cable machine is to use a fixed resistance band. The weight or resistance used should be light enough to allow smooth rotational movement at a controlled pace whilst standing at a distance which always keeps tension on the band.

MEDICINE BALL

Medicine ball exercises can be considered more advanced and more explosive rotational exercises. Any exercise performed using a medicine ball should always be as explosive as possible, with the aim being to throw or move the ball with as much power as possible.

For this reason, it's important to start with a light ball and to keep the exercises simple. Even athletes such as tennis players who place heavy emphasis on rotational training exercises will keep the weight of a medicine ball light, so most footballers will only need 1kg up to 3kgs to benefit from this type of training.

A good starting point is the half-kneeling medicine ball throw:

- Face a wall, or work with a partner who can catch the ball
- To throw to your left, position yourself with your right knee on the floor and your left foot out in front with a bent knee (just as you would in a half-kneeling hip flexor stretch)
- Hold the medicine ball in both hands, rotate to the right and then throw the ball to the wall or a partner as explosively as possible, keeping your lower half steady as you rotate both ways
- Complete 3 to 5 reps on each side for 2 to 3 sets

To progress from the half-kneeling throw, you would simply move to a standing throw.

Place your feet side by side and maintain a slight bend in your knees (athletic position) as you rotate away from the wall and then return in a fast, powerful rotation to throw the ball as hard as you can.

The standing throw can then be advanced to a more reactive exercise, but only after working on the above exercises and developing enough power to throw a medicine ball of 2kg to 3kgs forcefully.

- Get a partner to throw the ball at you from the direction you want to throw in (if you want to throw the ball to your left, get someone to throw it at you from the left)
- As you catch it, shift most of your weight onto the other leg (right leg if the ball is coming from the left) and then powerfully return the ball in an explosive throw

In summary, rotation exercises can effectively be split into two categories:

1. Control and Strength: Woodchops fall into this category and as such they can be done towards the end of a gym session when you're doing trunk stability
2. Power: Medicine ball exercises fall into this category and as with all power exercises (e.g. plyometric exercises or sprint training) they should be done when you're fresh, ideally at the start of a session after a warm-up. They could also be done before a football training session if you had a medicine ball available

HOW TO DECELERATE FASTER

Deceleration is key for enabling sharp changes of direction. You need to decelerate before you can turn and accelerate out again, so the better you can decelerate, the quicker you're going to be in and out of tight situations and the better your agility will be.

The technical abilities of good deceleration revolve around three simple things:

1. Being low in your body position
2. Having your feet in a wide base
3. Using lots of short aggressive steps to slow yourself down, rather than sprinting into a sudden stop from an upright position

EXERCISES TO IMPROVE DECELERATION

The best way to improve your deceleration abilities is to practice decelerating as often as possible in a controlled environment.

Cone Turns: A simple way to do this is to use a cone as a turning point.

- Sprint 10 metres at maximum speed towards the cone
- Decelerate as you approach to make the turn
- Then accelerate out of the turn to go back towards the start

The cone provides a marker, so you know exactly where you need to turn and therefore when you should begin to decelerate to make the turn. Keeping it controlled allows you to practice the technique and regular practice can lead to significant improvements in your ability to evade opponents and reach 50/50 balls first.

Deceleration Box: As you improve, another way to practice is to mark out a box on the ground. You sprint towards the box as you did with the cone, but this time you must wait until you're inside the box before you can begin to decelerate. Once inside, you must also come to a complete stop inside the box. The smaller the box, the more deceleration skill required to stop in a shorter space.

The next stage is to practice reactive deceleration in unpredictable environments.

Whistle Stops: Ask a teammate to blow a whistle or clap their hands at random intervals as you sprint. The sound is your signal to decelerate and stop as quickly as possible, but you no longer have the advantage of knowing exactly when you need to prepare to decelerate. Don't cheat by running slower in anticipation of the whistle!

Red Light Green Light: Another useful exercise is the red light green light drill. A coach or another player holds a red cone and a green cone. When they raise the green cone, you sprint as fast as you can and when they raise the red cone, you stop as quickly as possible. This type of deceleration drill is more sport specific in that you're looking up and around you for the signal to react, just as you would be in a game, rather than looking at your feet.

GYM-BASED EXERCISES

Practicing the skill itself is the most effective way of become better at doing it, but there are some exercises you can do in the gym to help improve your ability to decelerate.

Eccentric Strength: Lower body strength is needed to decelerate quickly, especially eccentric strength (strength as the muscles are lengthening). Working on this could be as simple as controlling a squat on the way down, rather than dive-bombing into the bottom of it. Keep the eccentric phase (going down) slow and controlled by giving yourself a 3 or 4 second count to the bottom of the squat each time.

Drop Lands: A large degree of eccentric force is produced to slow yourself down in a drop land. This is also a time-efficient way to train for deceleration if you're doing box jumps at the same time. Simply jump off the box and freeze in a wide, low landing position. It takes eccentric strength to freeze and avoid stepping forwards as you land.

Break and Lunge: This exercise helps to build eccentric strength within each leg individually. Step forwards to go into a lunge, but instead of gradually lowering yourself into the lunge, drop immediately into the bottom of the lunge position and then freeze. As with the drop lands, it takes eccentric strength to freeze the movement and this exercise can generate quite a bit of muscle soreness. For this reason, it's important to begin without added resistance. Only load up with dumbbells, kettlebells or a barbell if you have a good level of lower body strength.

KEY POINT

The above eccentric strength exercises should only be used to work on deceleration once a good level of lower body strength has been established. Work on developing general lower body strength first, then focus on improving your deceleration skills from a strong base.

The bottom line is that the ability to decelerate at speed (and safely) is crucial if you want to play at the highest level. There's an added injury prevention aspect to being able to slow down quickly and make changes of direction safely too. It can be relatively easy to make improvements with simple exercises, but to get the best results, training must be focused on the skill rather than an afterthought.

THE BENEFITS OF UPHILL SPRINTS

Uphill sprints can be a useful way of developing lower body strength and power for football. Short sprints on an incline are simply harder work than sprints on flat ground, so your body adapts to the extra workload in a way that transfers well to the movements you use on the pitch.

IDEAL INCLINE

A relatively gentle incline of 5 degrees up to no more than 10 degrees is ideal for hill sprints. This could be a grassy slope or a hill on a quiet street, but ideally the incline remains the same for a distance of at least 5 metres up to around 40 metres. Sprinting on a steeper incline will lead to a dramatic change in your running mechanics and therefore limits the usefulness of the exercise in terms of its transfer to football.

GYM EQUIVALENT

The type of force required to move your body at speed up a hill can be difficult to replicate in a gym environment. Many exercises in the gym are performed in what's known as the sagittal plane, meaning the movement is up and down rather than forwards. Running on a treadmill is one possibility, but it can be problematic to measure and manage short distances. Running with a heavy sled as resistance is another way, but not all gyms have this facility or suitable surfaces to pull on.

KEY POINT

Hill sprints on a slight incline are a simple and effective way to produce positive adaptations that will transfer to speed on the pitch.

SETS AND REPS

The best time to do this type of training is during pre-season. It could be done in season, but only if you're in a one game per week schedule and have plenty of recovery time between training and playing.

An ideal incline would be 5 to 40 metres in length, with a steady gradient of between 5 and 10 degrees.

- 2-3 sets of 3-5 reps
- Allow 30 seconds of rest for every 10 metres you sprint. So, if you sprint 10 metres each time, allow 30 seconds of rest between reps, if you sprint 40 metres each time, allow 2 minutes of rest between reps
- It's important to fully recover between sets, so give yourself a 5-minute rest each time

KEY POINT

Unless each rep is a high-quality sprint, you're no longer getting a good return for the work you're doing. If the gradient is too steep, you risk a drop in quality and if you fail to recover between sets, your sprint speeds (and therefore the benefits of the exercise) will also drop.

WHEN TO UTILISE DOWNHILL SPRINTS

Downhill running is also a training technique which can be used to help improve your running speed on the pitch. Many things can influence your speed as a player, but in terms of all-out sprint speed, it comes down to a combination of:

- Stride length
- Stride frequency
- The ability to produce as much force as possible in a short period of ground contact time

Elite sprinters can have a ground contact time of less than 0.1 seconds with each foot strike. The huge amount of force they're able to produce as they make contact with the ground propels them forwards and this (coupled with optimum stride length and frequency) generates speeds of over 20 mph on the track. Usain Bolt clocked a top speed of almost 28 mph during his racing career.

THE WHY, HOW AND WHEN OF DOWNHILL SPRINTING

WHY

Running downhill naturally increases your stride length as gravity pulls you into longer strides without having to consciously stretch forward into them. A decline also increases your stride frequency compared to running on a flat or an incline.

These differences lead to a shorter period of ground contact time as you'll be running faster than you naturally could on flat ground. If you currently lack sprinting speed on flat surfaces, it's predominately because your ground contact time is relatively long. Running downhill instantly pushes you into producing the force you need to move forwards at a much quicker rate. Your muscles adapt as you get accustomed to the feel of a longer stride and sharper ground contact. This is something you'll eventually be able to transfer into your sprints on the pitch.

HOW

Downhill running places greater forces on the working muscle groups. The steeper the gradient, the greater the braking forces and the higher the potential to experience DOMS (delayed onset muscle soreness) as a result.

For this reason, it's best to begin downhill running on a short, gradual slope. Some studies have used a 5-degree gradient, others a 3-degree gradient, the jury is still out over which is most effective in terms of increasing sprint speed. In another other study, a combination of downhill and uphill sprinting produced the greatest gains, but in the interests of staying injury free, the best approach is going to be to start small and then progress to slightly steeper gradients.

As a practical guide, if the decline gradient is causing your natural stride to shorten as you attempt to slow yourself down to stay in control and your arms are flailing wildly in the air, the hill is too steep. Focus on maintaining good posture, staying relaxed, quickening your leg turnover and allowing gravity to gradually lengthen your stride (rather than reaching for a longer stride and potentially over-striding into an injury).

WHEN

As a footballer, you must always be ready for your next team practice or match. Overdoing it and suffering DOMS or having to tell your head coach that you're not fit to train because you fell over and injured yourself running down a steep hill is not going to go down well. So, with this in mind, downhill sprinting should only be considered a small element of your overall training and the bulk of your speed work should be done on a normal, flat pitch.

A good time to incorporate some downhill running into your schedule is before a training session. Get out, warm up, do some downhill sprints (if you have an appropriate slope available), have a short rest and then you're ready to get into training and work on your sprint speed on flat ground.

KEEP IT FOOTBALL SPECIFIC

The principle behind including downhill sprinting in your football training programme is to increase your running speed in a match. As you adapt to the quicker leg turnover of downhill running, you learn to transfer the technique into running on a flat pitch. Plyometric exercises with suspension bands can also be used to help create the shorter period of ground contact experienced in downhill running. An example would be scissor lunges, using the band to provide greater lift in the jump as you switch legs.

Resistance bands can help to increase speed in football specific movements as the resistance created by a band increases the workload on the muscles involved, making the movements more explosive and powerful when performed without the band. Side-stepping through an agility ladder at speed with a resistance band in place around your thighs or a recoil bungee fixed at the waist are good examples of exercises designed to improve the lateral speed needed for quick changes of direction on the pitch.

Other methods of working against resistance to increase speed such using a prowler or running against parachute drag can also have their place, but you must be wary of significant changes in your running mechanics being created (like what we see when a decline gradient is too steep). Stick to downhill sprinting on a gradual slope and allow the gravity-assisted increase in stride length and frequency to crossover into your straight-line sprints on flat ground and then curved runs out on the pitch.

HOW TO INCORPORATE SLEDS & PARACHUTES

Tools such as sleds and parachutes can be useful in speed training and when used in the right way the benefits they bring transfer well onto the football pitch.

HOW IT WORKS

Using a sled or a parachute means having to produce more force to overcome the resistance created as you run and when the force is then taken away, you're able to run at a faster pace due to the training adaptation.

Improving your lower body strength correlates with jumping higher and sprinting faster, but it takes more than gains in strength alone to produce more speed. Training with resistance as you run is a specific way of training for increased speed.

BENEFITS OF SPRINTING WITH SLEDS

The main benefit of running with a sled is enhanced force production, especially in forward movements. Lower body training is typically done in the sagittal plane, meaning straight up and down movements, but achieving optimal acceleration into a sprint requires horizontal force production.

The resistance created by a sled puts you into an exaggerated forward lean (the position needed for efficient acceleration). Spending more time in this position can help to promote technical improvements, encouraging good posture in your trunk and a stiff foot and ankle in every ground strike, thereby creating a powerful strength-shortening cycle within the lower leg.

ARE SLEDS FOR ADVANCED PLAYERS ONLY?

Players of any level can train using sleds and parachutes; however, common sense needs to be applied. Loading yourself up with a 300kg sled if you're a relative newcomer to gym-training or not very strong would be counter-productive. As with all training, a progressive approach is needed.

TRAINING RECOMMENDATIONS

Sled and parachute training should not be at the core of your training programme, but it can be used as a supplementary exercise to help develop the strength and power needed to sprint faster.

Strength block: If you're in a strength block in the gym, adding a sled or parachute that gives heavy resistance can complement your weight-training exercises.

Power block: If you're in a power block, using a light sled or light resistance parachute provides the best match to complement this phase of your training programme.

Speed work: Mixing sled and parachute work into regular speed work can be very effective. After a warm up followed by some sprint drills, using a sled or parachute then creates a better stimulus, as running at the same speed with the added resistance involves producing much more force. When the resistance is removed, the force you've been creating will go straight into running faster in your next sprint (after a full recovery).

KEY POINT

As in all sprint training, the ATP system fuels your performance, so plenty of rest is needed between reps to ensure that each rep is a good quality maximal effort.

Training with sleds and parachutes is something that can be done in stand-alone speed sessions, or it could be done before football training if you have time. If done consistently, this type of training will go a long way towards helping you improve your sprinting speeds on the pitch.

ANALYSING RONALDO'S SPRINTING TECHNIQUE

In terms of sprinting technique, Cristiano Ronaldo doesn't conform to the high-knee, bent-arm image we'd expect to see in athletes competing in an Olympic 100m sprint final. In fact, his straight-arm running style goes against much of what would be considered optimal for both footballers and Olympic sprinters, but there can be no denying that he's one of football's fastest ever players. So, where does Ronaldo's speed come from?

ELITE SPRINTING TECHNIQUE

When you sprint, opposite arms and legs work together to help stabilise your torso. With a stabilised trunk (mid-section from your waist to your neck) there's a more efficient transfer of force from your body into the ground and back. It's this transfer that propels you forwards.

If you're unable to stabilise your trunk well, it leads to a side to side swaying effect as you run and the transfer of force to propel you forwards is diminished. Working opposite arms and legs together in a coordinated and synchronised way is going to help you maximise the transfer of force required to move at greater speed, but your leg turnover speed is also highly influential and this is limited by the speed of your arms.

A common training technique to help with the positioning of your arms when sprinting is to think of moving your hand from your hip to your cheek, aggressively switching from one arm to the other. Try jogging on the spot without moving your arms, put your hands on your head to keep your arms out of the movement. Now bring your arms into the movement, aggressively pumping them hip to cheek as if sprinting and you're going to notice that your legs are able to move faster.

INDIVIDUAL DIFFERENCES

Hip to cheek arm swings with an elbow bend of around 60 to 90 degrees can be considered optimal, but there are always going to be individual differences between players who have not been taught this technique from the moment that they started running and playing football. The way that Ronaldo moves his arms is different to the optimal technique which is taught, but it's not a technique he has intentionally developed to get faster, it's just his natural way of sprinting.

For this reason, attempting to imitate Ronaldo's sprinting style is not a smart idea. Remember that although very important, sprinting technique is not the only thing which helps to produce great speed out on the pitch. Ronaldo is also one of the most reactive and powerful men in football.

In a 2016 video, Ronaldo's counter-jump (vertical jump with hands on hips from a standing position) was shown to be 44cms. This gives a measure of the amount of power he can produce from a standing start and it's fair to say that a lot of athletes (even non-elites) could match his performance on this one. However, when he switches to a jump from just one leg, using his arms and with a brief run up, he achieves 78cms, a truly elite performance that very few can match. To put it into perspective, Ronaldo is 1.87m tall, but his vertical jump power would give him the same slam-dunking advantage as an NBA basketball player standing well over 2m tall.

Yes, there's a general set of rules that elite-level sprinters follow in terms of optimal sprint mechanics, but individual differences might see one sprinter use a slightly longer ground contact time compared to another with a springier style. Spending months making tiny technique adjustments that lead to straight line speed gains of only a fraction of a second can make the difference between a podium position in athletics, but in football, spending this much time focusing on trying to significantly alter your straight line sprint style will take you away from other aspects of training which are just as important for elite performance.

KEY POINT

Ronaldo probably could run even faster if he altered his sprinting technique, but spending time working on that one tiny aspect might negatively impact other areas of his game.

The energy Ronaldo can store in his Achilles tendon is largely responsible for the level of speed and agility that we see him perform week after week. He also has arguably some of the most powerful legs in the game, if he had a perfect sprinting technique but lacked these two qualities, then his speed capability would be significantly lower.

SPRINTING PRACTICE

For those of us who can only dream of Ronaldo's speed, sprint practice on the pitch and the development of strength, power and explosiveness in the gym holds the key. Of course, being mindful and practicing optimal sprinting mechanics whilst doing this is a smart idea and means you're killing two birds with one stone.

THE BOTTOM LINE

To get faster at running, you need to sprint often, allow for full recovery between each sprint and practice using optimal sprint mechanics. The lesson we can learn from Ronaldo is that it's extremely difficult not to allow for individual differences, as long as they aren't significantly holding you back (they may even be helping you in other areas of your game) it makes sense to embrace them and focus your training time on the areas which will move the needle the most.

KEY STRETCHES FOR ENHANCED PERFORMANCE

Stretching to enhance your football performance needn't involve hours of gymnastic bending and flexing. With just a little focused effort on the key muscle groups you can boost your performance on the pitch and help to prevent injuries.

The key areas are:

- Calves
- Hip flexors
- Hamstrings

CALF STRETCHES

The calves consist of two muscles: the gastrocnemius and soleus. The gastrocnemius originates above the knee, the soleus below the knee and both insert into the Achilles tendon. Having two different points of origin means that two different stretches are needed to stretch the calf muscles effectively.

STRAIGHT-LEG STRETCH FOR THE GASTROCNEMIUS:

- Stand on a step with a bannister or wall to hold onto for balance
- Place the ball of one foot on the edge of the step so that the heel is free to drop towards the floor
- Push the heel as low as possible to create the stretch, maintaining a straight leg
- Hold for around 1 minute, building up to 2 minutes, continuing to increase the stretch by dropping the heel lower if possible
- Switch legs to repeat the stretch

BENT-LEG STRETCH FOR THE SOLEUS:

- Stand facing a wall, about arms-length from it
- Drop down into a double-leg quarter-squat position (slight bend in both knees)

- Step forward with one leg, keeping the heel of the rear leg on the floor
- Using your hands on the wall for support, drive your weight forward over the front leg knee to create a stretch in the rear leg calf (soleus)
- Hold for 1 minute, building up to 2 minutes, keeping the heel of the stretching leg on the floor throughout
- Switch legs to repeat the stretch

Flexible calves are essential for good dorsiflexion, this is the ability to pull your toes up from the ground in a standing position. Dorsiflexion is a key movement in sprinting and running in football, allowing you to strike the ground and use stored elastic energy within the lower leg and ankle to run faster and more efficiently. The more efficiently you run, the more energy you have in reserve for later in the game.

HIP FLEXOR STRETCHES

Tightness in the hip flexors (often the result of long periods spent sitting down) can affect your pelvic position, leading to anterior pelvic tilt and lower back pain. Tightness in this muscle group can also prevent you from hitting a good figure-4 position when you run (picture an Olympic sprinter with a strong, upright posture and a high knee lift that brings the thigh in line with the waist).

From this position, you're able to hit the ground hard with every stride, creating a huge driving force. Think of your foot as a hammer and the ground as a nail; you're able to hit the nail harder when the hammer comes in from a distance compared to keeping the hammer close to the nail.

HALF-KNEEL HIP FLEXOR STRETCH:

- Kneel on the floor, then place one foot on the floor in front of you (as if in a lunge position but with your back knee still on the floor)
- Using your glute muscles, push the hip of the kneeling leg (rear leg) forward to feel the stretch in the hip flexor muscles (front of hip)
- Elongate your spine and maintain good posture by putting your hands up over your head (or rotate your hips inward towards the front leg to increase the stretch)
- Hold for 1 minute, building up to 2 minutes, gradually increasing the stretch if possible

- Switch legs to repeat the stretch

To advance this stretch (only if your hip flexors are not excessively tight), elevate your back foot on a bench to move into a couch stretch.

HAMSTRING STRETCH

The hamstrings are one of the most commonly injured muscle groups in football with both weakness and tightness increasing the risk of injury.

SEATED HAMSTRING STRETCH

This can be done as a double-leg or single-leg stretch.

- Sit on the floor with your legs straight out in front of you
- Bend forwards from your hips and extend your arms along the outside of your legs (or one leg at a time)
- Keep your legs straight (avoid bending your knees) and focus on lowering your chest towards the floor
- Hold each stretch for 1 minute, building up to 2 minutes

STAY RELAXED

For any stretch to be effective, your body needs to be able to relax into it. Many of the stretches that used to be seen in football involved your body remaining active, the standing hamstring stretch for example. If your body is having to work to keep you in a standing position, your muscles are unable to relax and benefit from the stretch being performed.

Deep breathing (diaphragmatic breathing) can also help to create a relaxed state for stretching. Focus on breathing in through your nose and out through mouth, trying to make your belly button move out and away from your spine as you inhale and then relax back into place as you exhale.

Stretching to enhance your performance need only take 10-15 minutes on a regular basis, especially at times when you become aware of tightness in your muscles. Whenever you have a small block of time, perhaps after training or after sitting in the car for a long period, take the time to relax into all or some of the above stretches. A little effort on a regular basis will go a long way towards keeping you performing at your best on the pitch and injury free throughout the year.

HOW TO RELIEVE HAMSTRING TIGHTNESS

Muscle tightness is a subjective feeling that might also be described as soreness, stiffness or simply not being able to move very well.

A common mistake made by footballers is to assume that because their hamstrings feel "tight", then focusing on stretching only the hamstrings is the answer. This often leads to a lot of time spent stretching for little to no gain, the feeling of tightness remains and this is because the hamstrings are only a part of the problem.

THE UNDERLYING ISSUE

The movements involved in playing football can cause the hip flexors and quads to become tight. The tightness in these muscles leads to them overworking, leading to even greater tightness which then forces the opposing muscles to lengthen. In this case, those muscles are the hamstrings.

This is known as lower cross syndrome (LCS) or anterior pelvic tilt and it means that your pelvis has rotated forward slightly due to your hip flexors and quads becoming tight and shortened and your hamstrings becoming lengthened.

FIXING THE ISSUE

Unless the underlying issues are addressed, your hamstrings are always going to feel tight, no matter how much stretching you do and they're also at greater risk of injury.

The first step is to work on releasing the tight muscles (the hip flexors and quads), foam rolling is a good starting point.

- Lie face down on a roller and position it under the hip flexors of one leg
- Roll backwards and forwards over the area to locate any tightness
- Focus the rolling pressure on any tight spots for 10 to 20 seconds or until the tension releases
- Repeat on the other leg

Once you've worked on both legs, move on to foam rolling your quad muscles in the same way.

The next step is stretching. A good way to stretch your hip flexors and quads at the same time is the couch stretch.

- Reverse yourself into position on your knees with a step, box, or the seat-cushion of your couch available to support the stretching leg
- Slide one knee back so that it fits into the angle between the box and the floor
- Your shin should be flush with the side of the box and your foot pointing upwards
- Slide your other leg out so that the foot is flat on the floor and the knee bent at 90 degrees
- Squeeze your glute muscles on the stretching leg (rear leg) as you drive the hip forward to increase the stretch
- Hold the stretch for up to 2 minutes, gradually increasing it by pulling yourself more upright as you push the hip forward

This stretch targets the hip flexors and the quads, but where you feel it most is an individual thing. Experiment with your hands above your head or rotate the stretching leg slightly inward towards the front leg to promote the ideal level of stretch for you. You can expect minor discomfort as you stretch, but it shouldn't be painful and it can be repeated several times throughout the day.

STRENGTHENING THE GLUTES AND ABS

Once the tight muscles are stretched, it's time to focus on strengthening the muscles that will hold your pelvis in the correct position. These are mainly the glutes and abs.

Suggested exercises:

- Glute bridges
- Loaded deadlifts or squats
- Dead bugs
- Ab wheel roll out
- Plank (on the floor or with elbows on a Swiss ball)

REDUCING HAMSTRING TIGHTNESS

Many of the above exercises can be built into your regular gym programme so that you're not trying to find extra time to focus on them.

Step 1: Lengthen your hip flexors and quads

Step 2: Strengthen your glutes and abs

Hamstring stretches can still be a beneficial element of your daily routine and with a little extra effort you will return your pelvis to its natural position, allowing you to continue training and playing without tightness and without the increased risk of picking up injuries.

WAYS TO IMPROVE HIP MOBILITY

The range of motion available around your hip joint influences the movements of your knee, ankle and lower back. It's important that your hips function well in order to avoid injuries in these areas and to be able to perform in an athletic and explosive way, but limited hip mobility is very common in footballers.

The three main muscle groups that can affect hip mobility are:

- Hip flexors
- Adductors or groin muscles
- Glutes

When these muscles become tight, they can cause pain in the hip and limit the range of movement in surrounding areas, negatively affecting your performance as a player.

HIP FLEXORS

The hip flexors are the muscles at the front of your hip that allow you to bring your leg in front of your body and lift your knee up towards your chest. If you have a job that keeps you sitting down most of the day, your hip flexors are going to become tight unless you work on maintaining flexibility with stretches.

A good static stretch is the half-kneeling hip flexor stretch:

- Kneel on the floor and then move one foot out in front to get into a half-kneeling position
- The knee of the leg in front should be directly over the ankle and the knee of the leg on the floor should be directly under the hip
- Keeping an upright posture, shift your weight forwards towards the foot on the floor to create a hip flexor stretch in the leg with the knee on the floor
- Squeeze the glutes (butt muscles) of the stretching leg to help push your hip forward and increase the stretch

Holding this stretch position for 2 minutes every day, or twice each day if you have the time, will help to lengthen the muscles and improve the sensation of tightness at the front of your hip.

KEY POINT

It's important to actively lean into this stretch for the first minute to keep increasing the stretch. Getting lazy with it or getting distracted by checking your phone will find you in a half-kneeling position without achieving any stretch at all.

ADDUCTORS

The adductors, or groin muscles, are used each time you cross your leg over in front of your body, so in movements such as passing the ball for example.

A good stretch for the adductor muscles is the frog stretch:

- Start on your hands and knees with your knees positioned as wide as you comfortably can (keeping your ankles in line with your knees)
- Sit back and lower your body towards the floor, aiming to sit between your heels
- Drive your backside as far back as you comfortably can to create a stretch on the inside of your thighs
- Relax into the stretch and hold this position for 2-4 minutes

This is a passive stretch that you can get comfortable in and the benefits of improving the muscle length will be noticeable as you become able to drop lower into a squat and keep good form.

GLUTES

Your glute muscles (or butt muscles) are used in sprinting and jumping movements, making them the powerhouse of the body when playing football.

A good stretch for the glute muscles is the pigeon stretch:

- Begin on your hands and knees, then bring your right knee forwards between your hands and sit onto your right hip
- Slide your left leg behind you, keeping the top of your foot on the floor
- Position your right foot in front of your left hip and relax into the stretch which is felt in the right side of your glutes
- Aim to keep equal weight on both hips to avoid tilting to one side

- Allow your upper body to lower towards the floor, resting on your elbows or with arms outstretched if comfortable

Like the frog stretch, this is a passive stretch that you can get comfortable in. Hold the stretch for 2 minutes on one leg before switching positions to repeat the stretch on the other leg.

KEY POINT

Doing all 3 of the above stretches daily for just 2 mins (or 1 min on each side) would take you less than 10 mins and noticeable improvements would be made quickly.

MAKING CHRONIC CHANGE

Daily stretches help to relieve tension by lengthening the muscles, but further exercises can be added to make lasting improvements.

GOBLET SQUATS

A goblet squat is essentially a standard wide squat holding a light weight close to your chest. The added weight helps to ease you lower into the bottom of the squat, increasing the mobility around your hips. At the lowest point, hold the squat and use your elbows to push outwards against your knees. With practice, your aim is to squat deep enough to get your hamstrings in contact with your calves and maintain a neutral spine throughout.

- Do 2 sets of 5 reps after a stretching routine
- Spend at least 2 seconds in the bottom of each squat

GLUTE STRENGTHENING EXERCISES

Weak glutes tend to lead into anterior pelvic tilt which puts the hip flexors in a chronically lengthened position, creating a tight sensation in the muscles.

If the hip flexors are tight, the glutes will become weaker, leading to an on-going anterior pelvic tilt and an increased risk of injury. Stronger glutes will help to correct the tilt and make the improvements in hip mobility lasting changes.

HOW TO OVERCOME IT BAND TIGHTNESS

The IT band (iliotibial band) is a thick band of connective tissue that runs down the outside of your thigh from the hip to the knee. When it gets inflamed and painful, it's known as IT band syndrome.

The pain is generally felt on the outer edge of the knee and it's caused by the IT band rubbing across the bony lump at the base of the femur (thigh bone). The main function of the IT band is to stabilise the knee, so IT band syndrome is an overuse injury that's common among athletes in running sports.

STRETCH OR STRENGTHEN?

It's a common belief that lengthening the IT band with stretches will help to prevent it from becoming too tight and causing pain. However, attempting to lengthen it is not the answer. In a medical experiment carried out on a cadaver, a 900kg weight was suspended on an IT band and left for 24 hours. At the end of the experiment, the IT band had only stretched by 1cm. This demonstrates that efforts to stretch the IT band are going to be a waste of time. IT band syndrome is the result of poor movement and weakness in surrounding muscle groups, so preventing it comes down to stretching and strengthening the muscles that contribute to stabilising the knee.

R.I.C.E

If you're experiencing IT band pain as you run or walk, the first thing to do is RICE it.

Rest, Ice, Compression and Elevation.

The RICE method should be applied over a 24-hour period to help reduce the inflammation and hopefully the pain. After this period, it's time to address the underlying issues that are really causing the problem.

MAINTAIN FLEXIBILITY

Tightness in your leg and hip muscles will contribute to poor movement, so it's important to maintain flexibility in the key areas. These are the glutes, hamstrings and quads.

A great stretch for the glutes is the pigeon stretch:

- Begin on your knees and then bring one leg in front of you with the knee bent as if moving into a sitting cross-legged position
- Stretch the other leg out behind you as you lean your upper body towards the bent leg
- Hold for 20-30 seconds and then switch positions to stretch the other leg

A good stretch for the hamstrings is the seated hamstring stretch:

- Sit on the floor with your legs straight out in front of you
- Bend forwards from your hips (waist) and extend your arms along the outside of your legs
- Keep your legs straight (avoid bending your knees) and hold the stretch for 20-30 seconds

A simple quad stretch is enough to help maintain flexibility.

- Lie face down on the floor with straight legs
- Bend one knee and catch hold of your ankle with the hand on the same side
- Gently increase the bend in your knee, bringing your foot towards your glutes and pushing your hips into the floor at the same time

This stretch can also be done lying on your side. Hold for 20-30 seconds on each leg.

FOAM ROLL

The TFL (tensor fasciae latae) is a muscle that inserts into the IT band. If the TFL is tight, it's going to pull on the IT band and this can lead to knee pain. Foam rolling the TFL is a simple way to release any tension and ease that pain.

- Place the roller under your hip on one side
- Roll backwards and forwards over the hip area and the outer edge of your thigh just below your hip for around 30 seconds
- Switch sides to repeat on the other hip

This can be done a couple of times each day which could be enough to relieve the IT band pain. It's worth noting here that directly targeting the IT band with a foam roller is unlikely to bring any lasting relief. Foam rolling the area is beyond uncomfortable (it's brutal) and the tension this causes in your muscles will make it almost impossible to relax the surrounding muscles.

STRENGTHENING EXERCISES

Increasing the strength in the muscles that contribute to good knee alignment will also limit the potential to experience IT band pain. These include your quads, hamstrings and glutes which help to stabilise your knee, keeping it in line with your foot as you run.

Simple exercises you can do to strengthen these muscles include:

- Double-leg and single-leg glute raises
- Single-leg deadlifts
- Single-leg squats (stand on one leg, bend your knee and hip at the same time, go as low as you can keeping your knee in line with your foot and then return to a standing position again)

Forget stretching the IT band. Concentrate on stretching the muscles around your hips and lower body, strengthening the muscles that help to stabilise your knee and foam rolling the TFL to ease tension and pain. Do it regularly and not only will you move better; you'll also stay free of IT band pain.

HOW TO SPEED UP THE RECOVERY OF SORE LEGS

In football, muscle soreness in your legs will have a negative impact on your performance both in training and matches. This means finding effective ways to boost recovery after a heavy leg-training session is essential to keep you performing at your best.

LEG SORENESS

In season, a heavy leg-training session might be in the gym using heavy weights of up to 90% of your 1RM (one rep max) and low reps of around 3 to 5. Compared to lower weight and higher rep sessions, the muscle soreness will be minimal, but it's crucial to recover fully after each training session so that your legs are fresh for the next game and the potential to pick up injuries is minimised.

Out of season, a heavy leg-training session in the gym will revolve around moderate weights of around 80% of your 1RM but with a much higher volume of reps and sets. For example, this could be 5 sets of 5 reps, creating much greater potential for muscle soreness. As it's out of season, most coaches factor muscle soreness into a training schedule and fresh legs aren't needed for a game at the weekend, but it's still important to boost recovery as much as possible to limit the potential to pick up injuries.

KEY POINT

Muscle soreness is the result of small tears in the muscle fibres after heavy training. The trauma and subsequent healing are part of the natural process of building bigger, stronger muscles, with soreness generally kicking-in around 24 to 48 hours after the session.

BOOSTING RECOVERY

Two essential elements of boosting recovery are eating and sleeping. In a nutshell, you need to eat as much nutritious food as you can (unless you've got excess weight concerns) and get as much sleep as you can.

EATING

Immediately after a heavy leg-session, drinking half a litre of whole milk will give you an instant supply of protein, carbohydrates and fat. A recent study compared full-fat to semi-skimmed milk and concluded that full-fat milk is more beneficial in terms of building muscle. Another benefit is that it won't fill you up too much and you'll then be able to closely follow this with a meal containing further sources of protein, carbohydrates and moderate amounts of fat (15g) within 30-60 mins of the session or match. Refuelling in this way helps your body to repair the muscle damage caused by heavy training and therefore aids recovery.

SLEEPING

The recommendation for a good night's sleep has always been 8 hours, but the ideal amount is going to be an individual thing. Recovery takes place overnight when the body is resting, so it's always going to be beneficial to get as much sleep as possible after a heavy training session.

KEY POINT

Delayed onset muscle soreness (DOMS) after training can take up to 72 hours to subside. However, recovery will only take this long if you're not eating well and sleeping well or if your workload is extremely high.

COLD BATHS

Immediately after a heavy training session, immersing the muscles in cold water of around 15 degrees Celsius or lower for 10 to 15 minutes constricts the blood vessels, helping to reduce inflammation and pain. Once out of the cold bath, the blood vessels dilate, helping to flush out waste products such as lactic acid.

Many of the claimed benefits of ice baths are yet to be proven scientifically, but there's strong evidence to support the psychological benefits. Feeling fresher the following day ultimately leads to playing with more energy and freedom.

KEY POINT

Cold baths are only recommended during the season when muscle soreness might limit your performance in an upcoming match. Muscle soreness is not so limiting in the off-season and reducing the inflammation after an off or pre-season training session also reduces the muscle growth and strengthening stimulus, so it becomes counterproductive to utilise cold baths in this phase of the season.

FOAM ROLLING

The day after a heavy training session, the hardest-working muscles will feel tight and sore. Foam rolling is essentially a form of self-massage that can help to release tension, improve mobility and thereby promote recovery.

To use a foam roller on tight hamstrings or calves:

- Sit on the floor with your legs straight out in front
- Place the foam roller under the affected muscles e.g. hamstrings or calves
- Place your hands on the floor on either side of your backside, using them to lift your weight from the floor
- Supporting your weight on your hands, roll back and forth over the affected muscle group

To use a foam roller on tight glutes:

- Sit with the right-hand side of your backside on a foam roller, using your left foot and right hand on the floor to support your weight and aid your balance
- Cross your right leg (ankle) over your left thigh
- Roll back and forth several times and then switch positions to repeat with the left-hand side of your backside on the roller

STRETCHING AND MOBILISATION

After releasing muscle tension with a foam roller, following-up with static stretches will help to regain flexibility in the affected muscle groups. After static stretches, progress to dynamic stretches in the form of movements such as lunges, leg cradles and deep squats. The purpose of dynamic stretches is to increase the blood flow to the working muscles, tendons and ligaments and improve the mobility of the joints involved in the movement.

Numerous studies have shown that dynamic stretches as part of a warm up routine before taking part in sport can boost performance and help to prevent injuries and those benefits extend to aiding the recovery of sore muscles in the days after a hard training session.

KEY POINT

If you can get yourself comfortably into the bottom of a deep squat position, it demonstrates that you have a good existing level of flexibility and mobility in the muscles and joints of the lower body. If you can't, it shows you that there's still room for big improvements and that further work needs to be done.

OPTIMISING RECOVERY IN SUMMARY

- Eat well: whole milk immediately, followed by a balanced meal within an hour to an hour and a half
- Sleep well: ideally 8 hours or more if you need it
- Utilise cold baths: in-season only
- Foam roll and mobilise: the day after a heavy training session, use foam roller exercises followed by static and dynamic stretches to ease tight muscles and promote recovery

USING BATHS TO AID RECOVERY

Hydrotherapy can be used as a recovery aid after a hard training session or game, the main benefit for football players is a reduction in the perception of muscle soreness the next day, allowing for consistency in training and less chance of picking up injuries. Some favour ice baths, others hot baths, but contrast baths using both cold and hot water can also be used. There's currently very little scientific evidence to support the effectiveness of baths in real terms, but many players swear by them, so it may be something that needs to be experimented with to discover the benefits for yourself.

ICE BATHS

Cold baths, also known as ice-water immersion baths or cryotherapy, use water temperatures of around 15 degrees Celsius or lower, but not below 10 degrees. The idea is to submerge the affected muscles in the water for anywhere from 10 to 15 minutes after training (something most people find mentally as well as physically challenging the first time around).

BENEFITS

Heavy training causes tiny tears in the working muscles, leading to inflammation and DOMS (delayed onset muscle soreness) the following day and up to 72 hours later. The theory behind submerging the muscles in cold water is that the cold constricts (narrows) the blood vessels, helping to reduce swelling and also lower pain as the nerve-endings are numbed. After getting out of the bath, the increased blood flow to the muscles as the body warms up brings nutrients to boost healing and aids the process of flushing out waste products such as lactic acid that cause soreness.

However, it's important to note that players who have been raised in hot climates can find a cold bath so traumatic that it actually triggers an increase in the stress hormone cortisol. This is exactly the opposite effect to what we want as cortisol impedes recovery. This highlights the importance of combining a number of recovery methods rather than relying on one alone, but no matter which strategies you use, the two key elements will always be sleep and optimal nutrition.

HOT BATHS

The water temperature for a hot bath needs to be around 36 degrees Celsius up to as hot as can be tolerated.

BENEFITS

The theory behind hot baths is that the heat dilates (expands) the blood vessels, thereby increasing blood flow to the muscles, helping to flush out the lactic acid and waste product build-up that leads to soreness the day after. Heat also increases the flexibility of the muscles, helping to ease muscle stiffness when combined with a stretching programme.

CONTRAST BATHS

This requires two separate baths, one at 15 degrees Celsius and the other at 36 degrees. The idea is to complete 3 to 6 cycles of being in cold for one to two minutes and then hot for one to two minutes, moving directly from one to the other and finishing with cold.

BENEFITS

In theory, contrast baths bring the combined benefits of both ice baths and hot baths. The cold constricts the blood vessels to reduce swelling and the heat dilates the blood vessels to increase blood flow and flush out waste products. An added bonus of a contrast bath is that the exposure to cold and heat is short-lived, so it's less of a mental and physical challenge to endure.

SCHEDULING HYDROTHERAPY

Ice baths: The tiny tears in muscle fibres caused by heavy training lead to hypertrophy, the body's natural response to a repetitive increase in workload. As the damaged fibres are repaired, the muscle grows bigger and stronger, so for this reason, ice baths should be limited to during the season and avoided in pre-season.

Pre-season training sessions are designed to promote muscle strength and growth, so reducing the inflammation that naturally occurs after a session will in fact hinder this process. Muscle soreness is to be expected after pre-season training sessions as this is one of the only times of the year where footballers can focus on adding lean muscle due to the soreness which is typically experienced which will hinder match performance during the season.

During the season, muscle soreness will limit performance and increase the potential to pick up injuries, so an ice bath after a heavy session can reduce the inflammation and the soreness it creates, helping you to stay on track in training and fresh for games.

Hot baths: This type of bath can be utilised at any point in the season, especially as part of a flexibility training programme. Studies have proven that muscles are more pliable after 10 to 15 minutes in a hot bath, so following up with a stretching routine can relieve tight muscles that are more prone to injury.

Due to the circulation-boosting effects of a hot bath, it's not recommended to take one just before going to bed. Allow time for your body to relax and return to normal body temperature to ensure a good night's sleep.

Contrast baths: The ice-water aspect of contrast baths limits their usefulness pre-season, but they can be helpful in terms of injury recovery. The dramatic change of temperature from cold to hot and back again can stimulate an injured muscle without adding the stress of movement. This way an injury can be rested but benefit from the tissue workout provided by the constricting and dilating blood vessels.

PSYCHOLOGICAL BENEFITS

There's limited scientific evidence to prove the physical benefits of hydrotherapy for footballers, but there's plenty of subjective evidence to support the psychological benefits. Those who swear by ice-baths report a lower rate of perceived exertion (RPE) in the following day's training session. There may be no measurable physical improvement, but feeling stronger or faster mentally has a positive impact on performance.

It's well-known that a soak in a hot tub can be a relaxing experience, so it's not surprising that many players find a hot bath therapeutic when their muscles are tired or sore. As with ice treatments, the psychological benefits of heat are closely linked to reports of feeling less physical pain in affected muscles.

PROS AND CONS OF BATHS IN SUMMARY

Ice or cold baths can help to reduce inflammation and associated muscle soreness. This is beneficial during the season to help keep training and match performance consistent, but ice baths should be avoided in pre-season training when the aim is to promote muscle growth.

Hot baths can help to relieve tight muscles, thereby reducing pain and promoting greater flexibility when combined with stretches. To gain maximum benefits, the water temperature needs to be kept above 36 degrees Celsius for at least 10 minutes.

Contrast baths can promote recovery in injured muscles. However, the logistics of keeping two baths (or wheelie bins) at the ideal temperature and the need to move straight from one to the other make contrast baths a less practical option (especially in a team environment).

DO EPSOM SALT BATHS AID RECOVERY?

Many players are led to believe that bathing in Epsom salt baths can aid muscle recovery...but does the science back up this commonly made claim?

WHAT IS EPSOM SALT?

Epsom salt isn't salt as you know it.

It's a naturally occurring compound of magnesium and sulphate (also known as magnesium sulphate). The high magnesium concentration in Epsom salt is believed to aid to muscle recovery as magnesium plays an important role in muscle and nerve function. Magnesium can also reduce inflammation and is an important co factor for many metabolic energy-related reactions.

The theory is that the magnesium ions in the Epsom salt can pass directly through the skin, into your blood stream and then into your muscle tissue. It's claimed that there's a 100% absorption of the magnesium into the muscle cells, which if true would mean that maximal magnesium uplift into your muscle stores could be achieved by taking just one Epsom salt bath.

This could be a game changer, as magnesium deficiency is extremely common in the general population and especially in athletic populations, with around 75% of people being magnesium deficient.

SCIENCE V ANECDOTAL EVIDENCE

However, scientific research on the effect of Epsom salts on the body is extremely limited. Only three studies have assessed the benefits of bathing in Epsom salts and only one of those studies found improvements in terms of increasing magnesium stores or any other muscle recovery related benefit. Interestingly that study was funded by the Epsom Salt Council...so the results of a study funded by an establishment selling Epsom salts may need to be taken with a pinch of salt itself.

The findings of the other studies concluded that magnesium ions are too large to pass through any sort of biological membrane, so magnesium is not able to pass through the skin. It might be possible in areas such as the sweat glands and hair follicles, but these areas represent only 0.1 to 1% of the skin surface, so any amount that's able to pass through is going to be insignificant in terms of effect.

As the research to back up the claims is very limited, it's true to say that any benefits to athletic performance reported from Epsom salt baths are psychological, from personal experience only and not backed up by concrete science.

FLAWED THINKING

The thinking behind bathing in Epsom salts may make some sense, but the claims don't add up. In an average bath, you're going to use around 35g of magnesium sulphate which equates to around 3.5g of magnesium. The current daily recommended intake of magnesium is only 300-400mg per day, so if 3.5g of magnesium was being absorbed through the skin, it would lead to toxicity issues and we'd have reports of people dying after taking Epsom salt baths – clearly, this is not the case!

One potential reason for Epsom salt bath fans claiming that they bring recovery benefits more likely than not stems from the positive effects of a hot bath alone, rather than the added salts.

It's known that sitting in a sauna after exercise can:

- Increase blood flow and thermo-regulatory performance during exercise
- Potentially increase muscle protein synthesis or even growth hormone levels post exercise

...so, it's possible that some of the same benefits are being experienced by sitting in a hot bath – but this is just a theory.

The bottom line on this one is that sticking to leafy green and cruciferous vegetables such as kale and spinach and oily fish such as salmon is the best approach to gain the benefits of magnesium.

THE IMPORTANCE OF SLEEP AND SCHEDULING RECOVERY TIME

Nutrition and good quality sleep are really the two biggest factors which will affect recovery over foam rolling, ice baths and almost any other recovery method you can name. Sleep is an incredibly important element of both cognitive and physical performance; it also has a huge impact on injury risk, with a 2014 study finding that athletes who slept less than 8 hours per night had a 1.7 x greater risk of injury than those who slept 8 or more hours.

Every potential positive adaptation that can come from your hard training (which provides only the stimulus for improvement) takes place during sleep. One of the roles of sleep is to help solidify and consolidate the information you've learnt throughout the day. Before you can store new information, it first needs to be processed, so if you really want to engrain that new 1v1 skill or striking technique, you need to have good quality sleep in order to solidify those experiences.

It's important to remember that when you're training, you're stressing and fatiguing the body. Straight after a tough session, your fitness is actually worse than it was prior to the session, you're not improving it during the session itself. In order for supercompensation to occur (which means to return to a level of fitness higher than you were previously at thanks to your training), optimal nutrition combined with good quality sleep is essential.

Human growth hormone (HGH) is released in pulses during sleep and plays a key role in muscle growth and repair, it's important to take advantage of this and not fall into the trap of sacrificing scheduled rest time for additional training sessions in the belief that more is always better. A common mistake which many players make is trying to mimic the training intensities of someone like Ronaldo whilst:

1. Not possessing fitness levels anywhere near the same level, so creating a huge spike in workload which can lead to injury and chronic fatigue
2. Not appreciating the key role that nutrition and sleep has in the whole training adaptation process
3. Not allowing enough recovery time between training and matches, therefore entering the match in a fatigued state and under-performing (remember the goal of all training, to improve match day performance)

So how is it that players like Ronaldo seem to be able to train hard day in day out and not break down?

Well the first factor is that all of their training is carefully planned and constantly monitored by sports science experts. This ensures safe increases in workload and reduces the chance of developing injuries related to overuse or fatigue. As for players at any level, sleep and optimal nutrition are still vital. The key difference is that a training schedule for someone like Ronaldo, would obviously cause a less trained player far more stress and fatigue than it would for Ronaldo because he has a higher base level of fitness.

So, whilst a top pro's training schedule might look intense on the face of it, the stress caused is relative to the level of conditioning of the player. Combine this with an ability to recover from any given training intensity quicker than a less trained player (thanks to years of conditioning) and it explains why top pros can consistently repeat such high levels of performance. They are simply conditioned to tolerate a greater workload and can also recover more efficiently.

This should hopefully highlight that achieving an elite level of fitness is done by repeating cycles of stress, optimal nutrition and recovery over long periods of time. Ultimately the primary goal is to be able to reach and maintain as high a level of fitness and performance as possible without getting injured. So, if you combine smart training with great nutrition and sleep, you're going to progress quicker and experience fewer setbacks in form from fatigue or injury.

It makes sense to get as much bang for your buck out of every training session and ensuring adequate sleep combined with great nutrition will provide this for you. You wouldn't accept being short changed for something you've paid for in everyday life, so why accept it in your training?

Post training naps are also a great strategy to utilise. If possible, schedule a 15-30 minute nap after your daytime training sessions, it's another opportunity to take advantage of increased HGH levels. If you often feel groggy after a nap, a common and affective strategy is to have a caffeinated drink such as coffee immediately prior to your nap, this won't work quickly enough to prevent you from getting to sleep but will help with alertness when you wake back up. Obviously, this strategy should only be applied to naps, don't do this one before going to bed at night.

NIGHT GAMES

Night games have been shown to negatively impact sleep quality and duration in elite players. Not only do flood lights hinder the release of melatonin (a sleep promoting hormone) and throw out your circadian rhythm (internal process which regulates the sleep-wake cycle) but it can also take hours to wind down after the final whistle due to increased levels of adrenaline. This undoubtedly has a direct and negative impact on the post-match recovery process.

Of course, you cannot avoid playing and training at night, but there are simple things you can do to mitigate the impact. These include meditation and going through a night time routine as soon as possible after ensuring good nutrition.

SLEEP RECOMMENDATIONS

- Sleep 8-9 hours per night
- Set a consistent lights-out and wake time
- Use the bedroom only for sleep
- Establish a relaxing pre bed time routine
- Stop looking at your phone at least 30 minutes before bed
- Create a quiet, comfortable and dark sleep environment
- Don't consume caffeine before night time sleeps
- Take one 20–30-minute power nap during the day or in between sessions if possible

WHY DO YOUR JOINTS CLICK?

Movements such as bending at the knee or flexing a hip as the knee is pulled towards the chest in a warm-up stretch can cause what's described as a clicking sound in the joint. For footballers, this is a noise that can raise concerns over whether there's a problem that might lead to injury, however, most of the time there's a simple explanation with a logical fix.

POTENTIAL REASONS FOR CLICKING JOINTS

- Gas build-up between the bones
- Rapid stretching of a ligament
- Tight muscles causing a tendon to rub on bone

GAS BUILD-UP

If you can crack your knuckles, the sound you hear is being made by the release of small bubbles of nitrogen in the joints. This gas build-up is quite normal between bones, so a similar noise in your knee or any other joint when you bend it is no cause for concern, provided there's no pain.

RAPID STRETCHING OF A LIGAMENT

Ligaments connect bone to bone across a joint. In some movements, the rapid stretching of a ligament can cause it to make a cracking noise as it snaps back into place. Again, provided there's no pain (or pain is very short-lived) there's little need for concern.

TIGHT MUSCLES

Tendons connect muscles to bones, so when a muscle becomes tight, it pulls on the tendon and this can lead to the tendon rubbing across the bone and a clicking sound.

Tight muscles are the most common reason for clicking joints and a simple way to test whether this is the cause is to repeat the move that created the sound after gently stretching the muscles around the joint. For example, if it's your knee that clicks when you bend it, gently stretch your quads and hip flexors and then repeat the move that created the click. If the click has gone, your muscles are just a bit tight and there's nothing to be concerned about. Tight muscles can be alleviated by following a regular stretching programme.

CAUSES FOR CONCERN

Clicking sounds without pain are generally nothing to worry about. However, if the sounds are accompanied by pain or swelling in the joint, it can be an indicator of an injury that needs to be checked out.

KEY POINT

Pain is the biggest indicator of a problem. Where there's pain, avoid stretching and visit a physiotherapist as soon as possible for an expert diagnosis.

POPCORN CRACKING

Another sound that can be heard around moving joints is a cracking that's almost like popcorn popping or bubble wrap being popped, so you no longer hear just one click but many clicks one after the other. For example, you might hear this type of popping in your hip joint when doing the opening and closing the gate warm-up exercise and if this is the case, you need the attention of a physio as it can indicate impingement.

If muscles around a joint become excessively tight, they can limit the normal range of movement and in some cases, if the joint is being prevented from moving as it should, it can lead to bone on bone contact. This type of cracking will generally cause pain and needs to be rectified before the risk of further injury increases.

LISTEN TO YOUR BODY

Cracking in your joints isn't necessarily a cause for concern, but it is important to look after your body. Some people get tight hips, other tight calves, so you need to listen to your body and build an awareness of your potential problem areas.

Use pain as your guide. If there's no pain, regular stretching and foam rolling should rectify it. If there is pain, get it looked at and take the advice of a physio.

HOW YOUR INJURY RISK CHANGES POST-MATCH

It's well known that there is an increased risk of injury in the 48-hour period after a tough match. This is due to residual fatigue and inflammation within your body that's part of the natural healing process. For this reason, you're not in the best state to train or play hard during this period and you should schedule your training to fit around recovery time.

The risk of injury is increased when your muscles are tired and when your body is working hard to repair the damage done in a game. Some professional teams measure counter-movement jumps pre-match and then every day post-match until the jumps return to the pre-match level. This can take anything from 48 to 72 hours, but a player won't return to full training until a satisfactory level is reached.

RECOVERY SCHEDULE

For most players, if the game is on Saturday, then the team will resume full training on Tuesday. This puts them on the other side of the higher injury risk period, so they can train hard in the gym and any residual fatigue from the Tuesday session should be long gone by the time the next match comes around on the following Saturday.

The 48-hour recovery period is a good time to work on foam rolling, stretching and mobility work. Releasing knots, maintaining flexibility and improving joint mobility in key areas such as the hips and ankles will help to reduce the risk of picking up injuries in training and in match play, it will also help to improve your performance.

Day 1: The day after the game should be a day of active recovery. This might be as simple as heading out and doing some light ball work just to raise your heart rate a little and get your blood flowing. Remember also that mental recovery is just as important as physical recovery, so adding variety to your normal training week during these days is key.

Day 2: If you're itching to train, this is a good day to do core stability work, or single-leg landing work. These exercises cause only a small amount of fatigue, so they won't hinder the recovery process or induce any further muscular damage. It's important to keep it light and avoid using heavy weights which could prolong your recovery from fatigue.

STRUCTURE YOUR WEEK

Players often don't structure their week to get the maximum benefits out of each training session. Without structure, there's potential for one training session to negatively impact the next training session and this approach can negatively impact your next game.

For this reason, it's useful to plan your week. Sunday night is a good time to think about the week ahead and make a clear plan of which sessions fit where, to ensure you're not training or playing with tired muscles that are much more susceptible to picking up injuries. As an obvious example, you know that a gym session involving leg work and heavy weights will likely lead to some muscle soreness, so you need to avoid this type of session on a Friday if you have a game on Saturday.

RECOVERY SCHEDULE IN SUMMARY

- Saturday: game
- Sunday: active recovery
- Monday: light training
- Tuesday: full training

The structure of your week is crucial if you are to avoid over-working tired muscles after a game and avoid scheduling heavy training immediately before a game. Your body needs recovery time and if you fail to plan your weekly training schedule, you could be putting yourself at a much higher risk of injury.

MAINTAINING FITNESS WHEN YOU'RE INJURED

FITNESS LOSS

When your life revolves around football, an injury at any stage of the season can be devasting, both physically and mentally. The first question asked by most injured players is, "When can I get back to training?" and when the answer involves more than a week or two of enforced rest, a huge sense of frustration kicks in at the thought of losing fitness and missing matches.

If this has happened to you, you will no doubt have questioned the effect that being unable to train will have on your hard-earned fitness levels, so let's answer those questions by taking a look at the body's response to rest and recovery in terms of strength, aerobic fitness and anaerobic fitness.

STRENGTH

The first thing to note here is that changes to your overall level of strength are going to be minimal in the first couple of weeks. If you're unable to get to the gym or lift weights for a week or two, you don't need to panic about your strength levels suddenly plummeting.

Once you're into week three however, your strength will begin to drop off, but even after a month of no strength training at all, you're still going to have maintained a level of strength that's above your initial baseline, so you're not going to be back at square one when you do resume training. You're also going to be able to regain your strength quicker than a complete beginner thanks to the solid muscle memory you'll have already developed (if you've been strength training regularly for at least a year prior to getting injured).

AEROBIC FITNESS

The aerobic aspect of fitness is perhaps the main concern for football players. As with strength, there's going to be minimal overall loss in the first week or two of enforced rest. After two or three weeks without aerobic exercise however, your VO2 max will start to decline and your heart musculature will begin to decrease (making it less efficient at pumping blood around the body to the working muscles).

One of the key benefits of aerobic training is an increase in the number of capillaries, the tiny blood vessels providing oxygenated blood to working muscles around the body, including the heart. After a month of no aerobic fitness training, decreased capillarisation means less oxygen getting to the heart, so everything begins to feel like harder work and you'll find it takes you longer to recover between high intensity efforts.

KEY POINT

The above losses in aerobic fitness may sound catastrophic, but the key to accelerating the recovery process is acceptance, being resourceful and doing what you can. Frustration and other negative thought processes will only sap your energy, so switch your focus away from what can't be changed and put it onto what can be achieved during this period.

ANAEROBIC FITNESS

Your anaerobic system provides your body with explosive, short term energy. It's utilised in moments such as breaking away from an opponent, defending in a 1v1 situation, sprinting back from a corner or aggressively protecting the ball. The good news is that even after a month of no training, the drop off in the intensity of these actions will be minimal (although you may struggle to sustain each effort for as long as you previously could), however your ability to keep repeating those same maximal efforts without a big drop off in intensity will be hindered due to a decline in aerobic fitness.

KEY POINT

The key to giving yourself the best chance of maintaining your all-round fitness level whilst injured comes down to answering these three questions:

1. What can you do to work around the injury and keep your lower body strong?
2. How can you keep your training load high? (What work can you do in this period to maintain fitness?)
3. What weaknesses can you work on in this period?

WORKING AROUND THE INJURY

The first thing to be aware of is something known as the cross-training phenomenon. In a nutshell, this describes the discovery that training one leg can lead to neural strength gains in the other leg, meaning that continuing to train your uninjured leg will help you to maintain strength in your injured leg.

This will not only help you to maintain strength levels whilst you're injured, it also means less training time will be spent on regaining strength once you've been given the all-clear to return to normal training, which will ultimately help you to return to peak performance a little quicker.

If you have a knee injury, the cross-training phenomenon can be useful, but if it's an ankle injury, you may be able to take a different approach. Exercise machines such as hamstring curls and leg extensions may still be useable as normal without affecting the injury. Split squats with the uninjured leg in front and the injured leg elevated in a comfortable position behind you could also be doable, but if any of these exercises cause pain or your physio advises you against them for your specific injury, then they should be avoided.

Being injured can be a blessing if you look at it positively. It gives you time to reflect and make big progress in weaker areas of your game and athleticism which may otherwise be pushed down the pecking order. For example, increasing your upper body strength and size isn't a priority during the season and even in the off-season the time available to make real progress can be limited. By increasing your upper body strength, you can increase your ability to hold off bigger players and be more dominant in the air, which might be something you've struggled with in the past.

KEEPING TRAINING LOADS HIGH

Your training load is essentially the amount of work you do in a week or given time period. If you're used to doing lots of training and you normally play two games a week, your training load is going to drop dramatically if you're suddenly unable to do any exercise due to injury. If you can't find a way to train in some way and then attempt to return straight back to the same training load, it's going to create a huge spike in workload which puts you at very high risk of re-injury and even developing a new injury.

Avoiding this type of workload spike requires either keeping your workload at a good level whilst you're injured or making gradual increases in training load once you're able to train again (and this requires time). So, if you can find a way to continue training in some form around your injury (in the gym for example) to try and keep your training load as high as possible, then you're simply going to return to play in better condition, decrease your risk of injury and have less of a mountain to climb to return to full match fitness. In the next article, we'll outline some great training options that you can utilise during this period and beyond as you return to full match fitness.

GETTING BACK TO MATCH FITNESS POST-INJURY

If you've been out of training for an extended period due to injury, the time it takes to get back to your pre-injury fitness level will depend on what that level was and whether you've been able to do any other form of exercise in place of training.

There's not a one size fits all answer and the time required to return to match fitness will vary from person to person. It essentially depends on:

1. How fit you were prior to the injury
2. How long you're going to be out for
3. What intensity of training you're going to be able to do without using the injured area

If you had a high level of fitness prior to getting injured, you're out for 6 months and unable to do any form of intense training at all, then obviously it is going to take you longer to build back up to your pre-injury level of match fitness.

It's also important to understand that if you were reaching a point of fatigue and training hard prior to injury, then it's likely that the initial extended rest time will actually allow your body to recover, adapt and super-compensate to a higher level of fitness. This is why when players are out for anything from a couple of days to a couple of weeks for whatever reason, they often return to training feeling lighter, fresher and fitter than before.

Of course, once supercompensation has occurred, the next stress and stimulus must be applied in order to keep progressing and avoid a decline in fitness, this may or may not be possible depending on the injury you have.

GETTING BACK TO PRE-INJURY FITNESS

When you've been out of action for a prolonged period, there's a huge temptation to launch straight back into training at the level you were pre-injury. Not only would this put you at risk of re-injury, you'd also be putting yourself at risk of picking up new completely different injury because your body is out of condition. The key to returning to fitness is to increase the workload gradually whilst ensuring good sleep, optimal nutrition and continually monitoring how your body is reacting to each training session or workout which is completed.

Having a goal to aim for (such as being available for a cup match) can be motivational, but it's important to ensure it's realistic and not going to put you at risk of re-injury, not to mention unnecessary stress. This can be very difficult when you're under pressure from coaches who want to have you back playing, but ultimately, it's in both of your interests to:

1. Return to match play and be able to play to your full potential (who knows who might be watching)
2. Return for the rest of the season and beyond, not just one match

It's important not to lose sight of that and avoid getting sucked into a dangerous cycle of playing through one injury which then leads to the development of a new injury.

KEY POINT

Take the advice of your physio and plan your return-to-fitness training schedule around a realistic timeframe. Getting back to fitness is going to require time and patience, every increase in workload must be made gradually to minimise the potential for setbacks and further injuries.

Research has shown that an increase of no more than 1.3 times the previous week's workload is the safest and most efficient way to make progress. Most studies revolve around distance running, as an example for demonstrative purposes this would mean an athlete running a total of 1000m in a week would not increase their workload to more than 1300m the following week and then 1690m the week after that.

Of course, this is harder to quantify in terms of football performance and there's no need to get your calculator out, but it demonstrates the need to avoid huge spikes in training-load when returning from an injury i.e. going from performing a non-contact rehab session which involves a 20m sprint every 2 minutes for 30 minutes, to full match play the next week which demands a 20m sprint every minute for 90 minutes.

The more time you give yourself to get back to full fitness after an injury the better, but one potential way of speeding up the process is to get resourceful and look for alternative ways to maintain fitness whilst you're unable to train with the team. Here's some examples:

CARDIO

Start by working continuously at maximal intensity using any of the options listed below until you can no longer sustain your speed, form and power. Make a note of this time and then rest until fully recovered, make a note of this time too. These are now your work to rest ratios. From here you can gradually progress the intensity by decreasing the recovery time between sets, extending the working time periods or adding more sets.

You could also switch between short periods of high intensity and longer periods of low intensity for a continuous workout (rather than stopping for complete rest between efforts).

- Battle ropes
- Assault bike (using arms only)
- Boxing (seated or standing depending on the injury)
- Swimming
- Rower (with the injured leg to the side on a sliding board)

STRENGTH

This is a great time to focus on stability work and single-leg exercises for the uninjured leg. Exercises such as single-leg deadlifts and single-leg squats to a box are effective exercises for improving ankle, knee and hip stability and can be done without incorporating the injured leg or using heavy loads.

In terms of upper body training, performing compound, seated/lying upper body exercises such as the bench press, seated dumbbell shoulder press and lat pull downs should also not be a problem. This is be a great opportunity to return from injury with increased upper body strength and power which will boost your ability to hold off opponents, be stronger in tackles and more physical in the air.

By using compound movements, you'll also be engaging the core. However, if you want to do some more targeted core training, then just be sure that you select exercises which do not require the injured area to become engaged. For example, trying to perform Russian twists whilst recovering from a hip flexor injury is only going to aggravate the area. Instead try to focus on core exercises which are more stable (less stable exercises could require sudden corrective movements) but still challenge the core in a dynamic and functional way across a session. These could include:

- Woodchops
- Hip raises

- Dead bugs
- Elbow plank
- Supine Toe Taps
- Wipers

MOBILITY & FLEXIBILITY

At the very least you should be able to work on your mobility, flexibility and tissue quality within the uninjured regions of your body on a daily basis. By focusing on these areas, you could actually return to training as a more athletic and powerful player than you were pre-injury thanks to a more optimal range of movement within your joints and increased muscle activation levels, allowing for a more efficient application, transfer and absorption of force. Similarly, an increase in flexibility and tissue quality can reduce your risk of future muscle strains and enable you to move with greater freedom. Combining all of these elements will enable you to utilise a greater percentage of the strength and power which you already possess within you. Some great options include:

- Assisted static stretching using a looped resistance band
- Regular static stretching
- Foam rolling
- Myofascial release using a massage ball or equivalent
- Yoga
- Massage gun

THE BOTTOM LINE

A month of no training will likely lead to a drop-off in all aspects of your fitness, however if you can get resourceful then you will slow this decline and return to match fitness faster once your injury is healed and rehabbed. The fastest route between two points is the path of least resistance, so don't let frustration prolong your journey from injury to recovery, accept the situation and do everything you can to maintain your fitness without risking re-injury.

NUTRITION

CAN YOU OUT-TRAIN A BAD DIET?

You may have heard it said that fitness is 80% nutrition and only 20% training, but statements like these are not based on any type of scientific evidence and they're nothing more than numbers pulled out of thin air. However, they do lead many to question whether it's possible to out-train a bad diet and the answer to this depends on the context.

WEIGHT LOSS

If you're training to change your body shape, whether it's fat loss or muscle gain, then you could potentially out-train a bad diet. However, it's certainly not advised and much depends on what is being defined as "bad".

For example, if you're trying to lose body fat and your diet is essentially huge quantities of junk food, your caloric intake is going to be very high, but you could still technically achieve weight loss if you increased your energy expenditure enough to compensate. At the end of the day, changes in weight are the result of changes in energy balance, so it's all about calories in versus calories out and burning off more calories than you're taking in.

KEY POINT

It is possible to lose weight on a terrible diet, but your exercise levels per day would need to be extremely high.

As a footballer, increasing your level of activity to compensate for a bad diet is not practical and it would likely hinder your recovery from other types of training done around your team sessions. It's possible to lose fat on a bad diet, but it's more than likely you'd also experience a relative loss in lean muscle mass. This would negatively impact your performance as well as your general health and well-being compared to dieting and losing fat with good nutritional habits.

MUSCLE GAIN

In terms of gaining muscle mass, you can get away with being slightly more lenient with nutrition. A bad diet will have less of an impact simply because your overall calorie intake needs to be quite high.

However, if you take this to a more extreme level, you might be adding lean mass whilst quickly gaining body fat at the same time. This will have a detrimental effect on performance, particularly agility and endurance. You're also much more likely to be deficient in micro-nutrients if your diet is poor and this will impact your health as well as your performance.

TRAINING ADAPTATIONS

Can you out-train a bad diet in terms of training adaptations? The answer to this one is no. Good nutrition is an essential element of making progress through training and improving your physical functioning. A complete beginner in an untrained state may experience some training adaptations and improvements despite a bad diet simply because the new training stimulus is huge compared to their previous state.

The more trained you are, the slower you will progress and the more essential it is to eat well to train well. As a footballer in a well-trained state, you can't maintain progress without good nutrition and you can't out-train a bad diet. Training only provides the stimulus and signals for the body to adapt, but it does not inherently cause adaptation. Adaptations and improvements will only occur when you match these stimuli and signals with the required nutrient availability to be able to take advantage of them.

For example, in a weightlifting session you are strategically breaking down your muscle tissue, providing the stimulus and signals that increase your potential to adapt and progress beyond your previous state. Your body may up-regulate signals during training, such as:

- The potential for protein synthesis
- The potential to generate new muscle cells and proteins
- The signals that promote an increase in the number of energy-producing mitochondria within your muscle cells

...but, the key thing to remember here is that these are just signals. In this example, unless you ingest the correct type and amounts of protein at the required time after training, you're not going to be able to take advantage of the training stimulus that will allow you to grow and improve.

KEY POINT

You need signals provided by training to adapt and the right nutrition to take advantage of the signals. You can't have one without the other and it's for this reason that statements relating to percentages are fundamentally flawed.

GENERAL HEALTH

Training and nutrition are of equal importance in terms of fitness and performance, but it can be argued that nutrition becomes more important in terms of general health. No amount of training will allow you to be healthy if you're not consuming the correct foods.

KEY POINT

In relation to health, you can't out-train a bad diet.

The more research that becomes available on nutrition, the clearer it becomes how critical the diet is in terms of health, well-being and disease prevention. Training can improve health but there is a growing body of evidence to support the effectiveness of correct nutrition in lowering blood pressure and reducing inflammation.

Common conditions associated with a poor diet include high cholesterol levels, elevated blood pressure and poor gut health. Training can reduce the extent to which these conditions harm you, but they will still harm you.

The bottom line is that if you want to be a fit, healthy footballer, training and playing to the best of your ability both physically and mentally, fuel your body and brain with good nutrition and don't try to out-train a bad diet.

THE IMPORTANCE OF NUTRITION FOR ADAPTATIONS TO TRAINING

One of the most important concepts that you should be aware of is that training does not inherently cause improvements to your physical capabilities or performances on the pitch. This is by no means a concept that diminishes the fundamental importance of training, but instead one that emphasizes that there is more to the puzzle than you may realise.

Correct training gives the "potential" for physiological systems (cardiovascular, nervous and musculoskeletal) to undergo specific adaptations that increase your bodies physical capabilities. As you are probably aware, training sessions themselves are actually physically detrimental when considering the large mechanical stress they place on the body.

However, athletes are of course fine with this reality when understanding that the acute physical detriment forces the body to rebuild, adapt and hopefully make them a better version of their prior self.

Provided the mechanical stress from training is sufficient, this stress will produce various signals that alters the expression and activity of your genes to give the intended result of that training session (improved speed or strength for example).

This all stems back to basic biology where your genes are fully responsible for the amount and activity of every single protein and cell that is made within your body. Although you may not know it, when you train you are communicating with your genes and demanding a certain response.

For example, as endurance capacity is mainly determined by the number of energy-producing mitochondria within your muscle cells, when you engage in strenuous endurance activity you are interacting with your genes to stimulate the production of mitochondrial proteins.

Alternatively, when you engage in resistance training to try and increase muscle mass, you are interacting with your genes to stimulate the production of multiple proteins which constitute muscle fibres. Further, the type of training you engage in influences the type of muscle fibres that can be formed (type 1 or type 2) because the proteins that the genes produce will vary based off the different training signals.

WHAT ROLE DOES NUTRITION PLAY?

In a simple sense, training is the lock and nutrition is the key.

For training adaptations to occur and for your genes to produce the proteins which you require to improve, you need the signal and you need the fuel. This follows on from the previous train of thought, as your genes need the signal to know which proteins to produce and the energy and amino acids to actually be able to make these proteins. So where do we get energy and amino acids from? You guessed it, the calories and dietary protein stored in food.

This concept explains why eating enough calories and protein is essential for training adaptations to occur. If you're under eating, you are not providing your genes with the substrates needed to produce the proteins that your training has signalled to be made.

This ultimately causes your physical framework to remain stagnant and you will not improve. On the other hand, providing your body with sufficient calories and protein will ensure training signals are taken advantage of (certain nutritional approaches can even influence the type and strength of the signals that are induced by training sessions).

THE CONNECTION BETWEEN NUTRITION & MENTAL PERFORMANCE

Your gut system is incredibly complex. Believe it or not, the health of your gut has the power to directly influence your psychology and mental function.

At any one time, you have thousands of different types of micro-organisms in your gut, collectively known as your gut microbiota or microbiome. These micro-organisms are living things, usually some type of bacteria. You have 100 trillion of them in your gut – about 10 times the number of cells in your body and approximately 200 times the number of human genes you have. If you think about it from a broad perspective, we are all just a super-organism that carries billions of living micro-organisms within it.

THE GUT-BRAIN NETWORK

Your gut microbiota is involved in a huge number of metabolic processes, including the:

- Metabolism and absorption of nutrients
- Decomposition of proteins
- Synthesis of vitamins and bioactive compounds

It plays a crucial role in maintaining a strong immune system. It's also recently been discovered that there's a crucial link between the gut and the brain, now deemed the gut-brain network.

The close communication between the micro-organisms in the gut and the brain is linked by what's known as the gut-brain axis and many recent studies have found that the gut microbiota develops simultaneously with the brain and your psychology. This means that the gut not only regulates the structure and function of the brain, it also influences the development and the behaviour of the brain.

Research has revealed that individuals with abnormal gut microbiota (abnormal composition of gut micro-organisms) have faster rates of brain dysfunction and mental disorders and this can include impaired learning capacity and even memory.

POOR GUT HEALTH

Something that's very important in relation to sport and football is that chronic fatigue is also known to be a consequence of poor gut health. The health of the gut barrier (surrounding the wall of the gut) is very important as this keeps micro-organisms within the gut and regulates the flow of nutrients and molecules from the gut into the bloodstream, ideally preventing any harmful micro-organisms and substances from entering the blood and causing an inflammatory reaction.

Without a strong and healthy gut barrier, a condition known as leaky gut can develop. Damage to the gut barrier prevents it from functioning properly, affecting its permeability and thereby its ability to prevent micro-organisms from passing through that wouldn't normally do so. This not only leads to damage and inflammation, it also impairs the blood-brain barrier, meaning harmful micro-organisms can reach the brain and induce neuro-inflammation, creating numerous poor psychological effects.

MAINTAINING A HEALTHY GUT

Maintaining a healthy gut comes down to two main things:

1. Making sure the micro-organisms within the gut are healthy and able to keep us functioning properly
2. Keeping the gut barrier strong and functioning properly to stop anything bad in the gut from leaking out and causing inflammation, or in terms of the brain, causing neuro-inflammation and damage to the brain

GOOD AND BAD GUT BACTERIA

So, what can be done from a nutritional perspective to keep your gut healthy?

What you eat and other lifestyle factors, dictates the composition of the micro-organisms in your gut and the function of the gut barrier. There are healthy gut bacteria and bad or unhealthy gut bacteria and what you eat is effectively providing living space and food for these micro-organisms in your gut. With your food choices, you are unconsciously regulating the type and the number of these micro-organisms.

The bottom line is that a terrible diet is going to feed the bad variety. If you're not providing enough dietary fibre for the healthy bacteria within the gut, your gut health is going to be bad in comparison to someone on a very wholesome natural food diet.

These different states in the gut have very different effects on the brain. When you start to deprive the healthy bacteria in the gut, you begin to see a disfunction in terms of gut function, including your digestive system, immune system, nervous system, the neural/brain systems that affect your behaviour, cognition and mental clarity.

Leading on from this, we know that human genes have not changed much over the last 100 years, but human microbiota has undergone tremendous change. This is due to agricultural changes and modern-day food processing which has led to higher levels of sugar, unhealthy fatty acids, chemicals and additives in the typical diet and a consequent change in the composition of gut bacteria. In more rural areas and in older generations, changes in gut bacteria are relatively small and this is because a more traditional diet of wholefoods has been maintained. This also means that these populations have lower incidences of modern-day diseases and the psychological issues which are increasingly prevalent in cities and urban areas.

A NATURAL DIET

To improve your gut health and maintain good gut health, it's important to start feeding your body with as many natural foods as possible. We have evolved to eat whole foods, so these are the foods that good bacteria like to feed on. As an athlete, there are times when convenience foods, processed foods or supplements have a place, but it's important to limit their use to those times when they meet an athletic purpose.

Natural foods will always have the best influence on your gut and therefore on your brain (not to mention the immune and digestive systems). This means basing your diet on foods such as potatoes, oats, fruits and vegetables, as these contain dietary fibre which is the main source of energy for healthy gut bacteria. We've also evolved to eat fish and meat, so these aren't damaging to gut health.

Foods to avoid include processed sugary products, sodas, sweets and things that are high in omega 6 fatty acids – mainly vegetable oils.

KEY POINT

It can be a good idea to analyse your diet and ask yourself how much of it is coming from whole, natural food sources and how much of it is high in sugar, oil and additives. From here, you can start to make some sensible swaps and see how this makes you feel.

WHAT'S THE IDEAL BODY FAT %?

There are many genetic differences in body composition. Some people stay lean, others hold more body fat, but there's no exact body fat percentage which is ideal in terms of optimising football performance. Science, so far, hasn't pinpointed a universal ideal body fat percentage for everyone. However, there is a body fat range in which most people are going to thrive in terms of their athletic performance.

We know that below a certain body fat percentage is potentially too low for optimal athletic performance and above a certain percentage can also limit performance, but there are always going to be outliers. Around 90% of people find optimal performance levels within the ideal body fat range.

TOO LITTLE BODY FAT

Fat stores in the body are essential for normal health, so improving your performance is never about attempting to eliminate all fat from your body. Fats help to:

- Support the skin
- Provide lubrication
- Cushion the joints
- Aid the central nervous system
- Store vitamins
- Provide the building blocks of many hormones

Too little body fat increases the risk of micronutrient deficiencies, especially the fat-soluble vitamins A, D, E and K and it can lead to a noticeable reduction in strength, an increased risk of infection and injuries and potentially some hormonal imbalances such as a reduction in testosterone and an increase in cortisol levels that may affect performance.

TOO MUCH BODY FAT

Science has shown that in males, a body fat percentage of over 10% (certainly over 12%) correlates with a decline in endurance performance. Too much body fat can hinder performance and as a footballer, excess weight through fat stores can be considered deadweight that will also potentially slow you down and affect your speed.

Football is a stop-go sport with aerobic and anaerobic components. Sprints, jumps, rapid stops and the general agility required in a game all involve moving your body mass against gravity, so any excess weight is an unnecessary load that's going to place an additional burden on the energy mechanisms being used (making it more difficult to perform the movements and keep performing them for the duration of a match).

OPTIMAL BODY FAT RANGE

The optimal body fat range is gauged through the performance of professional athletes and the range in which they're thriving. In the English Premier League for example, body fat percentages range from 9.9 – 12.9% and in Japan they range from 8.5 – 13.7% (dependant on playing position).

By looking at these figures, we can logically conclude that an optimal and desirable body fat percentage for an elite footballer is within the range of 8-12%.

KEY POINT

There will always be outliers. A player might be at 15% and others might be below 8% (Ronaldo, for example) but the majority of team players are going to be in the 8-12% range.

OPTIMISING FOOTBALL PERFORMANCE

Midfield players tend to have a lighter body mass to allow them to cover greater distances efficiently and defenders are generally slightly taller with more lean body mass, but despite these general differences in build, the body fat percentages remain within the 8-12% range.

Research has also revealed that players in teams which compete in leagues such as the Scottish League, Croatian League, or college football teams have slightly higher body fat percentages, with an average of 14.9%. This suggests that if you're currently in the upper-end of the optimal range and closer to 15%, lowering your body fat to within the 8-12% range could be of benefit in terms of optimising your performance as a player.

OPTIMAL BODY FAT RANGE FOR GOALKEEPERS

There's limited data available on the body fat percentages of goalkeepers, but current figures show a range of between 11-18%. Without further research, the optimum range for players in this position remains unknown, but goalkeepers need to be able to jump and accelerate quickly, suggesting that excess weight could potentially limit performance.

Until further data is available, aiming for the 8-12% body fat range is a sensible guide. If you're currently above this range, it could be a worthwhile experiment to see if lowering your body fat leads to overall improvements in your performance.

OPTIMAL BODY FAT RANGE FOR FEMALE PLAYERS

Women store more fat on their bodies than men. On average, this can be as much as 7% more and the reasons for this remain unclear. The best scientific guess is that women may have evolved to have greater fat stores in reserve in preparation for times of starvation when they're pregnant or lactating, therefore ensuring they're able to continue providing nourishment to a foetus or a child as well as themselves.

There is very little data available on body fat percentages in female footballers compared to male players. This is in part due to body fat measurements not being taken as a matter of course in elite female teams, with only lean body mass and BMI measurements being used. These measures don't give a good indication of body fat stores and body fat percentage, so in terms of providing an optimal body fat range to aim for, it comes down to educated guesswork.

Research across female athletes in all sports has concluded that less than 8% body fat can negatively affect menstruation, or stop periods altogether and lead to serious health issues. For health reasons, average body fat percentages in female athletes need to be higher than in male athletes and by looking at data obtained from other intermittent sports (field hockey, basketball, handball), a range of anywhere from 12% up to 22% becomes evident.

For this reason, an educated guess is that female footballers should aim for a body fat range of between 10-18%. However, with limited data available, a degree of flexibility is required and experimentation may be needed to help you find the optimal body fat percentage for you in terms of improvements in performance.

HOW TO LOSE FAT DURING THE SEASON

In season, footballers need to increase their carbohydrate intake to boost their energy stores in the lead-up to a match or intense training session.

However, if a player needs to lower their body fat during the season, they will also need to strategically decrease their caloric intake day to day so that more fat can be utilised as fuel. So, is it possible to lose fat whilst in season without negatively effective performance, energy levels and recovery?

The answer is yes, but to do it means being very strict with your diet. Losing body fat can help you to maximise your performance, but to maximise your performance on any given match day, you need to ensure your carbohydrate stores can fuel 90 minutes of intense activity. Losing fat in season and maintaining your performance on the pitch comes down to strategically timing your carbohydrate intake.

CARBOHYDRATE INTAKE

Carbohydrates are the primary source of fuel for moderate to high-intensity activity such as football and football training, so to fuel your performance you need to increase your carbohydrate intake.

Strategically timing your intake holds the key to boosting your energy levels ahead of a training session while simultaneously decreasing your overall calorie intake across the day to promote fat loss.

To initiate fat loss, take the daily caloric intake you need to maintain weight and then lower it by 250-500 calories. This figure is your overall calorie intake target for the day and from here it becomes possible to plan your meals to provide energy when you need it most and continue to lose weight.

Instead of spreading your carbohydrate intake across the day, switch to consuming the majority of your carbohydrates in the lead-up to training and immediately after training. In this way, you'll fuel your activity during the session and aid the recovery process after the session.

KEY POINT

Concentrate your carbohydrate intake into the 3-4 hours before intense training and within 1 hour after training to maximise your session performance and post-session recovery.

Reducing your overall caloric intake will lead to weight loss, but reducing your carbohydrate intake before training or a match will lead to entering a session with reduced energy stores and this will negatively impact your performance.

By reducing your carbohydrate intake outside of the window around your training sessions and sticking to normal pre and post-training meals, you help to minimise the potential for any deterioration in performance by ensuring your energy stores are boosted pre-training and then help to maximise post-session recovery by replenishing those stores.

PLANNING YOUR CARB INTAKE

This approach will get you the most bang for your buck in terms of carbohydrate intake (the primary influencer of your performance) and it ensures that you enter training in a well-fuelled state despite your daily caloric intake being reduced.

Known as a caloric deficit, you will be in a net negative energy balance over the course of a day, but by strategically planning your carbohydrate intake around your training, you ensure that you're in a positive energy state when you need it most. Your carbohydrate consumption must revolve around your energy needs, so consuming carbs as your primary energy source in the morning if you have training in the evening is not going to give you energy when you need it most.

For example, if you have a scheduled training session at 7pm, you should stick to the basic pre-training recommendations of eating 3-4 hours beforehand. At around 4pm, you would aim to consume 2g of carbs per kg of bodyweight (as normal) and then at the end of the session, follow the basic post-training recommendations of consuming 1-2g carbs per kg of bodyweight within 1-2 hours. You have a window of 6-7 hours in which to concentrate your carbohydrate intake, but your overall caloric intake across the day is going to be reduced due to eating less outside of pre and post-training meals.

KEY POINT

Concentrate your carb intake into pre and post-training meals and base other meals on proteins such as meats, vegetables and nuts.

CARB INTAKE FOR MATCH DAYS

Under normal recommendations, you should begin to fuel for a match in the 24-hours pre-game. This recommendation should still be followed, even when trying to lower body fat, because concentrating your carbohydrate intake into the 3-4 hours ahead of the match is not going to be enough to fuel your performance for 90 minutes on the pitch. Maintaining performance needs to be prioritised over reducing fat when it comes to competitive matches.

Increase your carb intake in the 24-hours ahead of the match and give yourself a day off from lowering your caloric intake. For 6 days of the week you're going to be in a caloric deficit, timing your carb intake around your training and for 1 day of the week you're going to be increasing your caloric intake to fuel your match performance.

This day of increased calorie intake each week will slow down weight loss. However, in the interests of preserving performance, it's an approach that will still lead to fat loss over time if you make sure the caloric deficit is maintained for the rest of the week.

CARB INTAKE ON REST DAYS

On rest days, the timing of your carb intake is a non-issue. With no training sessions to work around, your focus is on ensuring you maintain a caloric deficit, spreading your carbs across the day in whatever way fits your lifestyle.

SHOULD FOOTBALLERS DO INTERMITTENT FASTING?

Intermittent fasting is a method of eating in which you cycle between long periods of fasting (not eating food) and short periods of eating, known as your eating window.

THE 16:8 METHOD

The most common approach to intermittent fasting is known as the 16:8 method.

This revolves around 16 hours of fasting followed by 8 hours of eating, with the eating window planned to fit around your lifestyle and personal preferences. For example, you might choose to skip breakfast, eat as normal between 1pm and 9pm, fast as you sleep and then up to 1pm the following day when the cycle repeats.

This approach is a popular weight-loss method in the general population and in most cases, simply reducing the eating window to 8 hours tends to reduce the overall daily caloric intake, thereby making it effective. It can be a useful alternative for dieters who struggle to stick with more restrictive diet plans and there is some research behind it suggesting that it can also help to control blood glucose levels (making it useful for pre-diabetics and diabetics).

Other studies suggest intermittent fasting could be linked to longevity and increasing your life span, improving DNA repair within cells and improving the body's resistance to physiological stresses, which may help to lower inflammation in the body. However, it's still up for debate whether these benefits are the result of intermittent fasting or simply a secondary benefit resulting from fat loss.

INTERMITTENT FASTING AND FOOTBALL

In most cases, intermittent fasting is not going to be an appropriate choice for footballers.

There is a theory that it can increase HGH (human growth hormone) levels which could be considered an athletic advantage as this is linked to growth stimulation, cell reproduction and cell regeneration. One online report goes as far as to say that intermittent fasting can increase HGH levels by 5000%. Theoretically, this would lead to increases in muscle mass and increased muscle recovery as a result of increased rates of muscle protein synthesis and anabolism, but there's little to support this theory and it's not scientifically conclusive.

From an athletic stand-point, HGH generally only affects the connective tissue surrounding joints and organs, it has little effect on muscle tissue. Over and above this flawed theory, there are two reasons why intermittent fasting is not recommended for footballers:

1. IT INHIBITS YOUR ABILITY TO RECOVER

Intermittent fasting will decrease your daily muscle protein synthesis levels, meaning the amount of dietary protein available to rebuild muscles will drop. This is because the limited eating window won't be sufficient in terms of maximising the anabolic responses. When you consume a protein-based meal, there's generally only an increase in muscle protein synthesis for around 3-4 hours afterwards. For this reason, athletes are encouraged to consume another protein-based meal or snack every 3-4 hours and to consume 30-40g of protein each time to ensure they take in the nutrients needed to stimulate further muscle protein synthesis and anabolism. Over a 24-hour period, an athlete is getting the nutrition they need to sustain muscle growth synthesis at regular intervals, fasting only when they're sleeping.

Intermittent fasting would lead to no anabolic process stimulation during the fasting period (typically 16 hours) and thereby limiting the potential for a fast recovery. Missing breakfast and pre-bed snacks could lead to waking up in a state of elevated muscle tissue breakdown, potentially eating into muscle tissue more than someone following a traditional dietary approach and eating protein meals steadily and consistently.

2. IT BECOMES VERY INCONVENIENT DURING A COMPETITIVE SEASON

With matches once or twice a week, you'll need to increase your carbohydrate intake in the 24-hour period before each match to increase your energy stores. However, many people struggle to consume enough carbohydrate in that 24-hour period, so limiting the eating window to just 8 hours will only make achieving this even more difficult. Trying to consume more carbohydrates in a shorter time frame is a huge challenge unless you're a very good eater and you don't get full very easily. In most cases, intermittent fasting leads to under-eating and therefore fatiguing earlier in a match.

Another potential inconvenience created by intermittent fasting is not having the opportunity to recover fully post-match. For example, you may have an evening match and you've chosen a morning and afternoon eating window to accommodate the need to increase your carbohydrate intake. With this being the case, your eating window will not allow for a post-match meal later in the evening. This could mean having elevated muscle protein breakdown post-match but being unable to consume the carbohydrates and protein needed to aid recovery.

POTENTIAL USES OF INTERMITTENT FASTING

From an athletic stand-point, there's little to be gained from intermittent fasting and it effectively creates far more inconveniences than potential benefits. It leads to not being able to sustain protein synthesis at maximal levels and, as a result, it may even reduce your ability to recover.

However, with this said, there are two situations in which it could prove useful:

1. Weight loss going into season
2. Limiting weight gain coming out of season

Weight loss: if a footballer still has a higher than optimal body fat percentage at the start of the season, an intermittent fasting approach could prove to be more effective than a more restrictive weight-loss diet plan.

Limiting weight gain: if a footballer typically piles weight on in the off-season, an intermittent fasting approach can help to minimise the potential for binge eating and a 10kg weight gain which would be very hard to shift before the start of the next season.

It's important to note that both scenarios above relate to out of season. Intermittent fasting is never advisable for a footballer during the season.

SHOULD FOOTBALLERS EVER FOLLOW A LOW CARB DIET?

Whatever type of diet you might be on, the type of fuel or energy you're taking in through your diet will dictate the type of fuel you're burning out on the pitch. It's for this reason that a low-carbohydrate diet is not an ideal choice for footballers.

FUELLING PERFORMANCE

A player on a high-carbohydrate diet will be predominantly using carbohydrates to fuel activity, but a player on a low-carbohydrate diet will be burning a greater percentage of stored body fat or fat within the blood.

The type of diet you're on should be based on:

1. The type of fuel you want to be utilising out on the pitch
2. How well this type of fuel is going to support your performance and activity

No matter what type of diet you're on, you'll be constantly switching between fuel sources in a game depending on the type of activity you're performing and the intensity of the activity at any given moment.

For low intensity activities such as walking or light jogging, the fuel source used by the body is primarily fat stores. For high intensity actions such as short sprints, jumping or a duel, the body uses its carbohydrate stores for fuel.

The reason for this is that fat is an inefficient form of energy. Before it can be utilised and made available to burn as energy, fat must be released from your tissues and then transported to the muscle cells. On the other hand, carbohydrates are already located within the muscle cells, can be accessed very easily and burned at a much faster rate to fuel activity when the energy demand is much higher.

FUELLING FOOTBALL

Carbohydrate intake is a key element of a footballer's diet. To fuel your performance on the pitch, your intake must be high enough to maximise carbohydrate stores within the muscle cells, giving you a supply of energy that will allow you to perform at high intensity more often throughout a 90-minute match.

KEY POINT

If your carbohydrate stores are too low, you may find yourself with diminished stores at around the 45-60-minute mark and therefore struggle to perform at the same high intensity for the remainder of the match. Your body must switch to prioritising using fat for fuel, meaning you're now only able to support low-intensity activity. Matches are not won on the back of low-intensity activity.

WINNING MOMENTS

The winning, defining moments in any sport very often come down to those moments when you push yourself hard in the dying seconds. A great example can be seen in Kelly Holmes' 1500m triumph in the 2004 Olympics. Having stayed at the back of the pack for the entirety of the race, she had conserved her carbohydrate stores for when she needed them most. As the bell rang for the final lap, it's fair to say that Kelly had more carbohydrate stores available, allowing her to perform at a very high intensity for the remaining 200-300m in which she was able to sprint passed her competitors to take gold.

KEY POINT

The same can be seen in football. In the dying moments of a match, one team may look fatigued, whilst the other still has high energy. Time after time we see this slight edge winning them the game.

THE BOTTOM LINE

It is possible to incorporate a low-carbohydrate diet into football and training, but it will always be advisable to increase carbohydrate intake and therefore stores in the 24 to 48-hour period before a competitive match to help fuel your game.

A low-carbohydrate diet will present less of an issue on days when you're not in high-intensity training, although it's likely that your muscle glycogen stores are still diminished from the previous days training or match. In this scenario it still makes sense to make carbohydrate consumption a priority so that you can maintain a high level of performance in sessions which follow. This obviously is less of a concern if you're out injured, in which case it would be wise to lower your carbohydrate intake to avoid putting on unwanted body fat.

IS CARB CYCLING GOOD FOR FOOTBALLERS?

Carbohydrate cycling is a dietary approach which involves alternating between high and low carbohydrate intake on different days in your training schedule. It's an area of sports nutrition that has gained a lot of interest over the past few years and it's a concept that's currently being introduced into many elite football teams around the world.

CARBOHYDRATES AS FUEL

Carbohydrates are extremely important in a footballer's diet, especially when aiming for optimal performance in matches and training. The carbohydrate stores you have in your body provide the fuel for high-intensity activities such as sprinting and jumping. When these stores become depleted, your performance suffers because your body is forced to switch to other fuel stores such as body fat, but these stores can only fuel lower-intensity activities.

THE BENEFITS OF CARB CYCLING

Carbohydrate cycling is essentially manipulating your daily carb intake around your daily demands (meaning the demands of training and matches). This is known as fuelling for the work required.

For example, f you need to perform at your best in a match or you have a demanding training day ahead, your carb intake needs to be high in preparation for the workload. However, if you have a rest day or a low-intensity training session, your body requires less carbohydrates.

The main benefit of lowering your carbohydrate intake on days with lower levels of activity is the potential to gain better training adaptations. Research has shown that entering low intensity sessions with lower carb stores leads to an increase in the number of mitochondria in the body – a process known as mitochondrial biogenesis.

Mitochondria are the power source of your cells and they're responsible for converting fuel sources such as carbohydrates and fats into useable energy for your muscles. When you increase the number and size of mitochondria in the muscle cells, you increase your ability to produce energy. This allows you to compete and train at greater intensity for longer durations. This also leads to improvements in endurance and an increase in measures such as VO2 max.

FAT AS FUEL

Another benefit of reducing carbohydrate intake before low intensity sessions is that it helps to ensure you're still able to burn fat efficiently as a fuel source during exercise. Carbohydrate would normally be your primary fuel source, but by restricting availability, your body must switch to burning fat for fuel.

As a footballer, you'll primarily burn carbohydrates to fuel high-intensity activities such as sprinting during a match and primarily burn fat during low-intensity activities such as walking and light jogging. If you have an increased ability to burn your fat stores during a match, this can preserve your all-important carbohydrate stores for use when you begin to fatigue in the later stages and normally struggle to sustain high-intensity activity.

CARBOHYDRATE INTAKE

For footballers who want to train well, play well and recover well, but don't want to be too specific with their diet, the best approach is to maintain a high carbohydrate intake every day.

Carb cycling is a more advanced approach and as such requires more thought, manipulation and programming than a typical diet. But in both approaches, the key focus is to make sure your carb intake in the 24-hour period before competitive matches is high.

A high carbohydrate intake is 6-10g of carbohydrates per kg of bodyweight per day, so a 70kg footballer would need around 400-700g every day. A low carbohydrate intake is under 5g of carbohydrate per kg of bodyweight per day, so for a 70kg footballer, this restricted intake could be anything from zero carbohydrate up to 350g per day.

When carb cycling, the focus is on reducing carb intake on the lead-up to a low-intensity exercise session. This means the pre-exercise meal that's normally consumed 3-4 hours before the session should consist of proteins, fats, veggies and non-carbohydrate food sources. If the planned training session is in the morning, it could even be done fasted with no food intake at all.

CARB CYCLING IN SUMMARY:

- Carb cycling trains your body to utilise fat during lower intensity activities when carbs aren't necessarily needed, preserving them for times when they are needed
- With a high carb intake every day, your body is being trained to use carbs for fuel in all circumstances. even low-intensity activity, leading to stores becoming depleted faster and fatigue kicking-in earlier in a match
- Carbohydrates should only be restricted ahead of low-intensity training or on rest days
- Carbohydrates should still be the main component in a footballer's diet and players should fuel with carbs ahead of matches or intense training
- Carb cycling is an advanced dietary strategy and should only be considered once all other basic aspects of your diet are covered

THE PRO'S & CON'S OF A VEGAN DIET

A vegan diet is a plant-based diet in which all animal products (meat, fish, dairy, eggs, honey) are removed.

The main foods consumed include: beans, lentils, nuts, chickpeas (or any other type of legume), potatoes, oats, pasta, rice, quinoa and other starches and fruits and vegetables.

It's a diet choice that's becoming increasingly popular and several top footballers are known to be vegan or have experimented with a plant-based diet. They include Jack Wilshere, Chris Smalling, Jermaine Defoe, Sergio Agüero, Héctor Bellerín and Lionel Messi.

VEGANISM AND FOOTBALL

A common concern with a vegan diet is the difficulty in attaining all of the nutrients you need for good health and performance. However, the reality is that many people on an omnivorous diet lack balance in the foods they eat and therefore also fail to get the nutrients they believe might be missing in a vegan diet. Deficiencies can occur in any diet approach if there's a lack of nutritional knowledge.

Plants contain all the nutrients required for optimal performance, with the only exception being vitamin B12. The bioavailability of some plant nutrients may not be as good as some animal products, meaning the amount of an ingested nutrient that's actually absorbed and utilised for health and performance purposes might be slightly reduced, but there are certain nutrients where the opposite can be said.

KEY POINT

Potential deficiencies that could arise through a vegan diet can easily be corrected through an awareness of the nutritional values of each food you eat.

As a player, potential areas of deficiency that need to be addressed in terms of optimising performance when switching from an omnivorous to a vegan diet include:

- Daily caloric and energy intake
- Protein intake
- Vitamin D intake

- Intake of minerals such as iron, zinc and calcium

TIPS TO TRANSITION TO A VEGAN DIET

ENERGY INTAKE

Footballers have a high energy demand and a potential issue for players switching to a vegan diet is unwanted weight loss. Plant foods generally have a lower density of calories compared to animal foods, so to reach your daily calorie goal, you'll generally need to eat a much larger volume of food simply because plant-based foods are lighter in calories based on their volume. To get around this, athletes on a vegan diet just need to eat more. This will mean having more food on your plate than you may have been used to on an omnivorous diet, but including foods such as nuts in your meals can also help as they are higher in calories. It's going to be important to familiarise yourself with just how much food you'll need to eat on a vegan diet to hit your daily calorie intake recommendations, so downloading a nutrition tracker such as MyFitnessPal could be a useful tool as you transition.

DIETARY PROTEIN INTAKE

There are two concerns surrounding protein intake on a vegan diet:

1. The amount of protein you're taking in
2. The quality of the protein

Amount: The protein portion of your typical omnivorous meal will need to be replaced with a high-protein plant food. Examples include lentils, beans, chickpeas, nuts, tofu, soy products and meat replacement products such as vegan sausages or burgers (although these shouldn't be the focus of the diet). Familiarising yourself with these foods and the amount of each type you'll need to reach your daily target will be important. On an omnivorous diet, you may have taken in 40g of protein in an easily-measured portion of red meat or chicken, so you need to know how much of the alternative vegan food you will need to match that 40g intake.

Quality: It's a common misconception that plant foods have an incomplete amino acid profile (thereby making them an inferior source of protein compared to animal foods).

This is not strictly true as all plant foods have a complete amino acid profile, but they will generally be around 10% lower in amino acids, meaning they may have a slightly lower anabolic response compared to a given amount of animal protein. To compensate for this, you will need to eat slightly more than the protein recommendations given for players on an omnivorous diet. An omnivorous player will aim for 1.5g of protein per kg of bodyweight per day. A vegan player will need to compensate with a 10% increase, to around 1.6g-1.7g of protein per kg of bodyweight per day.

> **KEY POINT**

Don't be afraid to experiment with a vegan protein supplement if you have concerns about reaching your daily protein recommendation.

MICRONUTRIENT INTAKE:

- **Dietary Iron:** Iron can be deficient in a vegan diet. Focus on legumes, e.g. lentils, beans, chickpeas, as these will be your main source of iron. These foods are also your main source of protein on a vegan diet so ensure you're consuming them with each meal
- **Zinc:** Focus on fortified cereals, tofu, oats, any type of seed and quinoa to boost your zinc intake
- **Calcium:** Cruciferous vegetables such as kale and broccoli are good sources of calcium, also fortified plant milk, tofu and almonds
- **Vitamin B12 and vitamin D:** These micronutrients are not available through whole foods, so supplementation is needed. They can be deficient in vegans, but also in an omnivorous diet because they're not easy to attain through animal products either
- Supplement with 500µg (micro grams) of vitamin B12 in tablet form and 5000iu of vitamin D3 in tablet form. Make sure you have vitamin D3, not vitamin D2, because D2 is not so bioavailable. Also check that your tablets are vegan as some are derived from animal sources

THE PRO'S & CON'S OF EATING MEAT

The question of whether meat should be included in the diet is one that creates a great divide between meat-eaters and vegans. Putting this argument aside, there are numerous health benefits and issues to consider when choosing which meats to eat.

HEALTH BENEFITS

The first benefit to consider is that meat provides a high-quality source of protein. Athletes have an increased dietary need for protein due to:

1. Increased energy demands
2. The need for recovery from muscle damage
3. The overall goal of stimulating maximum muscular adaptations to benefit their performance

As a footballer, a high-protein food such as meat can go a long way towards making sure you reach your protein requirements for the day to help achieve the above benefits. Because meat has a great profile of amino acids which make it a high-quality protein source, this ensures the bio-availability of protein makes it ideal to facilitate your muscular adaptations and increase your anabolism.

KEY POINT

Meat sources of protein are generally superior to plant sources of protein which have a slightly inferior amino acid profile.

RED VS WHITE

In the battle for superiority as a protein source, there's no clear winner between red meats and white meats. Both types contain around 25g-30g of protein per 100g. The only thing separating these meats is that red meat tends to be higher in calories due to its higher fat content, whereas white meat such as chicken is predominantly protein and therefore perhaps a better choice for people avoiding extra calories.

The second health benefit to consider is that meat is dense in micronutrients which can help you to meet your vitamin and mineral requirements for the day. These include B vitamins, iron, phosphorous, zinc and selenium. When you compare red versus white meat, red becomes the superior option as it contains higher levels of these micronutrients. In this sense, there's a trade-off between red meat and white meat. White meat has a purer protein content with a lower fat content than red, but red meat is more micronutrient dense, containing more vitamins and minerals.

KEY POINT

Settling the argument between the meats comes down to your aims at the time. As a general recommendation, eat white meat on rest days and low intensity training days and eat red meat on high intensity training days and match days (when your caloric needs are higher).

HEALTH ISSUES

The above benefits highlight the important role meat can play in an athlete's diet, but there are also health issues to consider when meat consumption becomes excessive.

Epidemiological data (differences between different countries and populations) shows a correlation between meat consumption and various diseases. In short, meat-eating populations have a higher incidence of cardiovascular disease, CHD (coronary heart disease), cancer and diabetes when compared to vegetarian populations.

This creates a strong argument for not eating meat, however, the figures don't factor in lifestyle differences. For example, vegetarians are generally individuals who are more conscious of their lifestyle choices, so they may represent lower bodyweights with a lower obesity rate and non-smokers with a higher level of activity in daily life. This makes it difficult to pinpoint meat as the specific cause of the higher rates of disease compared to non-meat-eating populations.

SATURATED FAT AND CARCINOGENS

Two components of meat that may cause potential health issues when eaten in excess are the saturated fat content and carcinogenic content, meaning the number of cancer-causing substances within the meat.

SATURATED FAT

The saturated fat content of meat is more of a concern in red varieties as white meat tends to be quite low in fat. Saturated fat can be part of a balanced diet when kept to under 5-

10% of your total daily calories, but there are health issues connected to excessive amounts of saturated fat in the diet, especially with a high intake of red meat.

The two main health concerns posed by excessive saturated fat intake are:

1. It raises LDL (bad) cholesterol levels in the blood, which becomes embedded in the walls of your arteries and can lead to plaques that restrict blood flow. If a plaque breaks off, it can lead to a stroke

2. It leads to lipotoxicity, which is an accumulation of fatty acids in lean tissues such as muscle. These tissues have a limited amount of storage for fat, so the cells can become overloaded, causing inflammation that leads to the dysfunction and death of the cells. This is important because it may cause the death of beta cells found in the kidneys which are responsible for producing insulin and crucial for controlling blood glucose levels. The impairment of these cells can potentially lead to diabetes

There's counter evidence provided by separate studies on saturated fat intake and the rates of diabetes and heart disease in that not all studies show a clear consistent association. Much depends on the type of people used in the study and the amount of saturated fat they're given, but there is clear evidence to support switching your saturated fat intake to unsaturated fats or whole grains to significantly reduce risk of disease.

KEY POINT

What can be taken from current research on saturated fat is not necessarily that meat is bad, but that a balance needs to be struck between red meat and white meat consumption to ensure that protein sources are not excessive saturated fat sources.

CARCINOGENS

When cooked at high temperatures, meat may produce what are known as meat mutagens or carcinogens, which are essentially substances that might cause cancer.

These carcinogens are in all types of meat, but they are especially high in processed meats, making these types of meat more of a cause for concern than fresh, unpreserved meat.

The three main carcinogens that meat either contains or produces when cooked are:

1. Heterocyclic amines
2. Polyaromatic hydrocarbons

3. Nitrosamines

What's known about these carcinogens is that when used in animal-testing, two things become clear:

- They can promote the signalling for tumour or cancer growth and facilitate the survival of cancer cells
- They can cause a lot of DNA damage. This is important because they can accelerate the progression of a cancer tissue to other nearby cells

The counter argument for carcinogens in meat is that the current data only shows an effect in animal studies (there are few studies on humans as it's obviously quite hard to run a study that may result in a participant developing cancer) and much like saturated fat, the population level data on the association between carcinogens and cancer is not consistent. However, it is apparent that there's a greater issue surrounding processed meats. These contain higher amounts of carcinogens and this raises the risk of disease.

KEY POINT

Research indicates that meat does contain some carcinogens, so for this reason, it's not a bad idea to at least make sure you're not overconsuming meat and avoid processed meats as much as possible.

The current data cannot confirm that there is a direct relationship between meat and disease, but there is enough evidence to indicate that excessive meat consumption should be avoided, lowering your intake of high fat meats and avoiding processed meats whenever you can.

MEAT IN SUMMARY

Be smart. Don't consume meat three times a day or eat large portions of red or processed meats. Balance is the way forward.

As a recommendation, eat fresh meat once a day, stick to white meats on rest days and low-intensity training days, eating red meats on high-intensity training days and match days when additional calories may be needed. If eating red meats such as beef, you can lower the potential harmful effects by purchasing lean cuts that are 5% fat or less.

ARE NUTS REALLY THAT HEALTHY?

Some people consider nuts to be a health food, others a junk food...so are nuts a healthy choice for footballers?

NUTRITIONAL VALUE

In terms of nutrition, one small portion of around 30g (a normal handful) will provide 150-200 calories, making nuts calorically dense and ideal for anyone with a high caloric requirement or looking to gain weight.

Nuts also contain around 5g of protein, 15g of fat (meaning 50% of the weight of a handful is fat), a small amount of carbohydrate (mainly from dietary fibre) and they're also high in micronutrients such as vitamin E, magnesium, phosphorous, copper, manganese and selenium. These components can be considered beneficial to health, making nuts a nutritious food choice for footballers or anyone with a high caloric requirement.

Another healthy aspect of nuts is that they're very high in antioxidants, mainly in the form of polyphenols. These play a role in fighting oxidative stress, basically meaning they fight against cellular damage caused by harmful things such as free radicals.

Polyphenols may also help lower LDL (bad) cholesterol and with a good fibre content, they can act as a food source for healthy bacteria in the gut, producing short fatty acids that promote many positive functions and health benefits.

NUTRITIONAL CONCERNS

So far so good...but there are other components to consider.

The main concern with nut consumption is the ratio of omega 3 to omega 6 fatty acids – the only fats that must be sourced through the diet as the body is unable to synthesise them.

Fat has many important functions such as:

- Providing cell wall structure
- Aiding the transportation and absorption of fat-soluble vitamins A, D, E and K
- It's also needed for blood clotting, wound healing and inflammation

Omega 3s are typically anti-inflammatory, whereas omega 6s are pro-inflammatory and as most varieties of nut are high in omega 6, there's an increased potential for inflammatory issues.

KEY POINT

Inflammation refers to your body's natural response to things that harm it, including infections, injuries and toxins.

An inflammatory response (or immune response) is the body's attempt to deal with the damage and heal itself. The problem in modern-day society is that people have chronic inflammation, meaning the immune system becomes overactive and inflammation is then maintained for prolonged, sustained periods. This can lead to damage being done to healthy cells, tissues and organs which can mean DNA damage, cell death, internal scarring and potential links to just about every diet-induced disease.

OMEGA 3 TO OMEGA 6 RATIO

The main concern with a high intake of omega 6 fatty acids is that their chemical structure makes them very prone to oxidation, meaning they're prone to damaging your healthy cells.

In a typical modern-day diet, the ratio of omega 3s to omega 6s has become distorted and far from the ratio of around 1:1 up to 4:1 that nature intended. For every 1-4g of omega 6 we consume, we should be consuming at least 1g of omega 3 to help control inflammation in the body, but recent figures suggest that most people now consume an average 16:1 ratio of omega 6s to omega 3s, indicating that most people are in an unhealthy state.

BEST NUT CHOICES

Key contributors to a high omega 6 intake in the diet are processed vegetable oils (olive, coconut and palm oil represent better options) but nuts can also be added to the list.

Walnuts have the best ratio of omega 6 to omega 3 at 4:1, with the next best being macadamia nuts at 6:1. From here, the ratios become increasingly extreme and issues can begin to arise. Pecan nuts have a 20:1 ratio of omega 6 to omega 3, Brazil nuts come in at an alarming 1000:1 and almonds are all the way up to 2000:1.

The bottom line is that nuts do contain healthy components, so there's no need to stay away from them, but it's important to be aware of the high omega 6 to omega 3 ratio. High omega 6 intake can be an issue and could potentially cause some serious inflammatory problems, especially if eaten in large amounts, so choose walnuts and macadamia nuts first limiting the amount of other types consumed to a small handful only.

IS BREAD BAD FOR YOU?

There's a lot of misinformation surrounding bread, including that it's unhealthy, fattening and even harmful, but it's important to understand that blanket statements such as "bread is bad" don't take the context of every situation into account.

COMPONENTS OF BREAD

There are many different types of bread and they vary quite dramatically in their composition. The grains used to make bread consist of three parts:

Bran: The part that stores all the fibre.

Germ: The part that stores most of the micronutrients.

Endosperm: The part that stores the carbohydrate portion.

Each of these components has its own good health aspects, but not all breads contain all three. The type of bread you eat and how processed or unprocessed it is, dictates which of these components it contains. The more processed the bread is, the more likely it is that one of the components will have been removed, leading to it being labelled as an "unhealthy" option.

TYPES OF BREAD

Wholegrain: In this unprocessed variety of bread, all three components of the grain remain fully intact and other wholegrains such as barley, brown rice, oats (wholegrain or rolled) or seeds may be added. These breads have a rustic appearance.

Whole-wheat: All three components of the grain remain intact in this variety of bread, but there are no added grains or seeds. These breads are typically known as brown breads and have the same appearance as standard white bread other than colour.

White bread: In this processed variety of bread, both the bran and germ components of the grain have been removed leaving just the endosperm. This creates a lighter texture and flavour, but with fewer nutrients and a lower fibre content, this type of bread is generally labelled as the unhealthiest of the breads.

A further type of bread that's perhaps less well-known is sprouted bread. The grains in sprouted bread are soaked and rinsed over several days to mimic the natural germination process of a seed growing into a plant. This enhances the digestibility and nutritional value of the bread, making it a healthy option. A key health benefit of sprouted bread is that it contains phytase. This neutralises an enzyme and anti-nutrient known as phytic acid which can inhibit the absorption of many vitamins and minerals.

The removal of this anti-nutrient can also increase the absorption and bio-availability of the vitamins and minerals within the bread. Ezekiel bread is a good example of a sprouted bread.

NUTRITIONAL CONTENT OF BREAD

Compared to other foods such as green leafy vegetables and fruits, bread is quite low in essential nutrients. White breads and processed breads contain very few micronutrients, perhaps some types of B vitamins, manganese, selenium and iron, but not in quantities that will contribute significantly to daily micronutrient recommendations.

Wholegrain, whole-wheat, sprouted and other types of natural bread have a higher fibre content, also providing protein, beta carotene and possibly vitamins C and E, making them a healthier addition to the diet.

KEY POINT

The healthiness of a bread and its nutritional value is dependent on the type.

All breads are relatively high in carbohydrates, containing roughly 15g per slice and around 70-100 calories. The way the body processes these carbs depends on the type of bread. Processed breads contain less fibre, so they're going to be digested and absorbed faster than more natural breads. This can result in greater spikes in blood insulin and blood glucose levels, but this doesn't necessarily make them an unhealthy food.

There's nothing inherently harmful about foods that are digested quickly, despite the media tendency to demonise such foods, but fluctuations in blood glucose can cause spikes and crashes that affect your energy levels throughout the day so they should be eaten in moderation. Wholegrain and sprouted breads have a lesser impact on blood glucose and can therefore provide energy across the day.

SHOULD FOOTBALLERS EAT BREAD?

If you're someone who needs to eat quite a lot, whether it's the day before a match and you need to get some carbohydrates into your system, or you need to put on weight and require more calories in your daily diet, then white bread can be a good option because it's low in fibre and won't fill you up.

On the other hand, if you're dieting and lowering your calorific intake, then wholegrain or sprouted bread become better options as these will fill you up and stop you having cravings throughout the day.

GLUTEN IN BREAD

Gluten is a general term for the protein found in wheat. It has been demonised in recent years, but there's no data to prove that it should be of any concern in the diet of healthy individuals. However, gluten intolerance is an issue for a small portion of the population and these individuals struggle to digest and break down the protein found in wheat. It affects less than 5% of the total population, but if you have celiac disease or an intolerance, then wheat products need to be avoided or substituted with gluten-free options.

The bottom line is that a small percentage of people may struggle to digest wheat, but this doesn't automatically make wheat products bad for everyone. Not all bread is bad and irrespective of whether a bread is healthy or not, the type of bread that's most useful will depend on the individual and the situation.

IS COWS MILK BAD FOR YOU?

Several claims revolving around cow's milk and dairy products have circulated in the over the last few years leaving many to question whether the nutritional benefits of drinking milk are outweighed by the potential harmful effects.

So, is cow's milk okay for human consumption?

POPULAR CLAIMS

- Dairy contains animal hormones such as oestrogen and IGF-1 and this can then increase the levels of these hormones in humans and cause diseases such as cancer
- Dairy is acidic and this can cause calcium phosphate to be taken from the bones in order to neutralise the acidity, therefore lowering calcium levels which may lead to bone problems
- Dairy contains pus and antibiotics

SCIENTIFIC FACTS

ANIMAL HORMONES

Animal milk does contain hormones.

Just like human milk, animal milk is intended to accelerate the growth of the young, so in this case it's intended to accelerate the growth of young calves. In cow's milk, there is a notable amount of IGF-1 and oestrogen (predominantly a female hormone), however, the main issue with this claim is that there is no evidence to support the belief that these hormones have any cross-over effect into humans when milk is consumed.

No increase in human IGF-1 or oestrogen has been documented in studies surrounding the consumption of dairy, so we can assume that cow's milk is safe for human consumption.

> **KEY POINT**

If elevated levels of IGF-1 were to be found after consuming milk, then this could be linked to diseases such as cancer, but all evidence available to date shows consuming cow's milk has no effect on human hormones.

ACIDITY

Animal foods are inherently acidic and they do break down into acidic by-products, but the human body has a very tightly controlled system through which it can release bicarbonate ions from the kidneys to quickly neutralise these acids and then excrete the by-products either through urine or breathing. With this being the case, there is no need for the human body to leach calcium phosphate from the bones to neutralise the acidity.

> **KEY POINT**

This claim was based on the findings of a small population study which linked dairy-consumers with a rise in cases of osteoporosis (thinning bones). However, further research has concluded that this study was flawed and a high dairy intake remains beneficial for bone health.

PUS AND ANTIBIOTICS

To the surprise of many, this claim is not entirely untrue. Clearly, "pus" is not listed as an ingredient on the side of a milk carton, but there are legal limits in place in terms of the amount of pus a product can contain.

The somatic cell count is a measure of a milk's quality and is in fact a pus count. The allowable limit for pus and antibiotics found in milk is around 1 million pus cells per spoonful which, to be fair, can sound quite disgusting. However, this does not mean that all milk contains pus and as the milk we buy is pasteurised, these substances won't have a negative effect on the body even when they are present.

> **KEY POINT**

One way to effectively lower the chances of consuming pus and antibiotics is to buy organic milk. Modern-day farming methods encourage the highest yields of milk in the shortest space of time which can often lead to cows developing mastitis and the need for antibiotic treatment. Organic farming methods are more natural, meaning mastitis is largely avoided

IN CONCLUSION

The only real issue with dairy consumption is the possible high saturated fat content. If you're choosing whole fat milk rather than semi-skimmed or lower fat, the saturated fat content could lead to health problems such as an increase in LDL (bad) cholesterol in the blood, potentially leading to cardiovascular problems, or damage to the cells in the pancreas responsible for producing insulin and therefore controlling your blood glucose levels.

Is cow's milk okay for human consumption? The answer is yes, but low-fat organic milk is probably your best choice if you are concerned by any of the scientific facts.

UNDERSTANDING SUGAR

Is there a difference between glucose, fructose and sucrose and do they affect performance in different ways? Well, they are all types of sugar, but they do differ slightly in their chemical structures and the way the body digests and metabolises them, so they do have the potential to impact football performance in different ways.

GLUCOSE

This is the simplest form of a sugar, also known as a monosaccharide, meaning it's just one sugar molecule that cannot be further broken down into anything simpler. Glucose is very important to understand because all other types of sugar or carbohydrates eventually need to be broken down into glucose to be used for energy.

For this reason, glucose can be considered the body's preferred energy source because it can be accessed quickest. It doesn't need to be broken down during digestion and can simply pass through the gut into the blood and then travel to any cells that need energy. In the case of exercise, this will be your muscle cells.

However, glucose isn't found naturally in foods as a single molecule, it's normally part of other carbohydrates such as starch, which is basically just a long chain of glucose molecules bonded together. Or it's found in sucrose (table sugar), where it's bonded to fructose.

So, although glucose is naturally a part of many foods such as pasta, potato, rice and oats, it usually comes attached to other things and must be broken down into individual components during digestion. The only time glucose can be found by itself in food is in processed foods such as dextrose – a name for artificial glucose – or in sports supplements and sports drinks listed as glucose syrup.

As it's the simplest form of carbohydrate, it will be digested faster than any other type of sugar or carbohydrate, usually creating a very large spike in blood glucose and energy within 10 minutes of it being ingested (peaking at around 15-45 minutes). This is followed by a big drop in energy because glucose by itself can't sustain the large initial increase in energy for long periods. For this reason, the dextrose or glucose found in sports supplements is good, but it should only be used during exercise to provide a quick boost of energy when the muscles need it most.

KEY POINT

As a footballer, you could take sips of a glucose-based product throughout a match to provide a quick rise in energy while avoiding an energy crash, although it does need to be taken continuously throughout exercise to avoid the crash. It could also be taken at half-time, but that alone may or may not see you through the next 45 minutes plus extra time.

FRUCTOSE

Sometimes known as fruit sugar, fructose is another monosaccharide found mostly in fruits. It's metabolised similarly to glucose as it's also just one molecule which doesn't need to be broken down further during digestion and it also passes straight through the small intestine into the blood.

The big difference is that fructose must then travel to the liver to be converted into glucose before it can be used as energy by your cells. For this reason, fructose takes slightly longer than glucose to be absorbed, meaning it has a smaller impact on raising blood sugar levels and spiking insulin levels compared to glucose. However, fructose can maintain energy stores for slightly longer than glucose, resulting in less of an energy crash compared to glucose and sucrose.

Unlike glucose, fructose is found naturally in foods, including fruits, honey and agave. It's ability to increase energy levels in a more sustainable way makes it a good choice to incorporate into a pre-exercise meal approximately three hours before training or a match, with bananas being an easy option.

Fructose-containing snacks can also be eaten immediately prior to exercise as there's less chance of an energy crash due to the slower absorption rate, but it's a slightly inferior option compared to glucose as a source of more immediate energy during exercise.

SUCROSE

Sucrose is the scientific name for regular table sugar. It's 50% glucose and 50% fructose, making it a disaccharide (meaning two molecules).

The two types of sugar it contains need to be broken apart to then be metabolised individually as described above. Glucose will go straight to the cells, but fructose will go via the liver to the cells. Sucrose is a naturally occurring carbohydrate found in some types of foods, especially fruits, vegetables and grains, but it's mainly added to processed foods such as sweets, fizzy drinks, ice-cream, breakfast cereals...the list goes on.

Due to its glucose content, sucrose is going to have a large impact in terms of spiking energy and blood glucose levels at around 15-45 minutes after intake and then a noticeable reduction in energy levels kicks-in at around 30-60 minutes. This means it has a slightly slower rate of digestion than pure glucose, but slightly faster than pure fructose and for this reason it's best to treat it as glucose in terms of fitting it into sports nutrition, consuming it only during exercise when you really need energy fast.

STARCH

As mentioned earlier, starch is a long chain of monosaccharide molecules, making it your main carbohydrate source in most meals – oats, pasta, rice and potatoes.

While it's true that starches are just a long chain of sugar, they also contain fibre which is an indigestible type of carbohydrate that significantly slows down digestion. This means they have much less of an effect on blood sugar levels compared to sugar by itself and it's why starch is advised at the pre-exercise meal. Starch has a much more sustainable impact on energy levels and doesn't provide the huge instant hit that sugar would in isolation.

SUGARS IN SUMMARY

Glucose, fructose and sucrose will all spike energy levels quickly, usually within 15-45 minutes. Glucose is fastest, then sucrose, followed by fructose, although fructose will spike energy levels to a lesser extent and the energy will be slightly more consistent, partially avoiding the energy crash.

Take on fructose as part of the pre-exercise meal, approximately three hours prior, then potentially as a light snack just before you go out for a training session or match or even at half-time. Glucose and sucrose should only be consumed during exercise, perhaps sipping on a glucose or sucrose sports drink solution throughout training or a match, to consistently provide a quick source of energy.

THE DIFFERENT TYPES OF WATER

You may think of water as just water, but there are differences in terms of water quality from area to area and the level of purification a water supply goes through before you drink it. With this being the case, can different types of water provide different health and performance benefits?

TAP WATER

Across the UK, tap water is deemed safe to drink by environmental authorities and in your local area there will be regulatory procedures in place to ensure the water quality is within any contaminant limits.

However, the problem with tap water is that although it's deemed safe (the actual term used is relatively safe), there is always the potential for some type of contamination from natural sources or human activity, to affect the water's quality.

Under close examination, tap water may contain bacteria, algae, fungi, parasites, metals (such as copper and lead) and chemical pollutants. So, the question is perhaps not what's in the water, but how often and in what quantities do these contaminants feature in everyday drinking water and are they harmful to health?

It's very probable that the tap water in your home is safe and won't affect your health. There is however a chance that the water quality isn't what it's meant to be.

Nobody is going to come to your house and check the quality of the water, it's also known that many water systems across the country have not been properly maintained, leading to high levels of lead and copper in the water supply (and even incidents of Legionnaires' disease).

WATER PURIFICATION SYSTEMS

In a purification system, water generally goes through a filtering process to trap any impurities (like chemicals and other contaminants) in an absorbent type of medium before coming out of the tap. Chlorine may also be added to the water to act as a type of disinfectant.

Homes today usually have point of use treatment systems which purify the water used for cooking and drinking, so kitchen taps aren't generally a problem, but it's worth checking and finding out if the tap you drink from has a purification system in place. Another system used in some houses is a point of entry system. If your home has this, the water entering the house through all taps should be purified.

DISTILLED WATER

Distilled water is another step in the purification process, in which water undergoes distillation to further remove impurities. The distillation process involves boiling the water and collecting the steam, which then returns to water upon cooling. This process is proven to be very effective at removing contaminants like bacteria, viruses, chemicals such as lead and sulphate and chlorine, making distilled water a very pure source of water. It's for this reason that distilled water is commonly used in medical facilities and labs where safety is of paramount importance.

Distilled water is regarded as contaminant free, but is it really necessary to drink distilled water? The answer depends on many factors, but if you are someone who gets ill frequently for no apparent reason, switching to distilled water may be beneficial. Much depends on the strength of your immune system, but improvements in health or performance can be noticed by making the switch.

KEY POINT

The only counter argument to drinking distilled water is that the process also removes a lot of natural minerals and electrolytes. However, this is not an issue as water is not a dense source of nutrients and your vitamin and mineral requirements for the day should be fully covered by your diet.

IN SUMMARY

Distilled water is the best source of water and it's recommended if you're susceptible to illness. However, tap water or purified water is fine for most people if the system in place removes contaminants from the original water source. If you're not normally ill and you know your drinking water tap has a purification system in place, then there's no reason to make any changes.

PRE-MATCH NUTRITION

Pre-match nutrition is all about fuelling-up to allow for the best possible performance for the duration of the game ahead, but which foods provide the most energy and when should they be consumed in relation to your match?

CARBOHYDRATES

A footballer's main source of energy comes from carbohydrate-based foods. Carbohydrate is stored in the muscles (as glycogen), so the aim of pre-match nutrition is to ensure these stores are fully topped up before stepping out onto the pitch.

A common mistake made by many players is to consider the pre-exercise meal, eaten 3-4 hours ahead of the game, as the time to load up with extra carbohydrate foods, perhaps adding extra rice or potatoes or consuming a couple of bananas, but this one meal is not enough to maximise stores. Research indicates that carbohydrates consumed in a pre-exercise meal will boost the muscle stores by around 20%, but a much greater impact can be made by fuelling-up on carbohydrates 24 hours ahead of the match.

PRE-MATCH FUELLING

If you have a morning match, it's recommended that you start your pre-match fuelling the morning before (24 hours ahead of the match) and the evening before if you have an evening match.

To fuel up in this 24-hour period, you should aim to consume around 25-50% more than your current carbohydrate intake over a 24-hour period. If you're using a fitness and nutrition tracker such as MyFitnessPal, you can fine-tune your intake to ensure you take in around 8-10g of carbohydrates per kg of bodyweight within the 24-hour pre-match period.

KEY POINT

A player weighing 70kg would need to take in around 550-700g of carbohydrates to fuel 90 minutes of match play.

This can seem an overwhelming quantity of food initially, so switching to carbohydrate-dense sources of food (that you know you can eat a lot of) can be an efficient way to achieve your pre-match fuelling target.

For example, pasta or rice may be easier to eat in larger quantities than sweet potatoes, but as hitting the target is the primary goal, adding rice cakes, cereals, energy bars, fruit juice or smoothies may be necessary.

THE PRE-EXERCISE MEAL

The pre-exercise meal eaten 3-4 hours before the start of the match should be light on the stomach. High-glycaemic energy sources that are low in fibre and fat are good choices as these will be digested and absorbed into the muscle tissues faster, meaning they'll be available to fuel your performance during the game. Good options include white bread with jam, sports drinks, energy bars, cereals and some fruits.

For an evening match, white pasta or rice can be incorporated into a late lunch/early dinner. Foods to avoid include oils, red meats and high-fat dairy as these will slow down the digestion of the meal.

KEY POINT

Try to increase quantities of carbohydrates in the pre-exercise meal by around 25-50%, or 2g of carbohydrates per kg of bodyweight. If you are a 70kg player, you should aim for around 140-150g of carbohydrates in the pre-match meal.

You may be thinking "those food choices don't sound very healthy", but it's important to remember that within 24 hours of a match, the primary goal is to fully load your carbohydrate stores to enable optimal performance. This may not be as efficiently achieved with "healthier" foods depending on what you have available for your pre-exercise meal. Remember that these potential options make up only 1 meal from an entire week's worth of eating. Much healthier food choices will make up the rest of your week, ensuring you are getting all of the vital nutrients you need to remain healthy.

What's most important in your pre-exercise meal is the glycaemic index score of the foods you are consuming, the lower the score the longer it will take to top up your carbohydrate stores.

PRE-MATCH HYDRATION

As a general recommendation, aim to drink 500ml to 1 litre of water with your pre-match meal. Electrolytes can help to ensure you retain more of this water intake and many sports drinks contain sodium to help with this. To check your hydration levels, check the colour of your urine. If it's not pale in colour, continue to top up your fluids by sipping on water or an isotonic drink after your pre-exercise meal (until you step out onto the pitch).

HALF-TIME NUTRITION

The importance of half-time nutrition is often overlooked in football. It should be viewed as a free opportunity to put the nutritional protocols in place for maintaining energy, focus and hydration in the remaining 45-minutes (and potentially extra time).

MAINTAINING ENERGY

The primary aim of half-time nutrition is to prevent the onset of fatigue as much as possible in the second half. The foods of choice to allow for this should be carbohydrate-based. However, it's important to note that pre-match nutrition is much more important than half-time nutrition in terms of being able to sustain energy levels throughout the entire 90-minute period. Ideally, pre-match nutrition should set you up to walk out onto the pitch with enough energy in store to last the duration of the game, meaning half-time then becomes an opportunity to top up and replace the energy stores used in the first half.

KEY POINT

The carbohydrates consumed at half-time can't offer a magic formula if your pre-match meal was insufficient to fuel your performance for the duration of the match. Any carbs consumed at half-time can be considered a tool to give your stores a boost, but this can only work effectively if adequate stores were in place before the match. The carbohydrates you consume at half-time will help to maintain your energy levels until the end of the match, especially in the all-important last 5-10 minutes of the game (when others may be fatiguing).

Around 20-40g of carbohydrates should be sufficient for most players and this needs to be easily digested and quickly absorbed into the muscle. Isotonic products are favoured by most elite teams, with players consuming a carbohydrate-based gel or an isotonic sports drink specifically designed to provide the correct concentration of carbohydrates. If the ratio of carbohydrates to water matches the concentration within the cells of your body, this will be absorbed and made ready for use quickly. Products containing dietary fat or fibre should be avoided at all costs, as they will slow down digestion and therefore absorption.

KEY POINT

Most gels contain around 20-35g of carbohydrate and a 500ml sports drink generally contains 35-40g of carbohydrate, making these products convenient methods of obtaining 20-40g of carbohydrate at half-time.

MAINTAINING FOCUS

Focus refers to your mental state and it's fair to say that maintaining concentration until the very end of a match is something many players struggle with. To help with this, a caffeine supplement can be taken at half-time.

Caffeine is well researched and there's a lot of data behind its benefits in terms of boosting concentration and increasing adrenalin production which can be beneficial in high-intensity sports such as football. Caffeine also becomes active in the body very quickly, taking around 15 minutes to have an effect, making it perfect for half-time!

The amount of caffeine required depends on individual caffeine tolerances. The more caffeine you typically consume on a day-to-day basis, the greater the amount you will need to promote the desired effect. As a guide, most players notice a benefit at around 75-150mg of caffeine per serving and this represents a good half-time intake. You may need to take more, but it's not recommended to go above 300mg in one sitting. As a guide, a standard cup of coffee provides around 75mg of caffeine and a double espresso provides around 150mg of caffeine.

KEY POINT

The most efficient ways to add caffeine intake at half-time are to consume a carbohydrate gel or drink containing added caffeine. Caffeine pills are also another quick and convenient option. No matter which option you go for, be sure to trial it at training first before adding it to your match day strategy.

MAINTAINING HYDRATION

Many players will be around 5% dehydrated by the end of a 90-minute match. It only takes 2-3% dehydration to notice a significant decline in performance, making it extremely important to rehydrate fully at every opportunity. Aim to drink 500ml of water during half-time, but if you're feeling dehydrated as you come off the pitch, this could be increased to

1 litre, which obviously outlines the importance of starting the rehydration process as quickly as possible once the half time whistle blows.

KEY POINT

Adding electrolytes to your half-time water will help to boost water retention. Studies have shown that sodium can increase the amount of water your body retains rather than excreting it through urine, the recommended amount to take is between 0.5g and 1g of sodium per litre of fluid.

POST-MATCH NUTRITION

To understand what nutrition should look like in the 48-hour period after a game, it's important to begin with an understanding of what post-match recovery actually means. It's a belief shared by many that recovery relates only to the healing of damaged muscle tissue after a match or an intense training session, however, it's a much broader term than this. Muscle tissue recovery is just one aspect of complete recovery.

Complete recovery can be broken down into three simple components:

1. Healing and regeneration of damaged tissue, this being mainly muscle tissue
2. Restoration of energy stores lost during a match
3. Rehydration and the restoration of water stores lost during the game

HEALING OF DAMAGED TISSUE

It's this element of the healing process that usually causes delayed onset muscle soreness (DOMS) and recovery is promoted predominantly through protein intake. Again, it's a common belief that this can be achieved through chugging a protein shake at the end of the match, but complete recovery can take up to 48 hours, so it's going to extend beyond just one meal.

Protein requirements for recovery are going to be elevated above normal recommended amounts for the general population. For the day of the game and the day after, a total daily intake of 1.5g of protein per kg of bodyweight is recommended.

For example:

- A 70kg footballer should aim for around 105g of protein per day
- A 90kg athlete should aim for around 135g of protein per day

This amount has been shown to provide enough protein and amino acids (the building blocks for the generation of new muscle tissue) to fully repair damaged muscle tissue after intense exercise such as a football match. Around 30-40g of this protein intake should be consumed within the first hour after the match as this can immediately turn on the recovery mechanisms, helping to prevent any possibility of muscle tissue breakdown post workout.

The source of post-match protein should also be a fast-digesting variety such as whey protein, most likely your best and most convenient option as a protein shake or powder can be taken with you to the match ready for instant consumption afterwards.

A protein-containing meal should then follow every four hours or so, not including sleep time. This is because a single protein meal will only be effective in terms of synthesizing new muscle proteins for around three to four hours, so consuming at these intervals will ensure a consistently elevated state of muscle rebuilding. Each of these meals should contain approximately 20-30g of protein, allowing you to reach your protein intake target by the end of the day. High-quality protein sources such as meat or fish should be consumed (or dairy, lentils and beans if you're vegetarian). Reading labels or doing a Google search can help you to understand the portion sizes of each food source required to achieve a protein intake of around 30g. As a rough guide, this is usually around one regular fillet of meat or fish.

RESTORATION OF ENERGY STORES

Carbohydrate stores in muscle tissue are in the form of glycogen, the main fuel source used and degraded during a football match. A high-intensity football match can almost fully deplete all carbohydrate stores in the muscle, meaning the quicker you can replenish these carbohydrate stores, the quicker you'll be able to get back into training and performing at a high level.

As with post-match protein replenishment, a fast-digesting carbohydrate source in the one-hour period post-match is needed as this one-hour window has been shown to increase the effectiveness of replenishing carbohydrate stores when your body is in a diminished state. Consuming double the amount of carbohydrate in comparison to protein is recommended, meaning an intake of around 80-100g in the immediate post-match meal, equating to around 1g of carbohydrate per kg of bodyweight.

There are a few well-designed recovery shakes on the market that are convenient to use as they contain a blend of protein and carbohydrate in the correct amounts and ratios for post-match recovery. The carbohydrate in these products is usually in the form of maltodextrin which is relatively fast-acting, but alternatives include fruits. One large banana contains around 20-25g of carbohydrate or dried fruits such as raisins and cranberries offer denser sources. Another alternative is to stick with a traditional meal of pasta or rice when you return home, aiming for around 100g of uncooked weight which will roughly hit your requirements.

As with protein, your carbohydrate intake should be consistently elevated for around 24-48 hours post-match (not just for the post-match meal) to ensure complete replenishment of your lost carbohydrate stores.

To keep things simple, aim to increase the carbohydrate portion sizes in your day to day typical meals by around 25%, whether this is in the form of rice, pasta, potato, oats, or grains. If you'd like to be more precise, aim to consume around 8g of carbohydrate per kg of bodyweight, putting most footballers in the range of between 500-600g of carbohydrates per day. It's worth trying to get familiar with the carbohydrate content of the foods you eat to make sure you reach this target.

REHYDRATION

This is a highly overlooked aspect of recovery that's just as important as the rest. During a game, it's likely that you'll lose bodyweight in the form of sweat and it's essential that fluid intake post-match is sufficient to rehydrate effectively. As little as a 2% reduction in bodyweight due to sweat loss can cause dehydration, leading to the associated effects of an increase in heart rate and body temperature, along with decreased mental stimulation, concentration and overall performance.

A useful way of getting to know your post-match fluid requirements is to weigh yourself before and after a couple of matches to see how much bodyweight you typically lose. For most, this is going to be around 1-2kg, depending on variants such as environmental conditions. When you know how much you're losing, it's easy to ensure your post-match fluid intake is adequate to rehydrate properly. As a guide, aim for around 1 to 1.5ltrs of fluid per kg of bodyweight lost during exercise. This means that if you're losing 1kg, you need to drink around 1.5ltrs of fluid after the game, ideally within a few hours post-match.

REHYDRATION TIP

A tip to ensure you retain post-match fluid (and it doesn't just go straight through you) is to mix in a small amount of sodium. Sports drinks come with a good amount of sodium already in them, making them useful as part of your rehydration plan and as electrolytes such as sodium are also lost through sweat during the game, sports drinks can be an ideal way of replenishing stores.

UNDERSTANDING DEHYDRATION

Studies suggest that 90% of players are in a dehydrated state by the end of a match, so what steps can be taken to maintain hydration levels during a game?

THE MECHANICS OF DEHYDRATION

Dehydration describes the process of water loss from the body and in terms of exercise, it's generally defined as a loss in bodyweight. For example, 1% dehydration during exercise would be expressed as a 1% loss in bodyweight during exercise.

The cause of water loss is sweat. Sweat is used as a mechanism to release heat and to control your core body temperature. The amount of sweat lost during exercise will vary depending on environmental conditions (temperature, humidity, also exercise duration, intensity and individual genetic influences), but some people simply sweat more than others.

DEHYDRATION IN FOOTBALL

Studies carried out in amateur football have found that at least half of the players walking out onto the pitch at the start of a game are already in a dehydrated state and 90% of them are dehydrated by the end. Tests were done using pre and post-match urine samples and sweat-patch data analysis.

Other studies indicate that irrespective of conditions – hot or cold – players are generally at least 2% dehydrated by the end of a match (and even as much as 5%), with hotter conditions obviously leading to even greater dehydration.

KEY POINT

Scientific research has shown that it takes just 2% dehydration to impair football-specific performance. Dehydration impacts a player's ability to maintain high intensity sprints and around 2.5% dehydration can lead to a 5% decrease in dribbling ability. In general terms, dehydration depletes carbohydrate stores faster.

Carbohydrates fuel high-intensity activity, so this will impact your performance and increase your perceived rate of exertion (PRE), generating a sense of having to work harder just to maintain the same level of intensity you produced earlier in the match.

Sweating during exercise also affects the electrolyte balance within your body. Sweat contains electrolytes, including sodium and the sodium-electrolyte imbalance caused by sweating is linked to muscle cramps, although the exact mechanisms of why this is the case are yet to be discovered.

HYDRATION IN FOOTBALL

Entering a football game in a dehydrated state is something that can easily be avoided and it's probably only a lack of knowledge among players that's leading to it happening at all. However, becoming dehydrated during a match is probably the result of a lack of opportunities to rehydrate while the game is in progress.

Other than during half-time, opportunities to get some fluids on board can be quite rare, often limited to unscheduled breaks such as a player getting injured. In one recent study, it was found that players only replace around 50% of the fluid lost through sweating during a match.

Improving hydration can be done in two ways:

1. Ensuring you go into a match well hydrated
2. Looking for ways to replace the fluid lost through sweating during a match

PRE-MATCH HYDRATION

Keeping track of your urine colour is a useful way to gauge your hydration level prior to a game and at any other time.

If it's pale (similar to lemonade in colour), you're probably well enough hydrated, but if it's dark (more like apple juice in colour) then this gives a clear indication that you're in a dehydrated state. If this is the case, you need to drink at least 500ml of water as soon as possible. Anything from 500ml up to 1ltr should be enough to boost your body back into a hydrated state.

In more general terms, it's recommended that you drink 5-10ml of fluid per kg of bodyweight prior to a match, ideally in the 3-4 hours before kick-off. This could be achieved through filling a 1ltr bottle with water and ensuring it's finished in the time period between eating your pre-match meal and walking out onto the pitch. Sodium or electrolytes could be included in this fluid intake by adding 0.5g of salt to every 1ltr or by using a sports drink.

MATCH-PLAY HYDRATION

The amount of fluid lost during a game varies from player to player. The amount of weight you generally lose over the course of a 90-minute match will give you an indication of the fluid intake you personally need to maintain your bodyweight throughout the course of a match.

As a general recommendation, use every opportunity, such as a pause in play, to go to the side-lines and grab a bottle. Drink as much as you can whenever these opportunities arise and then at half-time, drink at least 500ml of water or a sports drink. The sodium, electrolyte and carbohydrate content of a sports drink could be useful later in the game and if you're someone who sweats a lot during a match, ideally try and aim for a fluid intake of 1ltr at half-time.

POST-MATCH HYDRATION

Rehydration is an important aspect of the post-match recovery process. Statistics show that most players are dehydrated by the end of a game, so it's important to replace the fluids and electrolytes that have been lost during a match.

To rehydrate effectively, you need to drink around 150% of the fluid that's been lost. For example, if you weigh 75kgs before the match and then find you weigh 74kgs when you get home after the match, you've lost 1kg. To replace this fluid, you need to drink 1.5ltr of water or a hypertonic drink (150%), as 1kg of bodyweight equates to 1ltr of water.

If you have a rest day following a match, rehydration can take place over the course of the evening, but if you have a scheduled training session or gym session within 24 hours, it's important to rehydrate as soon as possible so that you're not going into it already in a dehydrated state.

The bottom line, just 2% dehydration can have a negative impact on football performance, but going into a match or training session in a dehydrated state is completely avoidable. When in doubt, drink more fluids.

THE EFFECTS OF ALCOHOL ON RECOVERY

The effects of alcohol on physical and psychological performance are well known. It goes without saying that consumption pre-exercise is going to negatively impact balance, reaction time, strength, power, speed and endurance...but alcohol can also cause less obvious damage within the body.

NEGATIVE EFFECTS OF ALCOHOL

As a footballer the main unseen negative effect of alcohol is the impact it has on your body's ability to recover post-exercise. Full recovery requires rebuilding of muscle tissue, restoration of energy stores and rehydration. Alcohol has been proven to negatively affect all three of these aspects of recovery.

REBUILDING OF MUSCLE TISSUE

Alcohol decreases post-exercise muscle protein synthesis. Muscle protein synthesis is extremely important as it's the process by which the body builds new muscle proteins to replace the muscle proteins damaged in a hard or intense exercise session. Science has shown that post-exercise muscle protein synthesis can be decreased by up to 75% when alcohol is present in the body and the effects can last for up to 24 hours.

KEY POINT

As an athlete, a typical post-exercise recovery period is going to be around 24-48 hours. If alcohol can impact recovery for up to 24 hours, your recovery is going to be significantly delayed. Keep this in mind if you're going out for a drink after a game or a training session. If you have another game or training session scheduled in the next 24 hours, you may not be in an optimal state to perform at your best because your recovery is going to be prolonged.

The mechanisms of why alcohol has this effect on muscle protein synthesis are not yet fully understood, but there's a potential link to a reduction in testosterone levels and more testosterone being converted to oestrogen. Another possible reason is believed to be the suppression of anabolic signalling pathways which tell the muscle cells to generate new protein and to convert the proteins taken in through foods in the diet.

RESTORATION OF ENERGY STORES

Carbohydrate stores are predominantly utilised during a game of football. Alcohol reduces the amount of carbohydrates taken up into the muscle tissue to be stored for later use, whether that's your next training session or a match. The exact impact of this on the body is unknown, but studies so far show a dose-dependent relationship, meaning the more alcohol you consume, the more it's going to interfere with your muscle's ability to increase its glycogen stores. In extreme cases such as binge drinking, you can be reducing the amount of glycogen (muscle sugar) stored in the muscle by around 50%. This will significantly impact your next training session or match as you have only half the energy supplies normally available to fuel your performance.

REHYDRATION

Alcohol has a slight diuretic effect. It inhibits an enzyme called vasopressin, an anti-diuretic hormone, thereby increasing the amount of urine you excrete, making it harder to retain the water you take in post-exercise. Science has shown that for every 1g of alcohol you consume, you will increase your excretion of urine by around 10ml. This may not sound like much, but when you consider that a standard beer or shot of spirit has around 15g of alcohol, drinking six beers or six shots of vodka could increase the amount of urine you excrete by around 1 litre and this will have a significant effect on your ability to recover.

However, it's worth noting that even when drinking alcohol, you're generally taking in more fluids than you would normally post-game or exercise. This means the increase in urine excretion is being matched by an increase in fluid intake, so a useful tip is to stick to beers or ciders that have a high fluid content compared to their alcohol content.

KEY POINT

Shots represent less fluid, thereby they'll increase the negative impact of the alcohol content, leading to a dehydrated state.

OTHER POTENTIAL NEGATIVES

The negative effects of alcohol extend beyond its impact on post-exercise recovery, but the scientific data is not yet conclusive. Other potential negatives of alcohol include:

- Increasing the amount of inflammation in the body post-exercise
- Negatively affect sleeping patterns

- Compromising your immune system, leaving you more susceptible to illness or infection
- Negatively impacting thermoregulation and the body's ability to maintain the correct temperature

IN SUMMARY

The negative effects of alcohol on recovery performance post-exercise generally only present themselves when alcohol intake surpasses around 0.5g per kg of bodyweight. This means if you weigh 80kg, you will experience the negative impacts if you consume around 40g or more of alcohol in one sitting. A standard beer or shot contains around 15g of alcohol, so limiting your intake to 3 drinks is the best approach to reducing the potentially negative effects of a night out on your post-exercise recovery and your performance the next day.

NUTRITION DURING RAMADAN

As a footballer, Ramadan will require a few adjustments to be made to your eating and drinking schedule to help fuel your body for matches and training and promote effective recovery.

In all sports, nutrient timing is a very important aspect of nutrition, so maintaining your performance during this period of fasting will mean making the most of the available eating and drinking window each day.

The good news is that scientific research supports the potential to not only maintain performance levels during Ramadan, but also make improvements, provided a nutritional plan is in place.

Ensuring your performance doesn't suffer comes down to achieving two main goals:

1. Maintaining your daily caloric intake
2. Staying hydrated

MAINTAINING YOUR CALORIC INTAKE

Reducing the time in which you can eat will naturally often lead to a reduction in the overall amount you eat across a 24-hour period. However, as a footballer, your caloric intake (especially carbohydrate intake) is a top priority in terms of fuelling optimal performance. To be able to keep your energy levels high, you need to keep your caloric intake adequately high.

Nutritional plan: One way to approach this is to track what you eat in the week or two prior to Ramadan, either using an app or simply a written food diary. This will give you an understanding of the number of calories you normally take in each day to fuel your activities and provide a picture of the types of foods and quantities of each type you normally consume at each meal.

As you enter Ramadan, you then need to find ways to consume the same types of foods and achieve the same caloric intake within a shorter eating window each day.

OPTIONS FOR ACHIEVING THIS GOAL INCLUDE:

- Eating the foods and the quantities you normally would across three or four meals outside of Ramadan, in two large meals during Ramadan.

- Switching the foods you normally eat for higher calorie options at each meal, allowing you to eat less food but still gain the caloric intake you need. As an example, switching from oats to granola will provide a higher number of calories in the same volume of food. Nut butter on toast can add calories to a meal and switching low-calorie fruits such as strawberries for higher calorie options such as bananas will boost the daily intake. Starchy foods such as potatoes can be very filling, making it difficult to eat more in one meal, but switching to rice will allow you to increase your portion size and therefore increase the overall calories consumed in one meal.

KEY POINT

If you struggle to gain the calories you need in a short window, foods that may normally be considered a treat (flapjacks, fruit juices etc.) can be used to help bridge the gap. Getting the total number of calories needed to fuel your performance must remain your top priority during Ramadan.

MAKING THE MOST OF THE EATING WINDOW

Eating as close to dawn as possible and then as soon as possible after sunset will give you the best chance of meeting your caloric requirement within the eating window and spreading it across manageable meals.

Nutrition and training plan: The timing of your training sessions will influence your potential performance. In a morning training session, you will have more energy if you eat just before dawn, but you won't necessarily have the chance to refuel and recover optimally with appropriate nutrition after training.

If you train in the evening, you won't have the chance to fuel-up beforehand, but you will be able to refuel afterwards. Clearly, the timing of your training becomes an individual choice, but training in the morning will allow you to take advantage of the calories you've consumed the prior evening and it may make it possible to keep your pre-exercise meal within the optimal window of 2-3 hours beforehand.

KEY POINT

Scheduling strength and power sessions for the morning is recommended as these rely heavily on fuel stores. A lower intensity session may be more suitable for evening training.

STAYING HYDRATED

During Ramadan, fluid intake is arguably harder to manage than food intake. If you have evening training sessions or matches, you may find your performance suffers as you go into the sessions dehydrated or in a hypo-hydrated state, negatively impacting both physical and mental performance.

RECOMMENDATIONS:

- Make sure you take full advantage of the entire drinking window by taking on board a minimum of 500ml to 1 litre of water just before dawn and then immediately after sunset. In this way you are rehydrating optimally as soon as possible, but it's a good idea to have water available throughout the eating and drinking window and to keep a water bottle next to your bed at night

- It's also important to take steps to increase fluid retention during this period as drinking large quantities in one sitting can lead to extra urination. A typical recommendation would be to consume around 0.5g of sodium per litre of water, but as eating and drinking need to be squeezed into a shorter timeframe, simply adding 1g of salt to the food you eat at each meal will have the desired effect

- Avoiding unnecessary heat exposure or activity during the day will help to minimise water or sweat losses. This might mean wearing lighter clothing, keeping the temperature in your house cool, or limiting the amount of warm up exercise you do in training, but it's important to do enough to minimise the risk of injury

IN SUMMARY

As with nutrition, the earlier in the morning you can schedule your training, the more you can take advantage of the fluid stores you have in your body from the night before, but whatever time you train or play, maintaining your performance comes down to planning ahead and ensuring you make the most of the eating and drinking window to achieve your optimal daily caloric intake and stay well hydrated.

NUTRITION FOR GOALKEEPERS

Goalkeepers represent a unique position in football that often demonstrates distinct physical demands when compared to outfield players. Especially on match days, these demands are very apparent, with elite goalkeepers covering ~50% of the total distance relative to their teammates.

Not only this, but the frequency of intensive actions performed within this distance is far less than outfield players. Goalkeepers, on average, are only required to perform 2-10 saves per match, which often involve brief explosive actions such as diving, jumping and accelerating, despite the vital importance of these brief periods.

As for match day energy requirements for goalkeepers, when 62 goalkeepers in the English Premier League were monitored over 100 matches, it was found that 93% of the total distance covered was from either walking or jogging.

In fact, the average time per game spent running at a high-speed was just 67 meters, which conveys the stark differences to other positions. Considering this, experts in the field of sport nutrition have clearly stated that the energy intake required for goalkeepers to perform to their best in a match, specifically from carbohydrates which fuel high-intensity activity, is vastly lower than outfield players.

Whereas outfield players will look towards increasing their carbohydrate intake towards 8-10 grams of carbohydrates per kg of bodyweight in the 24-hour period before matches, high-level goalkeepers in the Premier League and Spanish First Division are only reported to consume ~3.5-4 grams per kg of bodyweight.

Importantly, although this is the current practice of high-level goalkeepers, there is no actual supporting evidence to suggest that this is an "optimal" universal recommendation. However, based on the knowledge of physical demands during match days, the current consensus from sport scientists is that there is no apparent need for goalkeepers to consume above or below the range of 3.5-4 grams of carbohydrates per kg of bodyweight.

This would require the average 70-85kg goalkeeper to consume approximately 250-350 grams of carbohydrates in the 24-hour period before a game, nothing too drastic from the average athletes' average dietary practices.

BUT WHAT ABOUT TRAINING?

The differences in physical demands are less obvious during training periods, as goalkeepers will be required to undertake similar intensive exercise programmes to outfield players to similarly achieve optimal body composition and physiological improvements.

This being said, there are still notable differences that will change the nutritional recommendations for goalkeepers during training. For example, the total distances covered by goalkeepers during training is ~3km, considerably lower than that typically observed (5-7 km) in outfield players.

This reduction in training load may be due to the common isolation of goalkeeper training that involves limited areas of the pitch (focusing on position specific attributes), with limited involvement in outfield player drills. As such, the daily energy expenditure of an elite Premier League goalkeeper, for example, is ~2900 kcal per day, compared to ~3500 kcal per day for team mates in the same week of training.

In general, a goalkeeper's carbohydrate intake should be between 3-5 grams per kg of bodyweight on training days (similar to match days as previously mentioned) and protein and fat intake recommendations remain the same for goalkeepers compared to other positions.

GREAT FOOD OPTIONS WHEN YOU'RE ON THE ROAD

Travelling to a match can present some issues if the journey means missing your normal pre-match meal or meal time. However, this is easily resolved with a little preparation.

OPTIMAL MEAL TIMES

The ideal time to eat a pre-match meal is 3-4 hours before kick-off. If your journey fits within this time frame then it's simply a matter of eating before you leave and you're covered, provided you've allowed time for the foods to be digested and absorbed.

A lot of footballers like to eat a pre-match meal just 1 or 2 hours ahead of kick-off, but it's in your best interests to get into the habit of allowing 3-4 hours for optimal absorption.

ON THE ROAD MEALS

If your journey is going to be longer than 3-4 hours, things are going to be more difficult and you will need to be a little more prepared ahead of time. The best option is going to be preparing a carbohydrate-based meal to take with you, ready to eat 3-4 hours ahead of kick-off or plan a stop-off at the right time to pick something up as you go.

Your pre-match meal should be a high carbohydrate, moderate protein, low fat meal. It needs to be something that travels well and is convenient to eat on the road. For this reason, sticking to the basics is your best bet.

EASY OPTION 1

A couple of sandwiches or a baguette is a go-to meal for most footballers on the road.

For example, take some whole wheat or Ezekiel bread and add sandwich meats or pre-cooked meats. Chicken or turkey is best as it won't slow down digestion too much. Add lettuce, tomatoes, a sauce of your choice (so long as it's low in fat) and this will cover most of your nutritional needs. Simply wrap it up in foil and you're good to go!

A bonus with this type of pre-match meal is that if you're in a rush and you don't have time to prepare it ahead of time, you can stop off and find something similar, whether it's in a supermarket or somewhere like Subway. Fast food options should always be a last resort, but Subway isn't a terrible choice as they offer healthier options using similar basic ingredients.

EASY OPTION 2

An alternative option is something pasta-based. This is quick to make, travels well and can be eaten cold.

For example, take 100-150g of pasta (pre-cooked weight) and add pre-cooked chicken breast, spinach, tomato sauce and peas, mix it together, put it in a Tupperware box and again, you're good to go.

SNACK OPTIONS

It's also a good idea to take some carbohydrate-based snacks with you.

These can be consumed alongside your pre-match meal or just as snacks on the journey. The best choices are high in carbohydrate, low in fat and light on the stomach (so they won't cause any gastro-intestinal upsets during the match). Fruits such as apples and bananas are good options, as are raisins, dried apricots and energy bars.

Choose low fat, low fibre options, so anything with oats, cereals or dried fruits is generally fine. Rice cakes, Nature Valley oat bars or Science in Sport energy bars are good examples. These snacks are easy to consume and light on the stomach and they're convenient to pack when on the road.

HYDRATION OPTIONS

Hydration is where many footballers go wrong when they're travelling to a game. The solution is simple – take at least a 2-litre bottle of water with you. The longer the journey, the more water you will need, so fill spare bottles and take those with you too. Starting a game in a dehydrated state is a very bad scenario and must be avoided because it's going to hinder your performance significantly.

It's also a good idea to take 1 or 2 sports drinks with you, which will help to top up your carbohydrate stores and get some electrolytes on board pre-match. This will help in terms of retaining the fluids you drink, thereby improving your hydration status for the duration of the match. In this sense, sports drinks should be considered an essential option and they should be taken with you not only for during the game, but also half time.

TRAVEL FOOD CHECK LIST:

- Pre-made whole wheat baguette with white meat (or beans if you're vegetarian) with some lettuce and tomato
- A pot filled with pasta, tomato sauce, chicken breast and spinach
- Banana
- Apple
- At least 2 litres of water
- A couple of sports drinks (for example, Lucozade Sport)

PROTEIN SHAKE

One last possible option is a high carb protein powder in a shaker, ready to just add water to before consumption. This could be used pre-match, but it could also be utilised post-match, taken immediately after the final whistle for recovery purposes.

WHAT TO BUY WHEN YOU'RE ON A BUDGET

It's one thing to be given recommendations in terms of foods for performance, but it's another to be able to afford them...so which foods represent the best nutritional buys when you're on a tight budget?

FOOD SHOPPING ESSENTIALS

Carbohydrates are the main source of energy for footballers and they're often the cheapest type of food to buy.

Starchy foods: Stock up on plain oats, plain rice, pasta and potatoes (both white potatoes and sweet potatoes). White or brown options are very often similar in terms of nutritional value so going with the cheapest option is still an adequate choice.

Fruits: These are going to be slightly more expensive carbohydrate sources, but bananas tend to be the most affordable. Finding the best value type of apple may take a little shopping around as costs can vary hugely across different varieties. Dried fruits often represent good value in terms of the amount of carbohydrate gained per pound or dollar spent.

Vegetables: Vegetable prices vary depending on where you shop, but it's important to note that frozen vegetables are generally much cheaper and represent a good source of energy as they remain nutritionally complete. They'll also last longer than many fresh vegetables. A bag of frozen mixed vegetables can be incorporated into most meals and they're very cheap, making them an essential for athletes on a budget. In terms of fresh vegetables, the best options are fresh spinach, broccoli and onions as these are inexpensive and versatile.

Protein sources are typically the most expensive element of a weekly food shop.

Non-meat sources: Stock up on these first as they tend to be less expensive. Egg and milk are good staples, but they can be quite high in saturated fat and cholesterol so mix them with tinned, plant-based sources of protein such as beans, lentils and chickpeas. These are good alternatives to meat sources and can be made even less expensive by buying dry versions and soaking them yourself if you have time.

Meat sources: Depending on your budget, fresh chicken thighs or frozen chicken breast represent the best value meat sources of protein. Frozen meats will generally provide a lower quality source of protein, but they remain nutritionally good enough and will give you meat protein on a budget.

Yoghurt products: These also provide protein, Greek yoghurts generally represent the best choice as they offer a slightly better nutritional profile for around the same price as a standard yoghurt.

Protein powder: Another option is to buy a protein powder as these provide a cheap but good source of protein and could be the cheapest option in terms of the amount of protein you get per gram.

Fat sources will be found in the carbohydrate and protein foods listed, especially meat, eggs and dairy. Other options include:

Flaxseeds or chia seeds: These provide a good source of omega 3s, a good alternative to often pricey fish and they can be easily incorporated into cereals or oats at breakfast.

Nuts: Nut products can also be high in omega 3s, with the cheapest type of nut generally being peanuts. A superior option in terms of health and nutritional value would be walnuts if affordable.

YOUR WEEKLY SHOPPING LIST

To eat a nutritious diet on a budget (appropriate for fuelling football performance and aiding recovery), add the following items to your shopping list:

Oats, rice, pasta, potatoes, bag of frozen mixed vegetables, fresh spinach and broccoli, frozen chicken breast or fresh chicken thighs, milk, eggs, canned beans, chickpeas, lentils, bag of flaxseeds and peanuts.

If you stick to these core ingredients, you may be surprised by just how cheap and affordable a weekly shop can be.

FOOTBALL "SUPERFOODS"

The term "superfood" is simply a marketing ploy, in sports nutritional terms there's no such thing.

However, the foods marketed as superfoods are generally quite high in nutrients, especially micronutrients such as vitamins and minerals and some contain phytonutrients such as flavonoids and glucosinolates which have antioxidative or anti-inflammatory properties, so these foods can be beneficial in a footballer's diet.

There's no single food that holds the key to good health, disease prevention, or optimum athletic performance – superfood or otherwise. The key to achieving these benefits is to focus on your diet as a whole. Exact dietary requirements are dependent on an individual's specific needs and any gaps they may have in terms of imbalances or deficiencies in their daily diet. As a football player, your focus should be on nutrient-dense foods which will include many of those promoted as superfoods.

SUPERFOODS TO INCLUDE IN YOUR DIET

Two "superfoods" that are of benefit to most people are sweet potatoes and salmon.

SWEET POTATOES

Sweet potatoes are high in carbohydrates and micronutrients, making them an overall well-rounded food to include in your diet. Many athletes, footballers included, fall short on daily vitamin and mineral intakes and just one large sweet potato can help to meet the recommendations for vitamin A, vitamin C, vitamin B6, pantothenic acid, magnesium, potassium and manganese (and they also contain small amounts of many other micronutrients).

Consuming 1-2 sweet potatoes per day in a single meal will help you to achieve the daily nutrient targets that are essential for health and the carbohydrate content will fuel you for training sessions and matches, making sweet potatoes a great option to include in pre-training and pre-match meals.

SALMON

Salmon is also high in vitamins and minerals, providing calories in the form of protein and dietary fat, especially omega-3s. The health benefits of omega-3s include the reduction of chronic inflammation, which could aid joint health and help to reduce recovery times after an intense training session. The essential amino acids within salmon's protein content also help to stimulate protein synthesis, thereby aiding muscle growth.

Micronutrients provided include thiamine, niacin, vitamin B6, vitamin B12 (this is very important for the function of the central nervous system and commonly deficient in an athlete's diet), phosphorous, potassium and selenium.

Including these two foods in your diet reduces the potential to be deficient in vitamins and minerals that could impact both your health and performance. Together they provide a good source of calories and nutrients in the form of proteins, carbohydrates and fats.

OTHER GOOD OPTIONS TO INCLUDE IN YOUR DIET

Greek yoghurt High in protein, making it a useful pre-bed snack and as a fermented dairy product, research has shown it to be beneficial to gut health.

Nuts or oats: High in calories, making them good as snacks between meals and especially useful for footballers in periods of intense training or match-play. Nuts and oats also mix well with other superfoods such as blueberries, making them a convenient way to boost your calorie intake with the added health benefit of containing powerful antioxidative and anti-inflammatory properties.

HOW BEETROOT JUICE CAN AID STAMINA

Beetroot juice is regularly consumed by many athletes, but can it be used to improve football performance?

HOW IT WORKS

Beetroot juice contains nitrates. These are compounds found naturally in many vegetables (specifically green leafy varieties such as spinach) and they're converted to a substance known as nitric oxide in the digestion process.

Nitric oxide has been shown to have performance-enhancing effects by improving the efficiency of muscular energy production in two main ways:

1. Acting as a vasodilator, thereby expanding the volume of blood vessels which increases the blood flow within the body, increasing the oxygen supply to the muscles
2. Increasing the number of mitochondria within muscle cells. Energy production takes place in the mitochondria, so more mitochondria will mean greater potential for energy production. It's also known that nitric oxide can promote greater efficiency in terms of energy production within the mitochondria

PERFORMANCE ENHANCEMENTS

In theory, if beetroot juice is taken appropriately, it can provide the double effect outlined above. If you have more mitochondria, there's more potential to produce energy and the more efficiently those mitochondria can produce energy, the less energy you need to fuel your performance. Add to this the increased blood and oxygen supply provided by vasodilation and it will have a positive impact on your endurance performance.

KEY POINT

Recent research has indicated that there may be potential anaerobic performance benefits. Nitric oxide can improve the effectiveness of calcium within muscle fibres to help produce a better contraction, but as this research is in its early stages, known performance enhancements remain endurance performance based.

FOOTBALL-SPECIFIC PERFORMANCE

In terms of football performance, the benefits provided by beetroot juice (nitric oxide) will mean you need a lower amount of oxygen to work at a given exercise intensity. For example, jogging around the pitch or putting in a brief sprint to get the ball will use less oxygen, making you more efficient as a player because you require less energy to produce each movement, effectively saving energy for when it's needed later in the match.

In one study, a potential power-based (anaerobic) benefit was demonstrated using the yo-yo intermittent recovery test which replicates the repeated sprint drills performed within football. This links to the research findings of improvements in muscle contraction and could lead to improvements in football performance through delaying fatigue.

HOW TO TAKE BEETROOT JUICE

Athletes currently taking beetroot juice use different approaches, but each one has shown benefits. The main methods are:

- Pre-exercise only: Beetroot juice is consumed pre-exercise, 3-4 hours before a training session or stepping out onto the pitch
- Daily dosage: Beetroot juice is consumed daily, including rest days

Studies show that acute doses have more of an effect on vasodilation, whereas consistent use promotes an increase in mitochondria, so a combination of these methods may help to maximise the benefits of beetroot juice.

The common recommendation for beetroot juice consumption is 90 minutes before exercise. However, it's known that the peak for nitric oxide concentrations in the blood occurs at around 2-3 hours after consumption and peak performance enhancements are noted at around 2 to 2.5 hours after consumption, therefore scheduling the time of consumption to around 2 hours before exercise will help to ensure those peak concentrations are taking effect as you begin training or are heading out for your pre-match warm-up.

HOW MUCH BEETROOT JUICE?

Research has revealed that the performance-enhancing effects of nitrate become noticeable at around 6-8 mmol or 300-400mg. To access this, you need to consume around 0.5 litres of beetroot juice. But, as many people find it hard to stomach this quantity, concentrated beetroot shots of around 70ml are useful alternatives.

KEY POINT

If you are an elite athlete, the amount of beetroot juice you need to consume to achieve the same effects noted in a non-elite athlete will be higher. The exact reason for this is as yet unknown, but one way to boost your intake is to consume beetroot juice every day rather than just pre-exercise, or you could up the quantity you consume by 25-50%.

KEY SUPPLEMENTS FOR FOOTBALL PERFORMANCE

The supplement market is enormous, with brands making bold claims about their products performance-enhancing benefits, it can be hard to know which supplements represent the best choice for footballers?

SCIENCE-BACKED SUPPLEMENTS

It's fair to say that many supplements available on the market today are as good as useless, but there are three products with extensive research behind them to substantiate their performance-enhancing claims. They are:

1. Caffeine
2. Creatine
3. Beta alanine

CAFFEINE

All athletes can benefit from caffeine. Studies have shown it to be beneficial in a variety of ways across endurance-based sports, power-based sports and in football specifically.

Improvements have been noted for both physical and cognitive aspects, including technical aspects such as sprinting ability, jumping performance, reactive agility and even passing accuracy when caffeine is consumed pre-exercise.

HOW IT WORKS

Caffeine can cross the blood-brain barrier and modulate the central nervous system. This increases the concentration of many hormones that are beneficial to performance such as adrenalin and dopamine.

The effects of this increase include:

- A delay in fatigue when you're out on the pitch (both physically and mentally)
- Improvements in concentration

- Decreased perception of exertion for a given intensity of exercise, meaning a movement such as a 10m sprint down the pitch will feel less intense

Caffeine can be taken in the form of a pill, as an energy drink, or in a simple cup of coffee. The amount of caffeine you need to take to achieve the beneficial effects varies from player to player and is largely dependent on your caffeine tolerance. The more caffeine you normally consume on a day-to-day basis, the more you will need to take to achieve the same benefits as someone who consumes less.

As a general guide, most footballers need between 75mg-200mg of caffeine around 15 minutes prior to exercise, but if you have a high caffeine tolerance, this could be taken up to 300mg. Intake beyond 300mg is likely to create unwanted side-effects.

CREATINE

Creatine, specifically creatine monohydrate, can benefit athletes by increasing the phosphocreatine stores within muscle tissue. This substance is essential in the enzymatic reactions that create energy during high-intensity activity (such as short sprints and jumping).

HOW IT WORKS

Creatine regenerates the body's phosphocreatine store, making it possible to produce more energetic, high intensity movements before fatiguing. This can also be beneficial for training purposes, specifically for players training to improve their strength in the gym or increase their power, even their lean body mass, as it allows for a higher overall work volume.

To have a positive effect, creatine needs to be loaded into the muscle tissue regularly every 24 hours. The best protocol is to start with 20g of creatine monohydrate daily for 5-7 days, then follow this with 5g of creatine daily to maintain the stores.

There is some scientific research that suggests taking creatine post-exercise may help absorption, but timing is not as important as simply ensuring that the daily dose is maintained.

BETA ALANINE

Beta alanine is a newer supplement compared to creatine and caffeine, but studies have shown that it can reduce or delay the onset of fatigue during high-intensity activity.

HOW IT WORKS

It does so by acting as an intra-cellular buffer to the accumulation of hydrogen ions, something that happens during intense exercise. Hydrogen ions put muscle into a more acidic state and this contributes to muscle cells failing to function correctly. By promoting a more neutral state in the muscles, fatigue can be delayed.

Currently, a dose of 2-5g per day is recommended. Some players prefer to take it pre-exercise as it can create a tingling sensation in the hands and/or feet. The tingling is easier to ignore whilst training compared to if you're trying to relax at home.

BEST SUPPLEMENTS IN SUMMARY

Ignore the marketing hype and stick to the supplements with scientifically proven benefits. Caffeine, creatine and beta alanine have the largest body of research behind them to support their claims. It's worth noting that other things such as protein powders and omega 3s are often mistaken for supplements, but these fall into the separate category of functional foods.

WHICH SUPPLEMENTS ARE SAFE TO TAKE?

Used by 50% of the general public and an even higher percentage of elite athletes, it's clear that supplement safety is essential. Supplements can be helpful for you as a footballer and they can give you a slight edge over your competition, but it's important to be aware of areas of concern in the supplement industry so that the choices you make are always informed.

INDUSTRY REGULATIONS

The supplement industry is NOT under the same regulations as the pharmaceutical industry...meaning there's no requirement for supplement manufacturers to produce a "safe" product, show safety records or even have some form of quality assurance for their product.

Just a few years ago, the Food and Drug Administration admitted that the current resources and protocols in place are insufficient for any type of comprehensive supplement monitoring. This leads to two concerns for you as an athlete:

1. Health and safety
2. The potential for banned substances and an accidental doping violation

CONTAMINATION

The current data available in scientific reviews indicates that 10-20% of dietary supplements tested in independent labs are contaminated with at least one substance that is not declared on the label. These substances include banned stimulants, anabolic agents, steroids and diuretics to name a few.

Contamination could be due to the contamination of raw materials being used by manufacturers and the ingredients they're sourcing from abroad, poor manufacturing practices and a lack of stringent regulations, or in fact purposeful alterations to enhance the effectiveness of the product.

KEY POINT

The level of contaminant or banned substance found in some products can be substantial. In one study, the prevalence of the anabolic steroid dianabol in an over the counter bodybuilding supplement was found to be 10-43mg per serving. The recommended therapeutic dose of dianabol is only 2.5-5mg per day...highlighting the potential health concerns of contamination such as this.

Some companies state that they third-party check their products for contamination, but even with these checks, there's no safety guarantee as many of the 10-20% of dietary supplements found to be contaminated were third-party tested products.

CONCERNS FOR FOOTBALLERS

As a professional footballer or a player who may be drug tested in the future, you may be competing under an anti-doping code, usually the World Anti-Doping Code.

Taking a prohibited substance, even if accidental, can result in an anti-doping violation if the ingredient is on the prohibited list. Many athletes have faced bans through inadvertently consuming prohibited substances found in supplements (although it's also known that many will hide behind this as a convenient excuse).

Even today 40% of elite athletes are unaware of supplements being related to doping violations, despite 10% of doping cases being caused by a tainted supplement.

SUPPLEMENT RECOMMENDATIONS

A world-renowned sports doping control and research laboratory known as the LGC, has shown that the instance of contamination among high quality products that are regularly tested for banned substances is approximately 0.0002%.

A high-quality product can be defined as a product that's Informed Sport certified. Informed Sport is a global risk management programme for sports nutrition products based on two fundamental pillars of quality assurance:

1. A rigorous pre-registration audit and every batch of product is tested before it's released to the market by the most accredited method possible
2. They test all ingredients in their raw state, during the manufacturing process and then after they've been processed

Examples of Informed Sport certified products include:

- Maxi Nutrition
- Nutrition X

- Science in Sport
- My Protein

That's not to say these are the only brands you should use, but be sure to always check for the Informed Sport logo on the packaging of any supplement you're looking to buy.

The bottom line is that higher quality brands are likely to be slightly more expensive, but paying a little extra may be the safest way to ensure the supplements you choose provide the benefits you're looking for without the risk of contamination.

WHAT SUPPLEMENTS CAN YOUNG PLAYERS HAVE?

The supplement market is enormous and with such a huge variety of products so readily available, the question of whether supplements are safe for use by young athletes must be raised.

Around 70-90% of adult athletes consume some type of dietary supplement. In adolescents and younger athletes, this drops to around 20-50%, so are younger athletes missing out? Or is there a large percentage of misinformed young athletes taking supplements?

In lower age brackets, the type of supplement taken tends to be health-related (such as vitamins and minerals) whereas adults tend to use ergogenic aids such as caffeine and creatine. The argument over whether young athletes should be exposed to the same performance enhancing supplements as adult athletes has two sides.

THE ARGUMENT IN FAVOUR OF SUPPLEMENTATION

The modern-day youth sports environment is ultra-competitive. Whether it's football or any other sport, young athletes are being pushed to the boundaries with packed training and match schedules that can be just as demanding as an adult schedule.

They're also being introduced to the world of strength and conditioning earlier (whilst dealing with the growth spurts which come with puberty), which adds to the increased demand for nutrients to aid recovery, energy levels and growth. For this reason, young athletes (and their parents) are becoming more and more concerned with proper nutrition and turning to supplementation to support their training.

With this being the case, experimenting with supplements that are safe and effective could potentially fill any gaps in a young athlete's diet and make reaching daily nutrient recommendations more convenient. According to the American Journal of Clinical Nutrition, optimising nutrition within adolescents is the key factor in their growth and development.

THE ARGUMENT AGAINST SUPPLEMENTATION

The argument against supplementation is based on safety issues surrounding there use with young people. The research on how safe supplements are and what dosage should be used is all done within adult populations, with very few studies including adolescents and young adults. For this reason, there's no solid understanding of what dosage is safe in this age group and what side-effects or health concerns there may be.

With this being the case, it's better to be safe than sorry and the general recommendation is that nutritional needs should be met through diet rather than supplementation.

DIET V SUPPLEMENTATION

Supplementation should be considered a potential added benefit once everything else is in place. This is true across all age groups and it's important to ensure that your diet is nutritionally complete before considering any supplementation that may help to improve your performance. The process of setting up and establishing a nutritionally sound diet can take a month or two as an adult and it's fair to say that not many teenagers have their diet really nailed down.

KEY POINT

Introducing supplements into a diet that's not nutritionally complete makes no sense no matter the age. The focus must be on diet and whole foods first, with supplementation only being considered once everything else is in place.

TRACKING IMPROVEMENTS

In the adult population, it's possible to track the influence of a supplement in terms of improvements in performance, but this is not the case with adolescents simply because there are too many variables. Whether its growth spurts, increases in lean mass, or any other changes in hormonal levels due to puberty, these changes are going to impact performance, making it difficult to know if the supplement is having any real effect.

POTENTIAL USES OF SUPPLEMENTATION IN ADOLESCENTS

There are two scenarios in which supplementation may be useful for young athletes:

1. Correcting a nutrient deficiency

2. Functional foods

CORRECTING A NUTRIENT DEFICIENCY

An annual blood test is a useful way of checking for nutrient markers, hormone levels, or any other markers of health in all age groups.

If a test shows a deficiency in vitamin A or vitamin C, it can be a good idea to introduce a supplement to overcome this. Of course, this could also be addressed through nutrition and wholefoods, but if it's proving difficult to overcome a deficiency, then supplementation could be useful. At this point, the potential negative effects of a clinical deficiency might outweigh any potential negative effects of supplementation.

FUNCTIONAL FOODS

A functional food is a processed food derived from a natural source, but unlike caffeine, creatine, or beta alanine, this type of supplementation is not necessarily aimed at enhancing performance. Examples include beetroot juice, omega-3 supplementation, or very finely cut oats that can be added to morning shakes or protein powders. Protein powders themselves can be defined as a functional food as they're derived from a natural source before going through a processing stage.

The main issue with this type of supplementation is the potential for contamination, especially when supplements are being sourced at cheaper price points. Always choose products that are Informed Sport certified, as these will have gone through the highest level of testing to check for any contamination, whether this is drugs or any other substance that shouldn't be in there.

Current research suggests that around 20% of products available on the market will be contaminated and contamination can be IGF-1 (insulin-like growth factor), steroids and any other variety of banned performance enhancing drug. When you take this into consideration, it becomes a question of whether you really want a young athlete to take the risk of being exposed to these contaminants, especially when most issues can be corrected through establishing a nutritionally complete diet.

The bottom line is that supplementation in young athletes under the age of 18 should only become a consideration if there is a dietary deficiency that can't be met through diet alone.

WHEN TO USE PROTEIN POWDERS

Protein powder can be considered a functional food rather than a supplement and while it's not essential, it can be a useful tool within a footballer's diet for two reasons:

1. It's convenient
2. It's a high-quality protein source

PROTEIN POWDER V REAL FOOD SOURCES

The quality of the protein provided by a protein powder depends on the type you buy, but all types serve the purpose of increasing muscle protein synthesis levels. They may be a functional food, but this doesn't make them inferior to other real food sources.

There are many types available on the market, but whey protein is the most popular and studies have shown it to be the most effective. Other types include casein, soy, rice and pea (there's a plethora of types and brands out there) but whey protein is considered the gold standard because it has the best amino acid profile, providing essential amino acids that the body can't synthesise.

Real food sources of protein and essential amino acids include meat, fish, beans and nuts and when looking at your diet as a whole, the majority of your protein intake should come from these sources. However, for increasing muscle protein synthesis and aiding recovery, protein powders provide an equally good source of protein in a convenient form.

Amino acids are the blocks of protein found in foods and the denser the amino acid content, the better the quality of the food as a source of protein. Whey protein is a dense source of essential amino acids and as the body can't synthesise these, they must be obtained from the diet. All protein powders provide essential amino acids, but whey protein consistently comes out on top when tested against other types and is therefore used as a gold standard measure in terms of promoting muscle recovery.

KEY POINT

Amino acids are mainly responsible for the anabolic response of a meal, increasing muscle protein synthesis levels, repairing damaged muscle proteins and speeding up recovery.

POST-EXERCISE RECOVERY

Liquid forms of protein supplement are easier to digest compared to eating and then breaking down solids. This leads to a faster rate of absorption, meaning the amino acids can be utilised faster for the purposes of recovery. It's not necessary to have this spike in anabolism across the day or after every meal, but consuming protein within 30 minutes post-exercise may help to boost recovery.

It's in this period after intense exercise that the greatest elevation in muscle protein breakdown occurs, so the quicker the breakdown can be reversed and the anabolic responses increased, the quicker the recovery mechanisms can be stimulated and the shorter the recovery time is likely to be. Shorter recovery times means a heightened chance that you're going to be ready for your next training session or match in a fully recovered state.

THE CONVENIENCE OF PROTEIN POWDERS

As an athlete, your protein requirement for the day is 1.5g of protein per kg of bodyweight (for most), but there can be days when you might struggle to meet this intake because of scheduling or simply not having time to prepare and consume meals providing a high-quality protein intake.

If you reach the end of the day and find you're 50g short of your protein requirement, a protein shake is a fast, convenient way to remedy the situation. Adding two scoops of powder to 500ml of water gives you the 50g intake you need and it can be prepared and consumed within minutes before going to bed.

A protein shake is also extremely convenient if you're going out for the day and you haven't had time to prepare or pack any food. Instead of relying on fast foods, you could take a shaker with you (which you've already put the powder into) and then just add water.

This can also be useful as a post-match or post-training snack. If getting home to cook a meal after a match is going to take quite a bit of time, you can have a protein shake (high carb version) with you ready to consume straight away at the end of the game, making it quick and easy to initiate the all-important recovery processes.

ALTERNATIVES TO WHEY PROTEIN

Whey protein has been found to be more effective than other types of protein powder in tests, but if you need to avoid dairy (whey is a type of dairy) then soy protein isolate is the next best option. Its amino acid profile is only slightly lower than whey, so soy is still a good-quality protein source.

Casein protein is popular as a pre-bed shake, it's commonly advertised as a long-lasting "drip-feed" for the muscles. It's a good quality protein source but it's not any better than whey, even in a pre-sleep scenario.

Scientific studies have concluded that the anabolic response provided by any protein powder is limited to just 3-4 hours after consumption, so any increase beyond the 4-hour mark is going to be insignificant.

THE BEST TIME TO CONSUME PROTEIN POWDER

There are 4 different times when protein powder is going to be beneficial:

1. POST-WORKOUT OR POST-MATCH

This is purely because it's convenient. You can take it with you, it's quick to consume and it's going to counteract any increases in muscle protein breakdown resulting from a training session or match, quickly stimulating the anabolic processes that aid recovery. It's very popular in a lot of professional teams to have a protein or recovery shake ready-prepared for the return to the dressing-room after a match, consuming it straight away to kick-start the recovery process as soon as possible.

2. BEFORE BED

Protein shakes offer a very quick and easy way to reach your protein intake for the day if you haven't quite achieved it before going to bed.

3. AS A SNACK

If you realise you've gone through a long period (6 hours or more) without consuming a significant source of protein, then a protein shake as a snack can help to ensure that protein synthesis levels stay elevated between meals.

4. BOOSTING A MEAL'S PROTEIN CONTENT

To achieve maximum recovery benefits, each meal should contain 30-40g of protein. If you realise that the meal you've cooked only contains 10g, not enough to maximally stimulate muscle protein synthesis and recovery mechanisms, you can use a protein shake to increase your intake at the meal.

As a footballer, you need to look at every meal as an opportunity to maximally stimulate protein synthesis and reduce recovery time. This is especially important if you're active most days and the recovery window between your sessions is short. Utilising protein shakes is a convenient and effective way to stimulate as much recovery as possible in the shortest possible time.

THE BENEFITS OF CREATINE

Creatine is a popular dietary supplement that's promoted as an aid to advancing sporting performance, but can it help football performance?

WHAT IS CREATINE?

Creatine is a compound that's found primarily in muscle tissue (around 90-100% of the body's creatine stores are found in muscle tissue.)

It can be synthesised in the body naturally from amino acids such as glycine and arginine, or it can be made available through the diet by consuming meat, fish, or milk. These dietary sources of protein are all animal products, so a typical omnivorous diet will provide around 1-2g of creatine per day. Of course, creatine is also available as a dietary supplement, coming in the form of a tasteless powder that can be dissolved in liquids to provide a drink.

KEY POINT

The average male has a creatine pool of around 120-140g in muscle stores and the average female stores slightly less at around 80-100g.

WHAT DOES CREATINE DO?

Creatine can serve as an energy substrate for the contraction of muscle tissue during very high-intensity exercise. This means creatine helps to fuel any bout of high-intensity exercise lasting up to 10 seconds, so this could be strength-based exercises in the gym or sprints during training. During these very high-intensity activities, your body needs to supply energy at an extremely fast rate and the usual energy sources such as carbohydrates and fat simply can't meet the rate of energy demand.

This rapid energy demand can be met by creatine because of something known as the creatine phosphate shuttle. In a nutshell, creatine is synthesised into another product called phosphate creatine which is then broken down again into creatine, with energy constantly being released during the cycle. However, this cycle can only be maintained for around 10 seconds, because we're limited to the pool of creatine stored in our muscle tissues and muscle cells.

KEY POINT

The theory behind creatine supplementation is that by increasing the amount of creatine and phosphate creatine present in our muscle stores, the creatine phosphate shuttle can be prolonged to meet energy demands for longer.

This may only amount to 1 or 2 extra seconds, but those seconds represent an advantage in terms of prolonging the time it takes to fatigue in high-intensity training or competition, which in itself has the potential to be game-changing.

CREATINE SUPPLEMENTATION STUDIES

Studies on creatine supplementation have proven it to be effective. The total creatine pool within the muscle cells can be increased by around 10-30% and phosphate creatine stores can also be increased by 10-40%. But, the question remains, can this physiological benefit translate to real-world results and real-world improvements on the pitch or in training?

The answer is yes. Scientific research centred on creatine supplementation has shown consistent results and the extent of the benefit is an increase of around 5-10% in strength and power due to the prolonged creatine phosphate shuttle and delay in reaching fatigue.

KEY POINT

Creatine supplementation allows you to increase your workload and an indirect effect of this can be an increase in muscle mass. The delay in reaching fatigue allows for progressive overload and the enhancement in training adaptations this brings.

In terms of sport-specific benefits, creatine can increase your work volume in competitive matches, meaning you're able to keep repeating high intensity bursts for a greater percentage of a full match.

As a player, it's not unusual to find your energy levels declining at around the 70 to 75-minute mark, so your performance in high-intensity activities such as sprinting or jumping for the ball begins to decline. The 5-10% benefit gained through creatine supplementation can have a significant impact during those final 5 to 10 minutes because it's those short bursts of high-intensity activity that will likely win or rescue a game.

As a side note, research has shown that the largest increases in terms of performance are seen in vegetarian or vegan players. This is because this population don't have the natural supply of creatine from animal products in their diet and muscle stores are typically lower compared to those eating an omnivorous diet.

WHAT TYPE OF CREATINE IS BEST?

There are many forms of creatine available on the market. The original (classic) formula is creatine monohydrate and this is simply a creatine molecule attached to a water molecule. There are many new and alternative versions to this and these are a creatine molecule attached to something else i.e. magnesium, alkaline powder, or a type of ester, for example.

These alternative forms are often promoted as being superior and more effective than the original formula, but there's no evidence to support these claims. In scientific research, creatine monohydrate consistently comes out on top and this is because it's able to completely saturate a muscle cell within muscle tissue, thereby it's able to elevate muscle tissue stores to a level which is physiologically impossible to go beyond.

Some of the alternative forms may be able to do the same, but they can't be any more effective, there's simply no room for any further saturation.

WHAT DOSE OF CREATINE MONOHYDRATE IS BEST?

The best way to begin supplementing with creatine is to go through a loading phase. For a period of around 5-7 days, you should take 20g of creatine monohydrate per day to accelerate the creatine storage within the muscle cells. Ideally this dosage should be split into 4 servings of 5g distributed evenly across the day. After the loading phase, take 3-5g per day to maintain the elevated levels within your muscle tissues.

It's worth noting that saturation can still be achieved without this loading phase, but by taking a standard dose, you lengthen the process to around 30 days.

A daily dose of creatine can be taken for as long as you want. It's sometimes suggested that there's a need to cycle off creatine periodically, but this is not the case. Creatine is found to be very safe and few side-effects of any concern have ever been recorded. The only safety concern relates to individuals with pre-existing liver or kidney health conditions, so if this applies to you, consult with your doctor before you begin supplementation.

COLLAGEN SUPPLEMENTATION

The structure and function of musculoskeletal tissues, such as tendon, ligament, cartilage and bone, are highly dependent on their collagen content. Collagen is the main structural protein found in these connective tissues with a job to provide strength and stability.

Although training is able to increase collagen synthesis to aid bone and joint strength, such consistent stresses from training and matches will inevitably place these tissues at a high risk of injury. Obviously, some injuries are just down to bad luck, especially in a contact sport like football, however it's the responsibility of the athlete to try and put themselves in the best possible position to reduce injury risk.

This is especially important when injuries have such major personal, competitive and financial costs in football. Preventing and treating musculoskeletal injuries still remains one of the most complex issues to fix and there are still very few scientific advances in this area. However, one nutritional approach which has recently started being implemented at major clubs is collagen supplementation.

This idea stems from a foundation of research within the last 10 years that shows nutritional insufficiencies significantly reduce the collagen content of musculoskeletal tissue and may leave it unable to withstand the mechanical demands of otherwise tolerable activity.

WHAT DOES THE RESEARCH SAY?

Collagen, just like muscle proteins, gets broken down during intense exercise bouts. Under normal circumstances, collagen within musculoskeletal tissues can be naturally replenished after exercise from certain amino acids that are sourced from dietary protein (or protein stores in the body).

But even better, new evidence has indicated that directly consuming collagen in its natural form may be able to increase collagen synthesis post-exercise to a larger extent. It is still unknown as to why musculoskeletal collagen synthesis is greater in response to collagen or gelatin (a food derivative of collagen) when compared to individual amino acids, but the important part is that it is!

Long-term research is lacking, but it appears there is a good chance that supplementing with collagen could improve the overall structure, strength and function of joint and bone tissue. One study from 2017 even found that athletes had 100% more collagen synthesis post-exercise when they consumed gelatin 1-hour pre-exercise, compared to a placebo.

Other findings on athletes have indicated that daily collagen supplementation results in an increase in collagen content within the knee and significantly decreases knee pain in those suffering with knee injuries. Limited research has even noted reduced markers of muscle damage, muscle soreness and inflammation when collagen is supplemented in high doses before strenuous exercise, but these findings are yet to be replicated.

And although it will likely take a few years for the research to make its way online, sport scientists within football clubs are already beginning to note the reduced prevalence of minor injuries since collagen supplementation has been introduced to their teams.

HOW TO BEST SUPPLEMENT COLLAGEN?

The benefits of collagen supplementation are becoming obvious, but the most "optimal" method to supplement with it are still being experimented with. Based on the information available to us now, it appears that consuming collagen within one-hour pre-exercise probably provides the greatest opportunity to gain the most benefits. This way by the time you finish with your workout, the collagen will be present in the bloodstream and available to support musculoskeletal recovery in the post-exercise period.

Most teams tend to use collagen peptides in tablet form, or if preferred, create gelatin "shots" which partly replicate jelly sweets (it might be worth finding some good gelatin recipes). Either way, it's best to aim for ~10 grams of gelatin from each serving. This can be increased to 15 grams if you are someone that frequently suffers with aches and pains from exercise.

SHOULD YOU BUY BCAA'S?

When they first burst onto the scene, branch chain amino acids (known as BCAA's) were advertised as doing two things:

1. They would signal to the body to grow new muscle tissue
2. And they would be a substrate for the building of new muscle proteins

They were thought to do this because BCAA's consist of three of the nine essential amino acids that are known to be essential to growing new muscle tissue.

WHAT ARE BCAA'S?

BCAA's consist of leucine, isoleucine and lysine.

Leucine particularly has a ton of research behind it to show how it can provide a signal for all the anabolic processes to start and out of the 20 amino acids (including the nine essential amino acids), leucine is probably the one that's most associated with muscle growth.

The original chain of thought was that if you consumed a lot of leucine through consuming BCAA's, then this would signal for more muscle protein to be synthesised and then for muscle growth to occur. On paper, BCAA's were looked upon as an alternative source to protein to stimulate new muscle proteins and new muscle tissue and because they contain such a high concentration of leucine, some people thought they might even be superior to all other sources of protein, including other protein supplements.

DO FOOTBALLERS NEED TO TAKE BCAA'S?

The answer to this question is definitely no.

The fact that they contain three of the nine essential amino acids was once thought to be the benefit of BCAA's, but this has since been discovered to actually be the problem with them.

In order to synthesise new muscle proteins and new muscle tissue, you need to have all nine essential amino acids present. BCAA's only contain three, so they're simply unable to do the job they were first intended to do.

When the research that shed light on this was first published, most sports nutritionists adopted the stance that BCAA's as supplements were not going to bring any additional benefit, but they were not harmful. However, the problem with them is bigger than first thought. The leucine content of BCAA's does provide a signal for anabolic processes to occur, but because these processes can only occur with all nine essential amino acids present, the body is forced to look elsewhere for the remaining six essential amino acids.

So, unless you're consuming another protein source along with your BCAA's, your body will source the missing six from the muscle stores within your muscle tissue. This leads to muscle tissue breakdown which is obviously the opposite of what you want.

KEY POINT

Science now tells us that your body will break down existing muscle tissue to release the six essential amino acids needed to join the three that are present in BCAA's. This has an overall damaging effect because within this process, you get around 30% more muscle breakdown than synthesis of new muscle.

Unless you're consuming other sources of dietary protein along with BCAA's, you're going to get greater muscle loss than muscle gain.

POTENTIAL USES OF BCAA'S

There are two sets of circumstances in which BCAA's could provide positive benefits.

The first is taking BCAA's alongside other complete protein sources to enhance the effect of these sources. Complete protein sources could be foods or a protein supplement. Men need around 30-40g of protein per meal to stimulate maximal anabolic processes and women around 20-30g, so if your meal provides only 10g, BCAA's could provide a boost. However, simply eating more of the complete protein sources on your plate would do the same job.

The second is taking BCAA's as a fuel source within low-intensity, fasted training sessions. Restricting carbohydrate intake during low-intensity training is a method used by some athletes to enhance the adaptations of training and it's favoured by Britain's Team Sky (INEOS) Tour de France cycling team, but there's no unique benefit to the use of BCAA's in this scenario as any complete essential amino acid product or a standard protein powder would do the same job.

The bottom line is that BCAA's could be useful in the above scenarios, but consuming other sources of complete proteins would be of equal if not more benefit.

WHAT'S IN A "PRE-WORKOUT"?

Pre-workout supplements are designed to be taken before a workout or competitive match. They're loaded with stimulants designed to increase your energy levels, both mental and physical, which can have a positive impact on your exercise performance, but are they beneficial to footballers?

The main ingredients are caffeine, creatine, beta alanine, l-arginine and citrulline malate.

Caffeine: Despite the list of ingredients, 90% of the effect provided by pre-workouts is down to the caffeine content and there's plenty of scientific research behind the benefits of caffeine as a stand-alone supplement.

Creatine and Beta Alanine: These also have proven benefits, but the problem with these ingredients in pre-workout supplements is that they don't have acute effects. The effects they have as stand-alone ingredients are the result of a loading phase followed by daily dosage, making their presence in a pre-workout supplement completely ineffective.

L-Arginine and Citrulline Malate: There's evidence to support the potential effects of l-arginine and citrulline malate, but nothing conclusive. L-arginine is an essential amino acid directly involved in producing nitric oxide within the body. This means it may help with vasodilation (widening of the blood vessels), thereby increasing blood flow and circulation. However, the research behind it is quite mixed and it appears only to be effective in individuals with an elevated blood pressure. Studies also show l-arginine is quite poorly absorbed within the intestines; therefore, it appears to not generate any appreciable physiological activity in the body.

Citrulline malate is an amino acid that works similarly to l-arginine, but it can also increase arginine levels in the blood. It may be able to help improve blood flow through vasodilation and it may also reduce ammonia build-up in muscle cells during exercise. Ammonia is a toxic by-product of high-intensity activity which appears to initiate fatigue by disturbing the metabolic pathways involved in energy production. This means a potential benefit of citrulline malate in football could be prolonging the time it takes for muscles to reach a fatigued state.

SHOULD FOOTBALLERS USE PRE-WORKOUTS?

To be frank, the answer is no (in my opinion). This is mainly because they represent an over-priced version of only one or two potentially beneficial ingredients:

1. Caffeine for mental focus
2. Citrulline malate for improved blood flow and elimination of potential by-products within the muscle cells

KEY POINT

Supplementing these ingredients separately (caffeine and citrulline malate) is not only cheaper, it allows you to control the dose to suit your needs.

When you buy pre-workouts, you're primarily paying for filler ingredients that provide no benefit.

TAKING PRE-WORKOUTS

If you are taking a pre-workout supplement, care needs to be taken over how often, because many athletes become too reliant on them to perform.

The same applies to taking caffeine in isolation, as people adapt to a frequent intake of these stimulants which dampens the perceived effect they're having. For example, a 200mg dose of caffeine given to someone who doesn't normally take caffeine will have a significant impact, but the same dose given to someone who takes caffeine every day will have a negligible effect, if any.

KEY POINT

Smart supplementation is needed. Ensure the product you use promotes the desired positive benefits. If you're taking a supplement simply to be able to function normally, you're no longer benefiting. To avoid dampening the perceived effect, take pre-workouts or caffeine on intense training days only and perhaps on competition days when maximising your performance is the main aim. It's also worth noting that, as with all supplements, it's important to be aware of the potential for banned substances being present in the product.

THE TRUTH ABOUT "FAT-BURNERS"

Fat-burning supplements are readily available in most supplement stores, with many brands making bold claims about their effectiveness. But do they really work and should footballers consider using them?

THE HYPE

Fat-burning supplements are targeted at individuals in a fat-loss phase, but it's extremely important to understand that these products will do absolutely nothing in terms of aiding fat loss if your diet and nutrition plan isn't dialled in to help you decrease your body fat. No matter what the packaging claims, the only way to drop fat is to follow the basic principle of eating 250-500 calories less than you are expending per day.

The bold claims put forward by many brands about promoting fat loss without the need to make any changes to your diet are not based on any scientific evidence and can be considered nothing more than marketing hype. However, there are certain ingredients present in some supplements that may give you a small amount of assistance, provided your diet is set up correctly to create the required caloric deficit.

POTENTIAL BENEFITS

To be of any benefit in terms of fat loss, an ingredient must work by doing at least one of the four following things. They might have the ability to:

1. Increase your resting metabolic rate, thereby increasing the total number of calories burned over a 24-hour period simply to function and survive. This is done by increasing thermogenesis, meaning the amount of heat energy produced by the body and it's one of the reasons why fat-burning supplements may also be referred to as thermogenic supplements

2. Increase activity or energy levels, thereby creating greater opportunities to remain active and expend more calories across the day

3. Reduce hunger levels throughout the day, thereby limiting the potential for cravings or binges, helping to reduce the overall daily caloric intake

4. Promote a switch to burning more fat tissue rather than carbohydrate stores, the body's usual primary energy source

The fat-burning ingredients that could potentially provide one or more of these benefits include caffeine, carnitine, green tea, conjugated linoleic acid (CLA), carnosine, phosphatidyl choline and chromium.

However, it only takes a quick look at the ingredients list on any fat-burning product to realise the list will generally be much lengthier, with brands claiming that their contents will work synergistically to generate a magical effect. To cut through the hype and get to the science behind these ingredients, the list can be shortened to just three: caffeine, green tea and carnitine.

CAFFEINE

Caffeine is the ingredient with the most evidence behind it in terms of being a potential fat-burner. Short-term studies have shown it can increase daily energy expenditure by between 3-10%. This may be due to stimulation of the central nervous system which provides the mental and physical boost needed to increase overall levels of activity throughout the day.

Other studies have shown it can increase an individual's resting metabolic rate by generating a thermogenic effect to increase the total number of calories burned per day and there's further evidence (as yet limited) to suggest that caffeine may also make fatty acids more available for use during exercise, potentially promoting a shift from carbohydrates to fat for fuel.

GREEN TEA

Despite the many bold claims surrounding the fat-burning potential of green tea, any effect it has is due to nothing more than its caffeine content, thereby green tea provides no additional benefit beyond caffeine from any other source.

CARNITINE

Carnitine is currently used by many elite endurance athletes for performance reasons and is not generally well-known for being a weight-loss supplement.

However, the performance benefits it brings to endurance athletes may lead to it becoming a good fat-loss option in the future (after further scientific research). Carnitine can increase the body's fat metabolism, making your source of energy during exercise lean more towards fat-based and away from carbohydrate-based (than it normally would). This is due to carnitine being a substance within the body that's responsible for transporting fatty acids across and into muscle cells, to be used for energy production. Normally, the body uses carbohydrates as its primary source of fuel for higher intensity actions (because stores are readily available within muscle cells) and carnitine stores would be more limited, creating a barrier to the number of fatty acids which are able to be transported into muscle cells. In simple terms, supplementing with carnitine can increase the carnitine stores in the body and theoretically aid the transportation of fat into muscle cells, therefore promoting greater fat-burning during exercise.

KEY POINT

The real effect of this theory on fat loss is questionable and further research on carnitine is needed, but some studies have shown that it can increase fat metabolism and this can provide a performance benefit.

THE BOTTOM LINE

Are fat-burning supplements effective and are they worth taking? Probably not. They may have a very small effect, but they're an overpriced product when you consider that any effect is essentially down to the caffeine content. If you do choose to experiment, a better approach may be to try a caffeine supplement, but in terms of fat loss, there can be no shortcut to success. Reducing your overall caloric intake is the only way to get noticeable results.

ENERGY DRINKS

The main purpose of an energy drink is to boost your energy, alertness and concentration. There are a huge variety of brands and products available on the market and they're becoming increasingly popular to use, not just in sport but in day-to-day life, so what role do they really play in terms of football performance?

The nutritional profiles of the main brands such as Red Bull, Monster and Rockstar are virtually identical, certainly in terms of their caffeine content. Most brands, including supermarket own brands, contain around 75mg of caffeine per 250ml of fluid. For example, a small Red Bull can is 250ml which contains 75mg of caffeine, but if you buy a larger Red Bull or a regular-sized can of Monster or Rockstar, they are usually around 500ml, so they contain 150mg of caffeine.

WHAT'S IN THE TIN?

Energy drinks contain caffeine, but they also contain sugar, unless you're choosing a zero-calorie option. One 250ml can of Red Bull contains 27g of sugar, while a 500ml can of Monster, Rockstar or a larger can of Red Bull contains 54g of sugar, double the amount. They also contain B vitamins. These are important for energy metabolism, but they're also cheap to incorporate and this is generally why they're used. Some brands contain amino acid derivatives such as taurine, others contain herbal extracts, but there's little evidence to back up claims of the effects these will have on the body and for this reason they can be considered filler ingredients used to bump up the price of the product and make it appear better than it really is.

In terms of whether energy drinks can have a beneficial effect on performance, the answer is potentially yes. However, there are various issues you'll run into with them and there definitely are better and cheaper alternatives. Energy drinks can provide a mental and physical boost, but the issue with them is that these effects are solely due to their caffeine content and the other ingredients can cause issues that negate the benefits of caffeine.

SUGAR CONTENT

The sugar content is likely to cause a considerable spike in your blood glucose levels, eventually leading to an energy crash as a consequence. For example, if you were to take an energy drink two hours before exercise, you would notice an initial spike in energy, but by the time you step out onto the pitch, your blood glucose levels may already be beginning to crash, meaning you'd be entering the game in a low energy state which would continue until your blood sugar levels begin to normalise or until you ingest further carbohydrates. Similarly, if you consumed an energy drink closer to exercise (around 30 minutes prior is advised when taking a caffeine supplement), this could also pose a problem. As you begin to exercise at high intensity, your body naturally reduces blood sugar levels in response to exercise and the glucose in the blood is shunted towards your muscles for energy. When this happens, you could experience what's known as exercise hypoglycaemia, meaning your blood glucose levels go from being extremely high to extremely low in response to exercise and you suddenly feel very tired and irritable. This will affect both your mental and physical performance until your blood sugar begins to normalise again during exercise, a process that could take between 5-25 minutes, or again until you consume further carbohydrates, it all depends on your individual metabolism.

HIGH GI VS LOW GI

Studies on high glycaemic (simple) carbohydrates versus low glycaemic (complex) carbohydrates as pre-exercise sources of energy have noted very few differences in terms of analysing performance, however, the timing of carb intake does raise issues with blood sugar fluctuations which can be better avoided by consuming complex carbohydrates. The effect an energy drink will have on you personally when taken pre-exercise is an individual thing and it will depend on how well you tolerate carbohydrates. In general, the safer and better option is to avoid carbohydrates within the immediate pre-exercise period and focus on taking in the final bulk of your carbohydrates with your main pre-exercise meal instead, approximately three hours before exercise. After that point, it's safer to avoid consuming further simple carbs (sugar/ high GI carbs), to eliminate the potential of an energy crash at kick off.

KEY POINT

The safest way to go about boosting your alertness pre-exercise is to consume caffeine 15-30 minutes before starting, rather than relying on an energy drink.

SUGAR-FREE ENERGY DRINKS

Sugar-free energy drinks will, of course, contain no sugar, but sugar-free energy drinks are still not recommended due to their fizziness, potentially giving rise to stomach problems. When the carbon-dioxide gas is dissolved in a drink to give it its fizziness, your body will try to expel the gas, resulting in one of two outcomes: expelling the gas through burping, or, if the gas gets trapped in your gastro-intestinal tract, bloating and irritation of your stomach. Neither of these outcomes would help you to achieve a best performance out on the pitch or in training.

KEY POINT

The benefits of energy drinks are virtually entirely due to their caffeine content, but they are not the most effective or convenient way to take on caffeine as they will likely cause energy crashes or stomach issues during exercise. This can be avoided by taking standard caffeine supplementation in pill form.

CAN AN ALKALINE DIET ENHANCE PERFORMANCE?

It's claimed that an alkaline diet can reduce inflammation in the body and alter your body's PH level to create an environment that's free from potentially harmful acids, but are these claims backed by science?

WHAT IS AN ALKALINE DIET?

As the name suggests, this is a diet that aims to create an alkaline state within the body, specifically within the blood. This is supposedly achieved by replacing acid forming foods such as meat, dairy, eggs and most types of processed foods, with alkaline forming foods which are most of your fruits and vegetables.

These dietary changes claim to lower the PH levels in the blood (the PH levels being a scientific measure of your body's acidity or alkalinity) and then create a better environment that's ideally free from potentially harmful acids.

This in theory can then reduce the chance of disease, improve health and from an athletic stand point, may even improve recovery and performance by reducing chronic levels of inflammation in the body which might typically hinder recovery and lead to issues such as:

- Joint pain
- Reduced blood flow
- Reduced oxygen flow through the blood vessels

ALKALINE FORMING FOODS

For people on an alkaline diet, around 70% of the foods they eat will be alkaline forming, so this includes all vegetables (apart from pickled vegetables which have acid forming components) especially green leafy varieties and root vegetables, also lentils, tofu, beans, chickpeas, nuts, seeds and oils. They do so in the belief that it creates a more alkaline environment in the blood.

THE ALKALINE DIET CONCEPT

When you consume foods, there's always a residue that's not needed for energy or health purposes and this residue is known as metabolic waste. Metabolic waste products can be defined as being either alkaline or acidic, depending on their PH value. It's from this physiological concept that some health enthusiasts (especially those promoting an alkaline diet) speculate that eating acid forming foods will increase the acidity of the blood, leading to the negative effects listed above and eating a diet rich in alkaline forming foods will create a more alkaline environment in the blood, thereby bringing positive health benefits.

THE SCIENCE

The crucial question is, do different foods produce different amounts of acid and different types of acid? The answer is yes.

Science tells us that diets containing meats and animal products do contain higher amounts of acids compared to vegetarian or vegan diets. This is mainly because omnivorous diets are generally higher in protein, usually sourced from sulphur-containing amino acids, specifically methionine and cysteine and these are oxidised into a substance called sulphuric acid which is a highly acidic waste product.

At the other end of the spectrum, most fruits and vegetables are alkaline-producing foods because their metabolic waste products are organic precursors usually known as citrate or succinate. However, a key thing to note is that a food might have an acid or alkaline waste product, but this doesn't necessarily mean it's going to have any real physiological effect in terms of altering blood PH values.

KEY POINT

Unless a food has a significant effect on the blood, then it's very unlikely that it's going to have any real effect on health, recovery or performance.

THE BODY'S BUFFERING SYSTEM

Science also tells us that the human body has a well-established and tightly controlled system in which acids produced from the ingestion of foods are rapidly buffered and excreted from the body. The kidneys produce bicarbonate ions which can neutralise any harmful acids within the blood, neutralising the PH of the blood and inhibiting any fluctuations in its acidity in the process.

The buffering system prevents PH fluctuations out of the normal range and even in studies where participants persistently ingested large amounts of acid forming foods such as processed foods and animal products, there was no change in the blood PH.

The only known cause of blood PH fluctuations is a medical condition known as acidaemia – and this is incredibly rare.

KEY POINT

Assuming you're an athlete and at least moderately healthy, then this issue isn't something you should even concern yourself with. In a healthy body, the production of bicarbonate ions by the kidneys will neutralise any potentially harmful acids in the body and then allow them to be excreted easily through urine or through breathing.

The takeaway is that even though you might consume different foods that produce different acid and alkaline levels, the overall balance of your net acid production versus your net acid excretion will remain neutral because of the tightly-controlled metabolic regulatory systems within your body.

THE BOTTOM LINE

There has been little research done on how acid forming foods might influence recovery or any other markers of athletic performance, but within scientific literature, it can be assumed that because the blood PH value remains stable throughout the day and because dietary changes can't alter this, an alkaline diet isn't going to change any of these markers, whether it's recovery, performance on the pitch or even just general health.

WHAT TO EAT TO STAY HEALTHY

With the primary focus being on performance, health is very often an overlooked aspect of football nutrition. It's important to consider that your overall health has a huge role to play in your ability to perform at your best consistently season after season.

NUTRITION FOR HEALTH VS NUTRITION FOR SPORT

It can appear that a divide between nutritionists and sports nutritionists exists, but in fact, the nutritional recommendations for health and those for sport are not so far apart, making it possible to strike a balance between nutrition for health and nutrition for performance.

Nutrition for health and overall wellbeing is centred on aspects such as lowering cholesterol, lowering blood pressure and reducing inflammation and these are all important components of nutrition outside of the sports performance mindset.

In this sense, nutrition for health means nutrition that can help to increase your lifespan and the longevity of your healthy years. Nutrition plays a key role in the prevention of diseases including cardiovascular diseases, diabetes and cancer. In the short-term, your diet helps to control markers of health such as the level of inflammation in your body, cholesterol levels, blood glucose levels and the amount of fat in your blood.

The research on nutrition for health is endless and discussions surrounding the many different types of diet people can choose are on-going in the popular press. However, nutrition for health can be broken down into three key factors which are consistent in scientific reviews of good health. These are:

- Controlling the level of inflammation in your body
- Avoiding potential deficiencies in vitamin and mineral intake
- Restricting your total calorie intake

CONTROLLING INFLAMMATION

Inflammation is the body's defence mechanism, stimulated by your immune system to remove any harmful substances and heal any damage to your cells. However, a growing problem in the modern world is excessive inflammation (known as chronic inflammation) in which your immune system begins to attack healthy cells, causing large amounts of damage within the body.

It's known that diet has an important role to play in controlling the amount of inflammation in the body and this is determined by the balance of anti-inflammatory nutrients consumed against pro-inflammatory nutrients consumed. Anti-inflammatory foods include vegetables, whole grains, omega 3s and dietary fibre. Pro-inflammatory foods include saturated fat, sugar, omega 6s and highly processed foods in general.

Pro-inflammatory foods are bad for your health in general, causing spikes in your blood sugar levels that will hinder your daily energy levels, as well as your concentration and mental clarity.

In the long-term, inflammation can cause damage to:

- Your blood vessels, which can lead to the development of cardiovascular diseases
- The cells responsible for producing insulin, which can lead to diabetes
- Brain cells, potentially leading to neurodegenerative diseases such as Alzheimer's disease

KEY POINT

Reduce inflammation by reducing your consumption of pro-inflammatory foods such as sugar and saturated fat.

AVOIDING VITAMIN AND MINERAL DEFICIENCIES

Vitamins and minerals are compounds within food that are essential to help maintain the body's natural processes, including:

1. Growth
2. Brain function
3. Energy production

In every case, there's a vitamin or mineral aiding the process, so any deficiency is going to have a negative impact, whether that's potential illness and disease, or on-going fatigue and drowsiness.

KEY NUTRITIONAL FACTOR

Ensure you eat a balanced diet and a wide range of foods to avoid any nutrient deficiencies.

RESTRICTING TOTAL CALORIE INTAKE

Restricting your calorie intake is important for two reasons. The first is that it will prevent excess body fat accumulation which is known to secrete pro-inflammatory molecules that can damage blood vessels and insulin-producing cells and even increase rates of cancer growth.

The second is that consuming calories and energy places some degree of stress and burden on your metabolism as it deals with the incoming energy intake. The processing of this energy can increase the rate of aging in your body. In simple terms, this is because normal aerobic energy metabolism causes the reaction of energy with oxygen. This process can produce harmful molecules known as reactive oxygen species, which can then cause chronic inflammation and cell damage (accelerating the aging process).

This is interesting when you consider that the chemical reactions keeping you alive are the same reactions that are killing you in the long-term, by causing cell damage as part of the natural aging process.

KEY POINT

Restrict your total daily calorie intake by balancing the calories you take in against the calories you burn off in daily activities.

NUTRITION FOR HEALTH AND SPORT

As an athlete controlling inflammation and avoiding vitamin or mineral deficiencies remain key nutritional factors for health and performance. As for restricting calorie intake, this is where nutrition for sport deviates from the nutrition for health recommendations.

A major component of sports nutrition is increasing your energy intake, mainly in the form of carbohydrates. This is to increase your energy stores before going into training or a match, thereby fuelling high-intensity activities and avoiding fatigue.

Clearly, this recommendation for sport nutrition contradicts the recommendation for health, but as a footballer, your calorie intake needs to stay relatively high to fuel your higher activity levels, so it's not a cause for concern. Nutrition for health recommendations are aimed at the general public and it must be remembered that being active and exercising will bring additional health benefits.

KEY POINT

It's important to remain aware of your bodyweight and ensure that your calorie intake is not excessive and causing body fat accumulation.

Of course, one area of concern with this is that the need to consume more calories to fuel greater levels of activity can lead to an increased intake of sugar and saturated fat, especially for athletes who are relying on calorically-dense foods or processed foods as a convenient way to bump up the overall calorie intake.

As an extreme example, some elite ultra-endurance runners can require over 7000 calories per day, a total that's impossible to achieve through eating whole foods alone, meaning high-calorie convenience foods such as sweets, sports drinks, chocolate, nuts and crisps become go-to foods to ensure the target calorie intake is achieved.

NUTRITION FOR HEALTH AND PERFORMANCE IN FOOTBALL

As a footballer, striking a balance between nutrition for health and nutrition for football performance can be achieved by incorporating as many whole foods as possible into your diet whilst ensuring you still meet your caloric requirement for the day.

When whole foods alone make it difficult to achieve your energy requirement, especially when fuelling up prior to a match, adding high-sugar or high-fat foods may be necessary within reason. The bottom line is that to support your performance on the pitch, your priority must be ensuring your carbohydrate stores are fully loaded to fuel 90-minutes of high-intensity activity.

THE BENEFITS OF BROTHS

Bone broth is a type of stock made by simmering animal bones and connective tissue on a low heat for around 24 hours. An acid such as vinegar or lemon juice is mixed in to help break down the collagen and connective tissue and the final product resembles a soup. The contents make it a nutrient-dense food source which is believed to improve gut health, but is this really the case?

BONE BROTH NUTRITION

Any type of bone can be used to make bone broth – chicken, lamb, pig, fish – and the nutrient content will vary depending on the ingredients used and their quality. In terms of general nutrition, the bone portion provides numerous minerals, including calcium, phosphorus, magnesium and potassium, also glucosamine and chondroitin, commonly found in dietary supplements for joint issues.

The bone marrow contains vitamin A, vitamin K2, some omega 3s and omega 6s, also iron, zinc, selenium and magnesium. Collagen is found in both the bone and the bone marrow and this turns to gelatine when cooked. It's clear from this nutritional information that bone broth can give you access to a lot of nutrients and therefore it's likely to provide health benefits, but bone broth is yet to be studied scientifically, meaning nutritionists at this point must rely on educated guesses based on what's known of its contents.

POTENTIAL BENEFITS

Any potential benefits to gut health provided by bone broth will come from the collagen content. Collagen is broken down into amino acids glycine and glutamine during digestion and these are known to promote gut health by strengthening the mucosal lining of the digestive tract.

Glutamine is also known to help maintain the function of the intestinal wall, preventing and potentially healing a condition known as leaky gut syndrome in which the barrier between the gut and the bloodstream becomes impaired, allowing bacteria and pathogens to leak out of the gut. This creates elevated inflammation in the body which can lead to chronic diseases.

Another notable way in which bone broth may be of benefit is through improving the composition and general health of your joints and bones. Again, this will be mainly due to the collagen content along with glucosamine and chondroitin which have been individually linked to improvements in joint health by preventing the deterioration of the cartilage tissue within the joint. They are also linked to improved bone health through the recycling of calcium in the body's natural bone remodelling process.

KEY POINT

It's highly likely that bone broth does have some beneficial impact on gut health as well as bone and joint health, but further research is needed to provide greater understanding. At this point, it's clear that bone broth provides a nutrient-dense source of vitamins and minerals that the body can benefit from.

STRENGTHENING YOUR IMMUNE SYSTEM

The foods you choose to eat and the overall quality of your diet can have a major impact on your health, essentially making the difference between good health and illness.

Malnutrition, or inadequate nutrition, is listed as the primary cause of immunodeficiency worldwide, with the immune systems of malnourished individuals failing to protect the body from infection and disease. Eating a nutrient-poor diet leads to the absence or insufficiency of protective substances and nutrients needed to help the immune system function properly and as your immune system is basically your internal network of specialised tissues, organs and cells designed to protect you from infectious bacteria and viruses, ill health results.

MICRONUTRIENT DEFICIENCY

Scientific research has shown that any type of micronutrient (vitamin and mineral) deficiency is closely associated with the function of your immune system and susceptibility to illnesses and infections.

This is very apparent in new-born babies, simply because a new-born hasn't had long enough to develop a strong immune system to protect itself from any harmful molecules. In young babies, there is a direct relationship between their vitamin and mineral intakes and their vulnerability to infections (and even the risk of death). This is because certain vitamin and mineral deficiencies in infants can have an exacerbating effect on immune health and to a lesser extent, the same can be applied to adult and athletic populations.

KEY POINT

What you eat can have a major impact on how well your immune system functions. It can lower your risk of infection and illness and lessen the severity of your symptoms if you do get ill, for example shortening the duration of a common cold. This is important as an athlete, as the less time you spend being ill the more time you have for training and the fewer matches you'll miss.

STRENGTHENING THE IMMUNE SYSTEM

The strength of your immune system comes down to two things:

1. Consuming the nutrients needed to improve the strength and activity of your gut barrier (or gut wall) as the gut is the primary base for your immune system. The gut wall acts as a barrier, taking responsibility for ensuring everything that enters or leaves your gut is not a potential toxin or virus that could cause an illness
2. Consuming the nutrients needed to improve your innate immunity, particularly the function of the immune system cells responsible for producing antibodies, natural killer cells and white blood cells, as these fight off various viruses and toxins

Current research has identified three micronutrients that play a strong role in helping to maintain the function of the gut wall and gut immune cells. They are vitamin A, vitamin C and zinc.

VITAMIN A

Vitamin A plays a crucial role in maintaining the integrity and functioning of the gut wall, making sure all toxins and bacteria are where they should be and not making their way into any areas of the body where they might be harmful.

Studies on vitamin A show a positive correlation between vitamin A intake and immune function. Keeping a high vitamin A intake through food or supplementation can successfully sustain gut integrity and reduce the incidence of diarrhoea.

Sources: To ensure your vitamin A intake is high, focus on foods such as sweet potato, squash, kale, carrots, spinach and animal liver if you're a meat-eater.

VITAMIN C

Vitamin C is particularly effective at preventing the common cold, but it can't treat a cold that has already started. An important function of vitamin C is aiding immune cells to generate helpful molecules that destroy any invading organisms or toxins, also protecting any nearby immune cells and structural cells of the gut wall from damage, thereby creating a positive impact on two fronts:

1. Maintaining the strength and activity of the gut wall
2. Boosting the activity and number of beneficial immune cells

KEY POINT

To be effective in the prevention of colds, vitamin C must be taken daily. Downing some orange juice once your nose is already running won't provide an instant "cure".

Sources: To ensure a daily dose of vitamin C, maintain a regular intake of fruits, especially blackcurrants, kiwis, oranges and lemons. Vegetables such as kale and broccoli are also high in vitamin C.

ZINC

Zinc is an important mineral required for many metabolic functions within the body and a crucial co-factor in the formation of many enzymes within the immune system.

It plays a role in the correct functioning of immune cells, helping them to recognise the presence of a virus within the immune system which can then be dealt with. The activity of immune cells and antibodies drops considerably in individuals with a zinc deficiency.

Sources: To ensure a healthy intake of zinc, include legumes, seeds, nuts and wholegrains in your daily diet. All types of meat are also good sources of zinc.

NUTRITION FOR ILLNESS IN SUMMARY

Illness is mainly caused by an impaired immune system. The health of your immune system depends on the integrity and functioning of the gut barrier and the immune cells within the gut that destroy any harmful viruses. To ensure the system can function properly, it's extremely important to consume enough vitamin A, vitamin C and zinc containing foods, with good options including sweet potato, kale, spinach, fruits, legumes and nuts.

WHAT TO EAT WHEN YOU'RE INJURED (TO AID REPAIR)

From a nutritional perspective, there are certain foods and supplements that have the potential to reduce recovery times in an injured athlete.

PROTEIN INTAKE

An increased protein intake can be beneficial to injured athletes. An injured area undergoes something called anabolic resistance, meaning a decrease in the ability of dietary protein to cause protein synthesis within your tissues and cells, most likely due to an impaired response to amino acids within proteins, or a reduced ability to initiate and signal anabolic signalling pathways.

If you're injured, you desperately want to heal and recover, so there's an increased need for protein synthesis to regenerate the damaged tissues. As an athlete, you may already have an elevated protein intake, but if you have a diminished response to the protein you're consuming through injury, this will be limiting its effectiveness in terms of muscle growth and repair.

RECOMMENDATION

If you are injured, increase the standard 1.5g of protein per kg of bodyweight to 2g of protein per kg of bodyweight. This increase will hopefully compensate for the diminished response and meet the higher demand for recovery and repair when you're injured.

OMEGA 3-OMEGA 6 RATIO

The predominant nutritional factor that can help to control the amount of inflammation in the body is the ratio of omega 3s to omega 6s in your diet. Omega 3s are anti-inflammatory fatty acids whereas omega 6s are pro-inflammatory fatty acids and both are types of fat found in certain foods.

If you are injured, a certain amount of inflammation is needed as this is ultimately responsible for repairing the damage. However, it's important not to create a state of chronic inflammation in the body as this can lead to damage in your healthy cells, or the potential for further damage in the already damaged cells. The best way to prevent excess inflammation from delaying recovery is to eat omega 3 fats and limit omega 6 fat consumption.

RECOMMENDATION

If you're injured, increase your omega 3 consumption with foods such as fish, avocados and seeds and nuts such as flax seeds and walnuts. Limit your omega 6 consumption by avoiding the use of vegetable oils, including corn oil, canola oil, cotton seed, soy and sunflower oil (substituting with olive oil if needed).

A further step to lower inflammation levels is to limit your intake of added sugars, typically found in sweets, non-diet drinks and juices. These can form advanced glycation end products when they combine with fat in the blood, negatively affecting the body by raising inflammation levels. You should also decrease your calorie and carbohydrate intake to match the decrease in activity levels, so this step shouldn't be too hard as lowering your sugar intake should naturally be part of the same process.

VITAMIN C INTAKE

Vitamin C helps your body to make collagen which helps maintain the integrity of your bones, skin, muscles and tendons. This means vitamin C could be effective in terms of promoting healing in injuries involving bones and joints, although no specific research has been done in this area as yet. However, vitamin C is known to have antioxidant and anti-inflammatory properties which may help speed up your recovery by preventing excessive levels of inflammation.

RECOMMENDATION

Foods with high amounts of vitamin C to include in your diet are citrus fruits, red and yellow peppers, dark leafy greens, broccoli, berries, tomatoes and mangoes.

ZINC INTAKE

Zinc is a component of many enzymes and proteins within the body and especially important in the protein needed for wound healing as well as tissue repair and growth. Studies have shown that a deficiency of zinc when someone is injured can impair wound healing and delay recovery times from injury.

RECOMMENDATION

If you're injured, include zinc rich foods in your diet. These include meat, fish, shellfish, seeds and nuts. Some people prefer to opt for zinc supplementations to ensure they meet their daily recommendations; however, most zinc supplements contain a very high amount of zinc and high doses can increase the likelihood of a copper deficiency as zinc competes with copper for absorption. For this reason, it's better to source zinc naturally through the diet.

GLUCOSAMINE SUPPLEMENTATION

Glucosamine is a natural substance found in the fluid around your joints which is heavily involved in the creation of tendons, ligaments and cartilage tissue. Your body naturally produces glucosamine, but you can further increase your levels through supplementation.

There's no concrete evidence to support the effectiveness of supplementation in non-injured athletes, but studies have shown that glucosamine supplementation can be effective in decreasing joint pain in arthritis sufferers. Further research indicates that glucosamine supplementation of 1-3g per day can reduce joint deterioration and one study carried out on animals has shown that a daily dose of glucosamine taken after a fracture may help to speed up bone reformation, potentially reducing recovery times.

RECOMMENDATION

If you are injured, experimenting with glucosamine may be helpful and it's not harmful to give it a try. Aim for a glucosamine dose of 1.5g per day.

WHAT TO EAT TO PREVENT & REDUCE JOINT PAIN

A joint in the body is simply where two bones meet. Between the bones, there's a gap which exists to allow the bones room for movement and to stop them rubbing together (this would cause pain). In this joint space, there's a fibrous tissue called connective tissue and within that is where cartilage is found (a rubber-like padding that protects the ends of the bones).

CAUSES OF JOINT PAIN

Joint pain is common in athletic populations and it stems from the high level of mechanical stress induced through training or competitive matches. This can damage the cartilage and as the protective cartilage on either end of a bone degrades, it leads to the bones rubbing together, resulting in joint pain.

KEY POINT

Joint pain is especially prevalent in athletes or footballers going through a period of overtraining. Not allowing the body enough time to recover between sessions means there's no time to repair and regenerate damaged tissue and bone.

Chronic inflammation is another cause of joint pain. Inflammation is a response by your immune system, acting as a defence mechanism against cells, pathogens or any sort of irritant that may cause damage in the body. Inflammation is part of the body's healing process, but if someone has chronic inflammation, this is an unnecessary persistence of the inflammatory reaction that begins to attack healthy cells. In the case of cartilage, chronic inflammation can cause it to degrade and something we know about cartilage is that it's particularly vulnerable to inflammation. This is because cartilage, unlike most tissues, is unable to send out the signals needed to stop chronic inflammation once it has started, making it an area that pro-inflammatory molecules can attack easily.

REDUCING CHRONIC INFLAMMATION

Foods in the diet can be pro-inflammatory or anti-inflammatory, so the choices you make can have an indirect effect on the amount of inflammation that's being directed at tissues (such as cartilage) in your body.

FATS

The first dietary change to make to reduce inflammation is to switch up your fat sources. Fats are extremely important because some of them are stored in cartilage and some are heavily associated with inflammation and the degradation of cartilage tissue.

Switch your fat sources from omega-6s, which are pro-inflammatory, to omega-3s, which are anti-inflammatory. Scientific research has concluded that diets high in omega-6 are correlated with joint pain and diets rich in omega-3 are associated with a decrease in cartilage loss and reduced joint pain.

The reason for this is that if there's a high ratio of omega-6 to omega-3 fatty acids in the diet, there's going to be a bigger number of pro-inflammatory molecules against a smaller number of anti-inflammatory molecules in the body, therefore the cartilage is going to be subjected to high levels of chronic inflammation. The more you can incorporate omega-3s into your diet and reduce omega-6s, the less chronic inflammation you're going to have and the lower the loss of cartilage.

A really simple way to make the switch is remove or limit the intake of processed foods which are high in omega-6s and introduce more foods that are rich in omega-3s into your diet.

Omega-6 food sources include processed meat, junk foods such as chocolate or crisps and vegetable oils. Omega-3 food sources include oily fish such as salmon, nuts (walnuts are especially high in omega-3), seed products such as flax seeds and try switching from vegetable or olive oil for cooking to flax seed oil because it contains a much greater amount of omega-3s.

CARBOHYDRATES

The second dietary change to reduce inflammation is to change up your carbohydrate sources.

Current research suggests that any type of refined or processed carbohydrate, especially those high in refined sugars, will cause rapid increases in blood sugar levels. When this happens, there will also be an increase in pro-inflammation molecules in the body, which can stimulate chronic inflammation and trigger cartilage loss within the joints.

Stay away from junk foods and any type of fruit juices or non-diet sodas as these are very high in processed sugars. Introduce carbohydrates with a higher dietary fibre content into your diet. These foods are good for the gut, can help to regulate the expression of anti-inflammatory molecules within the body and promote lower levels of inflammation (especially chronic inflammation). High dietary fibre sources include any type of whole grain such as oats, beans, any type of green vegetable, legumes and seeds.

SUPPLEMENTS FOR JOINT PAIN

Two supplements that are promoted as being helpful for joint pain are glucosamine and chondroitin, often packaged as a combined product.

Glucosamine is a precursor in the synthesis of proteoglycans which are present in the collagen fibres within cartilage, so it's thought that supplementation may stimulate cartilage cells to produce more of these proteoglycans and therefore promote more cartilage repair. Glucosamine is a popular supplement, but there's limited evidence to support this and only a few studies show any improvements in terms of improving or preventing joint pain. However, there is some evidence, so a glucosamine sulphate supplement could be worth a try in a daily dose of 1500mg.

Chondroitin, like glucosamine, is important for healthy joint structure and function. Some research suggests that supplementation may slow down the narrowing of joint space and therefore limit the joint degradation seen in elderly populations and athletic populations. The evidence to support this again is limited, but a few studies suggest it may be beneficial, so chondroitin sulphate could be worth a try in a daily dose of 500mg.

The bottom line is that supplementation will likely not have as large an effect in terms of reducing or preventing joint pain as dietary changes will. However, the mentioned supplements are generally safe so experimentation is an option that may be helpful for some.

NUTRITION TO PREVENT CRAMP

As a footballer, there are nutritional protocols you can put in place to help prevent cramp from cramping your style out on the pitch.

CAUSES OF CRAMP

There are two known mechanisms that can lead to muscle cramp:

- Localised muscle fatigue
- Dehydration

MUSCLE FATIGUE

Localised muscle fatigue is effectively overload on a muscle to the point where it can no longer cope with the demands being placed on it. Exercising at an intensity that's beyond your capability at the time leads to an alteration in the CNS (central nervous system). The mechanisms that are designed to inhibit muscular contraction are disrupted and depressed, triggering an involuntary muscle contraction experienced as "cramp".

From a nutritional perspective, preventing this type of cramp comes down to matching pre-exercise nutrition to the demands of the activity. The idea behind any pre-exercise nutrition is to prolong the time it takes for muscles to fatigue by extending the time your body can continue to perform high intensity activities. Increasing your carbohydrate intake pre-exercise fuels your energy stores so that you can maintain activity for longer before the risk of cramp sets in.

DEHYDRATION

Becoming dehydrated during a match, through excessive sweating and not taking on board enough fluids for example, can also lead to cramping. Exercising in high temperatures and sweating excessively leads to the water content in your blood (plasma) decreasing, because you're essentially sweating out your supplies.

To compensate for this, fluid is moved in from other spaces (such as just outside the cells), meaning the reduction of fluid in the blood plasma leads to a reduction in the volume of water outside the cells and this triggers nerve impulses and spontaneous contractions we know as cramp.

Further research is needed to clarify the involvement of sodium in this type of cramp and many questions remain unanswered, but from a nutritional standpoint, the aim is to prevent it from happening by ensuring hydration levels are high before the start of a game (both fluids and electrolytes). Theoretically, the better the supply of additional fluid, the lower the reduction in blood plasma volume and thereby the mechanisms that induce cramp are reduced.

HYDRATION PROTOCOLS

Pre-exercise: Around 10ml of water per kg of bodyweight is advised with a pre-exercise meal (around 3 hours before exercise).

So, if you're 70kg you need 700ml water and if you're 80kg, you need 800 ml. After the meal, continue to sip on water to ensure you remain hydrated right up to the start of the match. To test your hydration levels, check the colour of your urine. If it's pale, you're hydrated, but darker colours indicate dehydration.

Electrolytes: To optimise the hydration protocol, also consume electrolytes at the pre-exercise meal to ensure optimal sodium levels. Sodium increases water retention and can therefore improve levels of hydration from a given quantity of fluid, helping to retain more of the water and excrete less of it. Around 300-500mg of sodium is advised. One third of salt content is sodium, so if a food/product contains 1g of salt, this will provide around 300mg of sodium.

KEY POINT

Salt/sodium can be added to a meal, taken as a supplement or consumed through carbohydrate gels with added electrolytes. Some teams take salt tablets containing around 1g of salt. During a game, a further 300-500mg should be taken on board. Most sports drinks will cover this recommendation, but if cramp is becoming an issue, consume around 500ml of fluid along with 2-3g of salt.

As a final recommendation, if you tend to suffer with cramp, having fluids containing 2-3g of salt ready to drink at the side-lines has been shown to provide almost instant relief and can provide an effective cramp avoidance strategy.

WHY PROTEIN POWDERS CAN CAUSE STOMACH UPSET

Protein supplements provide a quick, convenient and high-quality source of protein, but they can cause stomach issues such as gas, bloating and stomach cramping in some people.

THE CAUSES OF STOMACH ISSUES

If protein supplements are causing issues for you, it essentially means there's something in the supplement you're taking which you're unable to digest. Typically, the foods you eat are digested in the small intestine, but if you have an allergy or an intolerance, certain substances within foods may not be digested efficiently in the small intestine and move on through the system into the colon.

Bacteria in the colon then feed on the substance you're unable to digest, fermenting it to get rid of it. This process produces gasses such as hydrogen, carbon dioxide and methane. It's the build-up of these gasses which can result in symptoms such as bloating and stomach cramping.

Common supplement ingredients that could cause stomach issues include:

- Dairy
- Dietary fibre
- Sugar alcohols

In 99% of cases, the three ingredients above will be the cause of stomach issues. By checking the ingredients list on the product or brand you use, you can then remove these substances from your diet one by one on an experimental trial and error basis to pinpoint which one (or two) is causing an issue for you. Once you've identified the culprit, you can look for alternative protein supplements that don't contain this substance.

DAIRY

Stomach issues caused by dairy products can be linked to a lactose intolerance. Some people are unable to digest dairy effectively because they can't digest lactose, the sugar contained in dairy products.

Everyone is born with an active enzyme in their body known as lactase. This enzyme digests lactose and the sugar within dairy, however, although we all have lactase as babies, levels can decline as we get older. It's this natural decline that can manifest as a lactose intolerance as dairy becomes harder to digest.

Intolerance levels vary from individual to individual, but it's estimated that around 70% of the population are lactose intolerant (but not everyone experiences stomach issues to the same extent).

Fixing a dairy issue: Check if your protein supplement contains dairy protein. Popular protein powders such as whey powder and casein powder are dairy-based products, so try switching to a plant-based protein supplement to see if this resolves the issue. Experiment with soy, hemp, pea, or rice protein (you could also try vegan supplement powders too).

DIETARY FIBRE

Commonly found in protein bars, a lot of companies use high amounts of dietary fibre in their products, advertising them as a healthier option. However, if you're not used to a high-fibre diet, consuming something that contains as much as 20g of fibre per bar can lead to issues, certainly in the short-term. Fibre is important for the digestion and absorption of food, reducing inflammation and improving the bacterial composition of the gut, but if you suddenly and dramatically increase your fibre intake, it's going to take time for your body to adjust.

Fixing a dietary fibre issue: One option is to just stick with the product of your choice and your body will adjust to the fibre content in around 2-3 weeks. Another option is to switch to a bar with a lower fibre content. You could of course simply limit the amount you eat, beginning with a quarter bar, building up to a half bar and then a full bar over a period of around two weeks.

SUGAR ALCOHOLS

Sugar alcohols are basically low-calorie sweeteners and they're mainly used in cheaper protein products. Check the ingredients list for contents ending in "ol".

Examples include: mannitol, maltitol, erythritol, xylitol, sorbitol, glycerol, the list goes on.

Fixing a sugar alcohol issue: Try switching to a product that doesn't contain any of these substances. This may mean paying slightly more, but a higher-priced product will contain more naturally-derived ingredients and the absence of sugar alcohols could be all it takes to resolve your stomach issue.

The bottom line is that a degree of experimentation is going to be required to identify the cause of your stomach issue. Remove dairy, dietary fibre and sugar alcohols one by one to discover which one is causing an issue for you and then look for alternatives. If the issue persists after removing all three elements, it's stemming from somewhere beyond your choice of protein supplement and experimentation may be needed elsewhere in your diet.

STOMACH ISSUES FROM COFFEE?

There's little scientific data to help give a conclusive answer to the question of why drinking coffee sometimes causes stomach issues but, based on our current understanding of coffee and its components and the experiences of coffee-drinking players, it's possible to come to some logical conclusions.

INDIGESTION

The stomach issues associated with coffee stem from the fact that coffee can lower the pH of the stomach and increase its acidity. The stomach is already naturally acidic to help with the breakdown of food, but coffee adds to this.

This may be due to coffee stimulating the release of gastrin which secretes gastric acid, potentially causing irritation in the stomach and stomach lining and also the lower part of the oesophagus (the tube connecting the throat to the stomach) which could promote acid reflux or indigestion – this is what happens when some of the acidic stomach contents go back into the oesophagus.

The reason why coffee has this effect hasn't been pinpointed. It may partly be the effect of caffeine, but other components in coffee include chlorogenic acids which may also be partly responsible The degree to which coffee-related stomach issues affect you personally is down to genetics, it's an individual thing. Some people have a zero tolerance to coffee, others have no issues at all. If you're noticing issues, switching to darker roasts can help as these have less of an acidic effect, but it's not necessarily going to eliminate all symptoms. For this reason, if you're using coffee pre-exercise as a caffeine boost, it may be worth considering alternate sources such as a caffeine pill or caffeine shot to avoid any stomach issues.

TRIPS TO THE TOILET

Trips to the toilet after drinking coffee can also be an issue. As well as the above, coffee stimulates colonic motor activity which basically means it accelerates muscle contractions in the large intestine, thereby speeding up the time it takes for food to be excreted. Caffeine in general works by blocking adenosine receptors and this creates the associated positive effects, but it also blocks adenosine receptors in the kidneys, creating the less desirable effect of causing the blood vessels to dilate and your body to produce more urine.

KEY POINT

As a footballer, making the switch to another source of caffeine may give you the benefits you expect from a cup of coffee without the potential side-effects. Avoiding stomach issues on the pitch will obviously allow for a better performance.

REFERENCES

FITNESS

Afyon, Y. A., Mulazimoglu, O., & Boyaci, A. (2017). The effects of core trainings on speed and agility skills of soccer players. *International Journal of Sports Science*, 7(6), 239-244.

Anderson, K. G., & Behm, D. G. (2004). Maintenance of EMG activity and loss of force output with instability. *The Journal of Strength & Conditioning Research*, 18(3), 637-640.

Andre, T. L., Gann, J. J., Hwang, P. S., Ziperman, E., Magnussen, M. J., & Willoughby, D. S. (2018). Restrictive breathing mask reduces repetitions to failure during a session of lower-body resistance exercise. *The Journal of Strength & Conditioning Research*, 32(8), 2103-2108.

Azevedo, A. P., Mezencio, B., Mochizuki, L., Valvassori, R., Amadio, A. C., & Serrao, J. C. (2018). 8-week training in partial minimalist shoe reduces impact force during running. *Human Movement*, 19(4), 20-28.

Baker, D. (2011). Recent trends in high-intensity aerobic training for field sports. *Prof Strength Cond*, 22, 3-8.

Barber, F. A., & Sutker, A. N. (1992). Iliotibial band syndrome. *Sports Medicine*, 14(2), 144-148.

Beals, C., & Flanigan, D. (2013). A review of treatments for iliotibial band syndrome in the athletic population. *Journal of Sports Medicine*, 2013.

Behm, D., & Colado, J. C. (2012). The effectiveness of resistance training using unstable surfaces and devices for rehabilitation. *International journal of sports physical therapy*, 7(2), 226.

Bezodis, I. N., Kerwin, D. G., Cooper, S. M., & Salo, A. I. (2018). Sprint running performance and technique changes in athletes during periodized training: an elite training group case study. *International journal of sports physiology and performance*, 13(6), 755-762.

Bieuzen, F., Bleakley, C. M., & Costello, J. T. (2013). Contrast water therapy and exercise induced muscle damage: a systematic review and meta-analysis. *PLoS One*, 8(4), e62356.

Booth, M. A., & Orr, R. (2016). Effects of plyometric training on sports performance. *Strength & Conditioning Journal*, 38(1), 30-37.

Chan, I. S., & Fu, L. L. (2018). Unstable Surface Training Effects on Balance and Lower Limb Power in Adolescent Female Soccer Players. *Medicine & Science in Sports & Exercise*, 50(5S), 781.

Chung, K. A., Lee, E., & Lee, S. (2016). The effect of intrinsic foot muscle training on medial longitudinal arch and ankle stability in patients with chronic ankle sprain accompanied by foot pronation. *Physical Therapy Rehabilitation Science*, 5(2), 78-83.

Cirer-Sastre, R., Beltrán-Garrido, J. V., & Corbi, F. (2017). Contralateral effects after unilateral strength training: a meta-analysis comparing training loads. *Journal of sports science & medicine*, 16(2), 180.

Comfort, P., Stewart, A., Bloom, L., & Clarkson, B. (2014). Relationships between strength, sprint and jump performance in well-trained youth soccer players. *The Journal of Strength & Conditioning Research*, 28(1), 173-177.

de Carnys, G. M. S., & Lees, A. (2008, August). 52 The effects of strength training and practice on soccer throw-in performance. In *Science and Football VI: The Proceedings of the Sixth World Congress on Science and Football* (p. 302). Routledge.

del Deporte, C. N. D. M. (2018). Strength Training in Children and Adolescents: Benefits, Risks and Recommendations. *Archivos argentinos de pediatria*, 116(6), S82-S91.

Earp, J. E., & Kraemer, W. J. (2010). Medicine ball training implications for rotational power sports. *Strength & Conditioning Journal, 32*(4), 20-25.

Ebben, W. P. (2008). The optimal downhill slope for acute overspeed running. *International journal of sports physiology and performance, 3*(1), 88-93.

Erdem, E. U., & Akbaş, E. (2020). Postural differences between professional soccer players and sedentary population. *Science & Sports, 35*(2), 99-e1.

Faigenbaum, A. D., Kraemer, W. J., Blimkie, C. J., Jeffreys, I., Micheli, L. J., Nitka, M., & Rowland, T. W. (2009). Youth resistance training: updated position statement paper from the national strength and conditioning association. *The Journal of Strength & Conditioning Research, 23*, S60-S79.

Faigenbaum, A. D., Lloyd, R. S., MacDonald, J., & Myer, G. D. (2016). Citius, Altius, Fortius: beneficial effects of resistance training for young athletes: narrative review. *British Journal of Sports Medicine, 50*(1), 3-7.

Foley, A., Hillier, S., & Barnard, R. (2011). Effectiveness of once-weekly gym-based exercise programmes for older adults post discharge from day rehabilitation: a randomised controlled trial. *British journal of sports medicine, 45*(12), 978-986.

Gabbett, T. J. (2016). The training—injury prevention paradox: should athletes be training smarter and harder?. *British journal of sports medicine, 50*(5), 273-280.

Granacher, U., Lesinski, M., Büsch, D., Muehlbauer, T., Prieske, O., Puta, C., ... & Behm, D. G. (2016). Effects of resistance training in youth athletes on muscular fitness and athletic performance: a conceptual model for long-term athlete development. *Frontiers in physiology, 7*, 164.

Granados, J., Gillum, T. L., Castillo, W., Christmas, K. M., & Kuennen, M. R. (2016). "Functional" respiratory muscle training during endurance exercise causes modest hypoxemia but overall is well tolerated. *The Journal of Strength & Conditioning Research, 30*(3), 755-762.

Gyarmati, L., & Hefeeda, M. (2016). Analyzing in-game movements of soccer players at scale. *arXiv preprint arXiv:1603.05583*.

Hammami, R., Granacher, U., Makhlouf, I., Behm, D. G., & Chaouachi, A. (2016). Sequencing effects of balance and plyometric training on physical performance in youth soccer athletes. *The Journal of Strength & Conditioning Research, 30*(12), 3278-3289.

Harrison, C. B., Gill, N. D., Kinugasa, T., & Kilding, A. E. (2015). Development of aerobic fitness in young team sport athletes. *Sports Medicine, 45*(7), 969-983.

Heisey, C. F., & Kingsley, J. D. (2016). Effects of static stretching on squat performance in division I female athletes. *International journal of exercise science, 9*(3), 359.

Hewit, J., Cronin, ., Button, C., & Hume, P. (2011). Understanding deceleration in sport. *Strength & Conditioning Journal, 33*(1), 47-52.

Hoff, J., Wisløff, U., Engen, L. C., Kemi, O. J., & Helgerud, J. (2002). Soccer specific aerobic endurance training. *British journal of sports medicine, 36*(3), 218-221.

Hohenauer, E., Taeymans, J., Baeyens, J. P., Clarys, P., & Clijsen, R. (2015). The effect of post-exercise cryotherapy on recovery characteristics: a systematic review and meta-analysis. *PLoS one, 10*(9), e0139028.

Huxel Bliven, K. C., & Anderson, B. E. (2013). Core stability training for injury prevention. *Sports health, 5*(6), 514-522.

Jagim, A. R., Dominy, T. A., Camic, C. L., Wright, G., Doberstein, S., Jones, M. T., & Oliver, J. M. (2018). Acute effects of the elevation training mask on strength performance in recreational weight lifters. *The Journal of Strength & Conditioning Research, 32*(2), 482-489.

Jeffreys, I. (2008). Movement training for field sports: Soccer. *Strength & Conditioning Journal, 30*(4), 19-27.

Jeong, T. S., Reilly, T., Morton, J., Bae, S. W., & Drust, B. (2011). Quantification of the physiological loading of one week of "pre-season" and one week of "in-season" training in professional soccer players. *Journal of sports sciences, 29*(11), 1161-1166.

Kownacki, B. R. (2018). *Effects of Barefoot Strength Training on Athletic Performance*. Southern Connecticut State University.

Lauersen, J.B., Bertelsen, D.M. andersen, L.B. The effectiveness of exercise interventions to prevent sports injuries: a systematic review and meta-analysis of randomized controlled trials. *Br J Sports Med*, 2014, 48: 871-877.

Little, T., & Williams, A. (2003). *Specificity of acceleration, maximum speed and agility in professional soccer players* (pp. pp-144). London, UK:: Routledge.

Lockie, R. G., & Lazar, A. (2017). Exercise technique: applying the hexagonal bar to strength and power training. *Strength & Conditioning Journal, 39*(5), 24-32.

López-Pérez, M. E., Romero-Arenas, S., Colomer-Poveda, D., Keller, M., & Márquez, G. (2020). Psychophysiological Responses During a Cycling Test to Exhaustion While Wearing the Elevation Training Mask. *The Journal of Strength & Conditioning Research*.

Los Arcos, A., Mendez-Villanueva, A., & Martínez-Santos, R. (2017). In-season training periodization of professional soccer players. *Biology of sport, 34*(2), 149.

Macadam, P., Cronin, J. B., Uthoff, A. M., Johnston, M., & Knicker, A. J. (2018). Role of Arm mechanics during sprint Running: A Review of the Literature and practical Applications. *Strength & Conditioning Journal, 40*(5), 14-23.

MacKinnon, L. T. (2000). Overtraining effects on immunity and performance in athletes. *Immunology and cell biology, 78*(5), 502-509.

Mahaboobjan, Viswejan, U. (2017). Impact of ladder training on agility balance and coordination among school students. *Physical education*, 6(1), 229-231

Mair, S. D., Seaber, A. V., Glisson, R. R., & Garrett JR, W. E. (1996). The role of fatigue in susceptibility to acute muscle strain injury. *The American Journal of Sports Medicine, 24*(2), 137-143.

Mathisen, G. E., & Pettersen, S. A. (2015). The effect of speed training on sprint and agility performance in 15-year-old female soccer players. *Lase Journal of Sport Science, 6*(1), 61-70.

McConell, G. K. (1991). The effect of reduced training volume and intensity in distance runners.

Myers, A. M., Beam, N. W., & Fakhoury, J. D. (2017). Resistance training for children and adolescents. *Translational pediatrics, 6*(3), 137.

Nédélec, M., Halson, S., Delecroix, B., Abaidia, A. E., Ahmaidi, S., & Dupont, G. (2015). Sleep hygiene and recovery strategies in elite soccer players. *Sports Medicine, 45*(11), 1547-1559.

Neto, W. K., Soares, E. G., Vieira, T. L., Aguiar, R., Chola, T. A., de Lima Sampaio, V., & Gama, E. F. (2020). Gluteus Maximus Activation during Common Strength and Hypertrophy Exercises: A Systematic Review. *Journal of Sports Science & Medicine, 19*(1), 195.

Odunaiya, N. A., Hamzat, T. K., & Ajayi, O. F. (2005). The effects of static stretch duration on the flexibility of hamstring muscles. *African journal of biomedical research*, *8*(2), 79-82.

Ott, T., Joyce, M. C., & Hillman, A. R. (2020). Effects of Acute High-Intensity Exercise With the Elevation Training Mask or Hypoxicator on Pulmonary Function, Metabolism and Hormones. *The Journal of Strength & Conditioning Research*.

Owen, A., Dunlop, G., Rouissi, M., Chtara, M., Paul, D., Zouhal, H., & Wong, D. P. (2015). The relationship between lower-limb strength and match-related muscle damage in elite level professional European soccer players. *Journal of sports sciences*, *33*(20), 2100-2105.

Pantoja, P. D., Carvalho, A. R., Ribas, L. R., & Peyré-Tartaruga, L. A. (2018). Effect of weighted sled towing on sprinting effectiveness, power and force-velocity relationship. *PloS one*, *13*(10), e0204473.

Paradisis, G. P., Bissas, A., & Cooke, C. B. (2009). Combined uphill and downhill sprint running training is more efficacious than horizontal. *International Journal of Sports Physiology and Performance*, *4*(2), 229-243.

Parr, M., Price, P. D., & Cleather, D. J. (2017). Effect of a gluteal activation warm-up on explosive exercise performance. *BMJ open sport & exercise medicine*, *3*(1), e000245.

Paul, M. (2019). The effects of core strength training on balance of soccer players. *Age (yrs)*, *3*, 15.

Polsgrove, M. J., Eggleston, B. M., & Lockyer, R. J. (2016). Impact of 10-weeks of yoga practice on flexibility and balance of college athletes. *International journal of yoga*, *9*(1), 27.

Prestes, J., De Lima, C., Frollini, A. B., Donatto, F. F., & Conte, M. (2009). Comparison of linear and reverse linear periodization effects on maximal strength and body composition. *The Journal of strength & conditioning research*, *23*(1), 266-274.

Pretz, R. (2006). Plyometric exercises for overhead-throwing athletes. *Strength and Conditioning Journal*, *28*(1), 36.

Raja Azidin, R. F., Sankey, S., Drust, B., Robinson, M. A., & Vanrenterghem, J. (2015). Effects of treadmill versus overground soccer match simulations on biomechanical markers of anterior cruciate ligament injury risk in side cutting. *Journal of Sports Sciences*, *33*(13), 1332-1341.

Riley, P. O., Dicharry, J., Franz, J. A. S. O. N., Della Croce, U., Wilder, R. P., & Kerrigan, D. C. (2008). A kinematics and kinetic comparison of overground and treadmill running. *Medicine & Science in Sports & Exercise*, *40*(6), 1093-1100.

SA, H. K., Kianigul, M., Haghighi, A. H., Nooghabi, M. J., & Scott, B. R. (2020). Performing Soccer-Specific Training With Blood Flow Restriction Enhances Physical Capacities in Youth Soccer Players. *Journal of Strength and Conditioning Research*.

Sánchez-Ramírez, C., & Alegre, L. M. (2020). Plantar support adaptations in healthy subjects after eight weeks of barefoot running training. *PeerJ*, *8*, e8862.

Schoenfeld, B. J. (2010). The mechanisms of muscle hypertrophy and their application to resistance training. *The Journal of Strength & Conditioning Research*, *24*(10), 2857-2872.

Self, B. P., Beck, J., Schill, D., Eames, C., Knox, T., & Plaga, J. (2006). Head accelerations during soccer heading. In *The engineering of sport 6* (pp. 81-86). Springer, New York, NY.

Sellers, J. H., Monaghan, T. P., Schnaiter, J. A., Jacobson, B. H., & Pope, Z. K. (2016). Efficacy of a ventilatory training mask to improve anaerobic and aerobic capacity in reserve officers' training corps cadets. *The Journal of Strength & Conditioning Research*, *30*(4), 1155-1160.

Sheppard, J. M., & Young, W. B. (2006). Agility literature review: Classifications, training and testing. *Journal of sports sciences*, *24*(9), 919-932.

Slimani, M., Chamari, K., Miarka, B., Del Vecchio, F. B., & Chéour, F. (2016). Effects of plyometric training on physical fitness in team sport athletes: a systematic review. *Journal of human kinetics*, *53*(1), 231-247.

Small, K., McNaughton, L. R., Greig, M., Lohkamp, M., & Lovell, R. (2009). Soccer fatigue, sprinting and hamstring injury risk. *International journal of sports medicine*, *30*(8), 573.

Styles, W. J., Matthews, M. J., & Comfort, P. (2016). Effects of strength training on squat and sprint performance in soccer players. *The Journal of Strength & Conditioning Research*, *30*(6), 1534-1539.

Suarez-Arrones, L., Lara-Lopez, P., Torreno, N., Saez de Villarreal, E., Di Salvo, V., & Mendez-Villanueva, A. (2019). Effects of strength training on body composition in young male professional soccer players. *Sports*, *7*(5), 104.

Teodoro, C. L., Gáspari, A. F., Berton, R., Barbieri, J. F., Silva, M., Castaño, L. A., ... & Moraes, A. C. (2019). Familiarization With Airflow-Restriction Mask During Resistance Exercise: Effect on Tolerance and Total Volume. *The Journal of Strength & Conditioning Research*, *33*(7), 1762-1765.

Timmons, J. A. (2011). Variability in training-induced skeletal muscle adaptation. *Journal of applied physiology*, *110*(3), 846-853.

Toninato, J., Casey, H., Uppal, M., Abdallah, T., Bergman, T., Eckner, J., & Samadani, U. (2018). Traumatic brain injury reduction in athletes by neck strengthening (TRAIN). *Contemporary clinical trials communications*, *11*, 102-106.

Wilson, J. M., Lowery, R. P., Joy, J. M., Loenneke, J. P., & Naimo, M. A. (2013). Practical blood flow restriction training increases acute determinants of hypertrophy without increasing indices of muscle damage. *The Journal of Strength & Conditioning Research*, *27*(11), 3068-3075.

Wisløff, U., Castagna, C., Helgerud, J., Jones, R., & Hoff, J. (2004). Strong correlation of maximal squat strength with sprint performance and vertical jump height in elite soccer players. *British journal of sports medicine*, *38*(3), 285-288.

Young, W. B. (2006). Transfer of strength and power training to sports performance. *International journal of sports physiology and performance*, *1*(2), 74-83.

Zetou, E., Papadakis, L., Vernadakis, N., Derri, V., Bebetsos, E., & Filippou, F. (2014). The effect of variable and stable practice on performance and learning the header skill of young athletes in soccer. *Procedia-Social and Behavioral Sciences*, *152*, 824-829.

Zouita, S., Zouita, A. B., Kebsi, W., Dupont, G., Abderrahman, A. B., Salah, F. Z. B., & Zouhal, H. (2016). Strength training reduces injury rate in elite young soccer players during one season. *The Journal of Strength & Conditioning Research*, *30*(5), 1295-1307.

NUTRITION

Aird, T. P., Davies, R. W., & Carson, B. P. (2018). Effects of fasted vs fed-state exercise on performance and post-exercise metabolism: A systematic review and meta-analysis. *Scandinavian journal of medicine & science in sports*, *28*(5), 1476-1493.

Allan, G. M., & Arroll, B. (2014). Prevention and treatment of the common cold: making sense of the evidence. *Cmaj*, *186*(3), 190-199.

Alsunni, A. A. (2015). Energy drink consumption: beneficial and adverse health effects. *International journal of health sciences*, *9*(4), 468.

Ansari, R. M., & Omar, N. S. (2017). Weight loss supplements: boon or bane?. *The Malaysian journal of medical sciences: MJMS*, *24*(3), 1.

Azoulay, A., Garzon, P., & Eisenberg, M. J. (2001). Comparison of the mineral content of tap water and bottled waters. *Journal of general internal medicine, 16*(3), 168-175.

Barnes, M. J. (2014). Alcohol: impact on sports performance and recovery in male athletes. *Sports Medicine, 44*(7), 909-919.

Barr, S. I. (1999). Effects of dehydration on exercise performance. *Canadian Journal of Applied Physiology, 24*(2), 164-172.

Bennett, B. J., Hall, K. D., Hu, F. B., McCartney, A. L., & Roberto, C. (2015). Nutrition and the science of disease prevention: a systems approach to support metabolic health. *Annals of the New York Academy of Sciences, 1352*, 1.

Biesalski, H. K. (2005). Meat as a component of a healthy diet–are there any risks or benefits if meat is avoided in the diet?. *Meat science, 70*(3), 509-524.

Binnie, M. A., Barlow, K., Johnson, V., & Harrison, C. (2014). Red meats: Time for a paradigm shift in dietary advice. *Meat science, 98*(3), 445-451.

Bo, S., Seletto, M., Choc, A., Ponzo, V., Lezo, A., Demagistris, A., ... & Gambino, R. (2017). The acute impact of the intake of four types of bread on satiety and blood concentrations of glucose, insulin, free fatty acids, triglyceride and acylated ghrelin. A randomized controlled cross-over trial. *Food research international, 92*, 40-47.

Burke, L. M. (2010). Fueling strategies to optimize performance: training high or training low?. *Scandinavian journal of medicine & science in sports, 20*, 48-58.

Burke, L. M., & King, C. (2012). Ramadan fasting and the goals of sports nutrition around exercise. *Journal of sports sciences, 30*(sup1), S21-S31.

Calder, P. C., Albers, R., Antoine, J. M., Blum, S., Bourdet-Sicard, R., Ferns, G. A., ... & Løvik, M. (2009). Inflammatory disease processes and interactions with nutrition. *British Journal of Nutrition, 101*(S1), 1-45.

Camera, D. M., Smiles, W. J., & Hawley, J. A. (2016). Exercise-induced skeletal muscle signaling pathways and human athletic performance. *Free Radical Biology and Medicine, 98*, 131-143.

Carling, C., & Orhant, E. (2010). Variation in body composition in professional soccer players: interseasonal and intraseasonal changes and the effects of exposure time and player position. *The Journal of Strength & Conditioning Research, 24*(5), 1332-1339.

Cava, E., Yeat, N. C., & Mittendorfer, B. (2017). Preserving healthy muscle during weight loss. *Advances in nutrition, 8*(3), 511-519.

Clark, K. L. (2007). Nutritional considerations in joint health. *Clinics in sports medicine, 26*(1), 101-118.

Close, G. L., Sale, C., Baar, K., & Bermon, S. (2019). Nutrition for the prevention and treatment of injuries in track and field athletes. *International journal of sport nutrition and exercise metabolism, 29*(2), 189-197.

Cooper, R., Naclerio, F., Allgrove, J., & Jimenez, A. (2012). Creatine supplementation with specific view to exercise/sports performance: an update. *Journal of the International Society of Sports Nutrition, 9*(1), 1-11.

Correia-Oliveira, C. R., Bertuzzi, R., Kiss, M. A. P. D. M., & Lima-Silva, A. E. (2013). Strategies of dietary carbohydrate manipulation and their effects on performance in cycling time trials. *Sports Medicine, 43*(8), 707-719.

Cuenca, E., Jodra, P., Pérez-López, A., González-Rodríguez, L. G., Fernandes da Silva, S., Veiga-Herreros, P., & Domínguez, R. (2018). Effects of beetroot juice supplementation on performance and fatigue in a 30-s all-out sprint exercise: a randomized, double-blind cross-over study. *Nutrients, 10*(9), 1222.

Deng, Y., Misselwitz, B., Dai, N., & Fox, M. (2015). Lactose intolerance in adults: biological mechanism and dietary management. *Nutrients*, *7*(9), 8020-8035.

DiNicolantonio, J. J., & O'Keefe, J. H. (2018). Importance of maintaining a low omega–6/omega–3 ratio for reducing inflammation. *Open Heart*, *5*(2).

Domínguez, R., Maté-Muñoz, J. L., Cuenca, E., García-Fernández, P., Mata-Ordoñez, F., Lozano-Estevan, M. C., ... & Garnacho-Castaño, M. V. (2018). Effects of beetroot juice supplementation on intermittent high-intensity exercise efforts. *Journal of the International Society of Sports Nutrition*, *15*(1), 1-12.

Eichner, E. R. (2007). The role of sodium in 'heat cramping'. *Sports Medicine*, *37*(4-5), 368-370.

Fenton, T. R., & Huang, T. (2016). Systematic review of the association between dietary acid load, alkaline water and cancer. *BMJ open*, *6*(6).

Ganesan, K., Habboush, Y., & Sultan, S. (2018). Intermittent fasting: the choice for a healthier lifestyle. *Cureus*, *10*(7).

Gibson, M. E., Schultz, J., & Glover, D. (2016). To Supplement or Not. *Missouri Medicine*, *113*(4), 305.

Gimbar, M. (2017). A Sip Above the Rest... Is Bone Broth All Its Boiled up to Be?. *Journal of Renal Nutrition*, *27*(6), e39-e40.

Goulet, E. D. (2012). Dehydration and endurance performance in competitive athletes. *Nutrition Reviews*, *70*(suppl_2), S132-S136.

Gröber, U., Werner, T., Vormann, J., & Kisters, K. (2017). Myth or reality—transdermal magnesium?. *Nutrients*, *9*(8), 813.

Hall, M., & Trojian, T. H. (2013). Creatine supplementation. *Current sports medicine reports*, *12*(4), 240-244.

Harty, P. S., Zabriskie, H. A., Erickson, J. L., Molling, P. E., Kerksick, C. M., & Jagim, A. R. (2018). Multi-ingredient pre-workout supplements, safety implications and performance outcomes: a brief review. *Journal of the International Society of Sports Nutrition*, *15*(1), 1-28.

Hawley, J. A., & Leckey, J. J. (2015). Carbohydrate dependence during prolonged, intense endurance exercise. *Sports Medicine*, *45*(1), 5-12.

Hespel, P., Maughan, R. J., & Greenhaff, P. L. (2006). Dietary supplements for football. *Journal of Sports Sciences*, *24*(07), 749-761.

Hills, S. P., & Russell, M. (2018). Carbohydrates for soccer: A focus on skilled actions and half-time practices. *Nutrients*, *10*(1), 22.

Howell, S., & Kones, R. (2017). "Calories in, calories out" and macronutrient intake: the hope, hype and science of calories. *American Journal of Physiology-Endocrinology and Metabolism*, *313*(5), E608-E612.

Hsu, D. J., Lee, C. W., Tsai, W. C., & Chien, Y. C. (2017). Essential and toxic metals in animal bone broths. *Food & Nutrition Research*, *61*(1), 1347478.

Ibrahim, N. K., & Iftikhar, R. (2014). Energy drinks: Getting wings but at what health cost?. *Pakistan Journal of Medical Sciences*, *30*(6), 1415.

Impey, S. G., Hearris, M. A., Hammond, K. M., Bartlett, J. D., Louis, J., Close, G. L., & Morton, J. P. (2018). Fuel for the work required: a theoretical framework for carbohydrate periodization and the glycogen threshold hypothesis. *Sports Medicine*, *48*(5), 1031-1048.

Inoue-Choi, M., Oppeneer, S. J., & Robien, K. (2013). Reality check: there is No such thing as a miracle food. *Nutrition and cancer*, 65(2), 165-168.

J. Boekema, M. Samsom, GF van Berge Henegouwen, AJPM Smout, P. (1999). Coffee and gastrointestinal function: facts and fiction: a review. *Scandinavian Journal of Gastroenterology*, 34(230), 35-39.

Jagim, A. R., Harty, P. S., & Camic, C. L. (2019). Common ingredient profiles of multi-ingredient pre-workout supplements. *Nutrients*, 11(2), 254.

Jahic, D., & Begic, E. (2018). Exercise-associated muscle cramp-doubts about the cause. *Materia Socio-Medica*, 30(1), 67.

Jeukendrup, A. E., & Randel, R. (2011). Fat burners: nutrition supplements that increase fat metabolism. *Obesity reviews*, 12(10), 841-851.

Kanter, M. (2018). High-quality carbohydrates and physical performance: Expert panel report. *Nutrition today*, 53(1), 35.

Kerksick, C. M., Arent, S., Schoenfeld, B. J., Stout, J. R., Campbell, B., Wilborn, C. D., ... & Willoughby, D. (2017). International society of sports nutrition position stand: nutrient timing. *Journal of the International Society of Sports Nutrition*, 14(1), 1-21.

Levitt, D. E., Luk, H. Y., Duplanty, A. A., McFarlin, B. K., Hill, D. W., & Vingren, J. L. (2017). Effect of alcohol after muscle-damaging resistance exercise on muscular performance recovery and inflammatory capacity in women. *European Journal of Applied Physiology*, 117(6), 1195-1206.

Levy, E., & Chu, T. (2019). Intermittent Fasting and Its Effects on Athletic Performance: A Review. *Current Sports Medicine Reports*, 18(7), 266-269.

Mäkinen, K. K. (2016). Gastrointestinal disturbances associated with the consumption of sugar alcohols with special consideration of Xylitol: scientific review and instructions for dentists and other health-care professionals. *International journal of dentistry*, 2016.

Marangoni, F., Pellegrino, L., Verduci, E., Ghiselli, A., Bernabei, R., Calvani, R., ... & Giacco, R. (2019). Cow's milk consumption and health: A health professional's guide. *Journal of the American College of Nutrition*, 38(3), 197-208.

Martinez, N., Campbell, B., Franek, M., Buchanan, L., & Colquhoun, R. (2016). The effect of acute pre-workout supplementation on power and strength performance. *Journal of the International Society of Sports Nutrition*, 13(1), 29.

Martínez-Sanz, J. M., Sospedra, I., Ortiz, C. M., Baladía, E., Gil-Izquierdo, A., & Ortiz-Moncada, R. (2017). Intended or unintended doping? A review of the presence of doping substances in dietary supplements used in sports. *Nutrients*, 9(10), 1093.

Mathews, N. M. (2018). Prohibited contaminants in dietary supplements. *Sports health*, 10(1), 19-30.

Maughan, R. J., Zerguini, Y., Chalabi, H., & Dvorak, J. (2012). Achieving optimum sports performance during Ramadan: some practical recommendations. *Journal of sports sciences*, 30(sup1), S109-S117.

McCartney, D., Desbrow, B., & Irwin, C. (2017). The effect of fluid intake following dehydration on subsequent athletic and cognitive performance: A systematic review and meta-analysis. *Sports medicine-open*, 3(1), 13.

McDowall, J. A. (2007). Supplement use by young athletes. *Journal of sports science & medicine*, 6(3), 337.

Mielgo-Ayuso, J., Calleja-Gonzalez, J., Marqués-Jiménez, D., Caballero-García, A., Córdova, A., & Fernández-Lázaro, D. (2019). Effects of creatine supplementation on athletic performance in soccer players: A systematic review and meta-analysis. *Nutrients*, *11*(4), 757.

Miller, K. C., Stone, M. S., Huxel, K. C., & Edwards, J. E. (2010). Exercise-associated muscle cramps: causes, treatment and prevention. *Sports health*, *2*(4), 279-283.

Milsom, J., Naughton, R., O'Boyle, A., Iqbal, Z., Morgans, R., Drust, B., & Morton, J. P. (2015). Body composition assessment of English Premier League soccer players: a comparative DXA analysis of first team, U21 and U18 squads. *Journal of sports sciences*, *33*(17), 1799-1806.

Morton, J. P. (2015). Increasing lean muscle mass: nutritional and periodization strategies. *BMC Sports Science, Medicine and Rehabilitation*, *7*(S1), O9.

Mul, J. D., Stanford, K. I., Hirshman, M. F., & Goodyear, L. J. (2015). Exercise and regulation of carbohydrate metabolism. In *Progress in molecular biology and translational science* (Vol. 135, pp. 17-37). Academic Press.

Nikolaidis, P. T., & Karydis, N. V. (2011). Physique and body composition in soccer players across adolescence. *Asian journal of sports medicine*, *2*(2), 75.

Nikooyeh, B., & Neyestani, T. R. (2017). Higher bioavailability of iron from whole wheat bread compared with iron-fortified white breads in caco-2 cell model: an experimental study. *Journal of the Science of Food and Agriculture*, *97*(8), 2541-2546.

Oliveira, C. C., Ferreira, D., Caetano, C., Granja, D., Pinto, R., Mendes, B., & Sousa, M. (2017). Nutrition and supplementation in soccer. *Sports*, *5*(2), 28.

Parr, E. B., Camera, D. M., Areta, J. L., Burke, L. M., Phillips, S. M., Hawley, J. A., & Coffey, V. G. (2014). Alcohol ingestion impairs maximal post-exercise rates of myofibrillar protein synthesis following a single bout of concurrent training. *PLoS One*, *9*(2), e88384.

Rasmussen, O., Winther, E., & Hermansen, K. (1991). Glycaemic responses to different types of bread in insulin-dependent diabetic subjects (IDDM): studies at constant insulinaemia. *European journal of clinical nutrition*, *45*(2), 97-103.

Richardson, R. A., & Davidson, H. I. M. (2003). Nutritional demands in acute and chronic illness. *Proceedings of the Nutrition Society*, *62*(4), 777-781.

Riesberg, L. A., Weed, S. A., McDonald, T. L., Eckerson, J. M., & Drescher, K. M. (2016). Beyond muscles: The untapped potential of creatine. *International immunopharmacology*, *37*, 31-42.

Rogerson, D. (2017). Vegan diets: practical advice for athletes and exercisers. *Journal of the International Society of Sports Nutrition*, *14*(1), 36.

Rondanelli, M., Miccono, A., Lamburghini, S., Avanzato, I., Riva, A., Allegrini, P., ... & Perna, S. (2018). Self-care for common colds: the pivotal role of vitamin D, vitamin C, zinc and echinacea in three main immune interactive clusters (physical barriers, innate and adaptive immunity) involved during an episode of common colds—practical advice on dosages and on the time to take these nutrients/botanicals in order to prevent or treat common colds. *Evidence-Based Complementary and Alternative Medicine*, *2018*.

Russell, M., West, D. J., Harper, L. D., Cook, C. J., & Kilduff, L. P. (2015). Half-time strategies to enhance second-half performance in team-sports players: a review and recommendations. *Sports Medicine*, *45*(3), 353-364.

Schwalfenberg, G. K. (2012). The alkaline diet: is there evidence that an alkaline pH diet benefits health?. *Journal of environmental and public health*, *2012*.

Seal, A. D., Bardis, C. N., Gavrieli, A., Grigorakis, P., Adams, J. D., Arnaoutis, G., ... & Kavouras, S. A. (2017). Coffee with high but not low caffeine content augments fluid and electrolyte excretion at rest. *Frontiers in nutrition*, *4*, 40.

Seo, A. Y., Kim, N., & Ch, D. H. (2013). Abdominal bloating: pathophysiology and treatment. *Journal of neurogastroenterology and motility*, *19*(4), 433.

Shenkin, A. (2006). Micronutrients in health and disease. *Postgraduate medical journal*, *82*(971), 559-567.

Simopoulos, A. P. (2002). The importance of the ratio of omega-6/omega-3 essential fatty acids. *Biomedicine & pharmacotherapy*, *56*(8), 365-379.

Singh, R. K., Chang, H. W., Yan, D., Lee, K. M., Ucmak, D., Wong, K., ... & Bhutani, T. (2017). Influence of diet on the gut microbiome and implications for human health. *Journal of translational medicine*, *15*(1), 73.

Slimani, M., Znazen, H., Hammami, A., & Bragazzi, N. L. (2018). Comparison of body fat percentage of male soccer players of different competitive levels, playing positions and age groups: a meta-analysis. *J Sports Med Phys Fitness*, *58*(6), 857-866

Sobsey, M. D., & Bartram, S. (2003, January). Water quality and health in the new millennium: the role of the World Health Organization Guidelines for Drinking-Water Quality. In *Forum of nutrition* (Vol. 56, pp. 396-405).

Sutton, L., Scott, M., Wallace, J., & Reilly, T. (2009). Body composition of English Premier League soccer players: Influence of playing position, international status and ethnicity. *Journal of Sports sciences*, *27*(10), 1019-1026.

Thomas, D. T., Erdman, K. A., & Burke, L. M. (2016). Position of the Academy of Nutrition and Dietetics, Dietitians of Canada and the American College of Sports Medicine: nutrition and athletic performance. *Journal of the Academy of Nutrition and Dietetics*, *116*(3), 501-528.

Thomas, S., Browne, H., Mobasheri, A., & Rayman, M. P. (2018). What is the evidence for a role for diet and nutrition in osteoarthritis?. *Rheumatology*, *57*(suppl_4), iv61-iv74.

Thorning, T. K., Raben, A., Tholstrup, T., Soedamah-Muthu, S. S., Givens, I., & Astrup, A. (2016). Milk and dairy products: good or bad for human health? An assessment of the totality of scientific evidence. *Food & nutrition research*, *60*(1), 32527.

Tipton, K. D. (2015). Nutritional support for exercise-induced injuries. *Sports Medicine*, *45*(1), 93-104.

Tsarouhas, K., Kioukia-Fougia, N., Papalexis, P., Tsatsakis, A., Kouretas, D., Bacopoulou, F., & Tsitsimpikou, C. (2018). Use of nutritional supplements contaminated with banned doping substances by recreational adolescent athletes in Athens, Greece. *Food and chemical toxicology*, *115*, 447-450.

Valdes, A. M., Walter, J., Segal, E., & Spector, T. D. (2018). Role of the gut microbiota in nutrition and health. *Bmj*, *361*.

van Loon, L. J., Greenhaff, P. L., Constantin-Teodosiu, D., Saris, W. H., & Wagenmakers, A. J. (2001). The effects of increasing exercise intensity on muscle fuel utilisation in humans. *The Journal of physiology*, *536*(1), 295-304.

Verma, K. C., & Kushwaha, A. S. (2014). Demineralization of drinking water: Is it prudent?. *medical journal armed forces india*, *70*(4), 377-379.

Vos, E., & Weir, E. (1999). Nuts, omega-3s and food labels. *Circulation*, *99*, 733-5.

Wall, B. T., Morton, J. P., & van Loon, L. J. (2015). Strategies to maintain skeletal muscle mass in the injured athlete: nutritional considerations and exercise mimetics. *European journal of sport science*, *15*(1), 53-62.

Williams, C., & Rollo, I. (2015). Carbohydrate nutrition and team sport performance. *Sports Medicine*, *45*(1), 13-22.

Williams, C., & Serratosa, L. (2006). Nutrition on match day. *Journal of sports sciences*, *24*(07), 687-697.

Wittich, A., Oliveri, M. B., Rotemberg, E., & Mautalen, C. (2001). Body composition of professional football (soccer) players determined by dual X-ray absorptiometry. *Journal of Clinical Densitometry*, *4*(1), 51-55.

Wolfe, R. R. (2017). Branched-chain amino acids and muscle protein synthesis in humans: myth or reality?. *Journal of the International Society of Sports Nutrition*, *14*(1), 1-7.

Wyness, L. (2016). The role of red meat in the diet: nutrition and health benefits. *Proceedings of the Nutrition Society*, *75*(3), 227-232.

Zhu, X., Sang, L., Wu, D., Rong, J., & Jiang, L. (2018). Effectiveness and safety of glucosamine and chondroitin for the treatment of osteoarthritis: a meta-analysis of randomized controlled trials. *Journal of orthopaedic surgery and research*, *13*(1), 170.

Thank you for reading, I hope you've gained many valuable insights which have both inspired you and will serve you well for the rest of your football career. If you did find value in this book, please help our mission by sharing what you've learnt with one of your coaches or teammates. Thank you and keep training smart!

James - Matchfit Football

Printed in Poland
by Amazon Fulfillment
Poland Sp. z o.o., Wrocław